Tasting the Essence of Tantra

Tasting the Essence of Tantra

Buddhist Meditation for Contemporary Western Life

Rob Preece

Mudra Publications
Devon, 2018

Mudra Publications
1 Church Park Cottages
Holne
Devon TQ13 7SG
UK.

www.mudra.co.uk

ISBN: 978-1-5272-1498-9

Edited with Anna Murray Preece
Cover design by Rob Preece

Contents

PART TWO: A JOURNEY OF DEPTH

PART THREE: GUIDANCE

I dedicate this book to my wife Anna who has supported me in the journey of my own work and helped in so many ways through sharing her insight and experience of this wonderful path. I wish to express my huge gratitude for all the time and energy she contributed to helping clarify and edit this book. Her help has made its final emergence possible.

I wish to express my profound gratitude to my primary teacher Lama Thubten Yeshe who passed away in 1984. May this work help to keep the flame of Lama's vision alive and be of benefit to many Westerners who were not fortunate enough to meet him during his life and experience his gift of guidance and inspiration.

I also offer my gratitude to Lama Thubten Zopa Rinpoche whose impeccability shines brightly and whose kindness in the early years of my journey was extraordinary. May his life be long.

Lastly, I would like to dedicate this book to those I have worked with over the years in the context of retreat and mentoring. Your openness and courage to share your experience on this journey has been of immeasurable value in helping me understand more deeply how this path can become a Western experience. May your awakening be swift and of infinite benefit to others.

Thank you.

Introduction

WHEN WE MEET TIBETAN BUDDHISM we inevitably see that the Tibetan tradition is permeated by possibly the most complex and elaborate aspect of Buddhism, namely the practice of tantra or Vajrayana. The tradition of tantra emerged in India before, during and after the time of the Buddha. In the years that followed his passing the Buddhist form of tantra travelled into parts of Indonesia, Japan, Nepal, China and eventually Tibet where it became well established. In the enclosed mountains of Tibet, it flourished and became shaped, such that Tibetan culture, Tibetan Buddhism and tantra are inextricably interwoven. The Tibetans have created an extraordinarily rich and profound literary, artistic and musical masterpiece with highly experienced and deeply realised masters.

The term *tantra* in sanskrit is often translated as *weave*. One could understand this as the weave or play of reality or perhaps the weave of many practices. In Tibetan, the word *gyu*, generally translated as *continuity*, gives a very different connotation. We could see this to imply the underlying continuity of our innate nature. It can also imply the continuity of a lineage and transmission that has been passed down for hundreds of years. Another name for tantra is *vajrayana* sometimes translated as the *diamond vehicle*. Here the meaning of *vajra* relates to what is indestructible and pure in our nature and *yana* means vehicle or vessel as a way of moving along a path.

While it is no simple matter to understand the meaning of the word tantra or vajrayana, it is, I feel, through actual practice rather than intellectual knowledge that we begin to gain a taste of its meaning and effectiveness. At the heart of tantra is the liberation of our innate pure nature, our buddha-nature, from the veil of obscurations that are an expression of our ignorance and confusion. Tantra recognises that rather than trying to get rid of aspects of ourselves that are not acceptable, all that we are can transform and be purified into its natural innate potential in the process of awakening. This is an alchemical process that particularly orientates around the use of deity practices. These are an expression of our innate nature that act as a catalyst or vehicle for transformation. The practice of tantra is a powerful and profound path that has been cultivated with great expertise by the Tibetans and remains a living lineage of experience to this day.

As the tantric tradition comes to the West it is important to consider how it can be integrated into Western psyche and Western life so that we might experience its full potential. Many of us find this approach to Buddhism both fascinating and awe inspiring, but also extremely complex and sometimes confusing. For some people, the connection to tantra may be immediate and natural as though there is a deep-rooted resonance with the tradition. One might consider that this was a past life connection, although we cannot necessarily know. Others may feel a powerful attraction and yet need some means of bridging the profound nature of this Eastern tradition with our Western mind. Unfortunately, there are also times when people can be overwhelmed by its elaborate richness and the apparent need for so much study, and as a result feel somewhat alienated. This is a tradition that is undoubtedly not for everyone and those that prefer simplicity may struggle with it.

We can be very enthusiastic and have genuine desire to practise but may be surprised at the complexity we encounter. It is challenging to bring tantric practice into a busy, demanding and often stressful Western life, where it is hard to find time and space to devote to meditation. It is not surprising then that there can be times when we lose our way and our inspiration and wonder what we are doing.

There are aspects of tantra that many of us find immediately inspirational such as the relationship to the archetypal forms of deities. They will often fascinate us even though we may not always understand their actual meaning. Many of us feel a very natural connection to the nature of the energy-body that is so central to tantra, because we have encountered it through practices such as qigong, tai chi, acupuncture and so on. There is also within tantra a relationship to the sacred, expressed in a rich and creative way that responds to what many of us long for to restore something absent in our secular world. At the heart of tantra is the recognition that this is not something external we have to find but is all within our nature and can awaken if given the right conditions.

Through my own practice and work over many years as a meditation teacher and mentor of Western practitioners, it is clear that tantric practice can touch us very deeply if we learn to work with it skilfully. This does not mean we can instantly find the depth of connection that is possible unless we receive careful guidance in meditation. This is why the teacher is so important in this tradition. Today there is so much information available such that we can gain a huge amount of knowledge. But intellectual study alone will not bring experience. It is through the deeper process of meditation that we begin to wake up to our natural potential. In my own studies, there was a lot of opportunity to receive commentaries on the *sadhana* practices of various deities. These are the texts describing the often complex and detailed rituals, visualisations and prayers composed to 'accomplish' the deity. It was not always easy, however, to find someone who could teach me to meditate deeply within this process. This tended to mean my practice was at first primarily the recitation of these sadhanas, until I received some very specific guidance from my primary teacher, Lama Thubten Yeshe, and one of my retreat teachers, Gen Jhampa Wangdu. They began to explain a way of meditation that radically changed what I was doing.

In my own journey there have been periods when I felt my practice become dry and mechanical. I have spoken with friends who said they have felt the same and yet have faithfully continued. When this happened it usually meant I had lost the connection to what is at the heart of my practice. I needed to look at how I was practising and find ways to restore my connection to the 'juice' in my practice. Lama Yeshe would often emphasise that tantric practice is not about adopting Tibetan culture, nor about intellectual knowledge, it is about truly gaining a taste of what the essence of tantra is. He felt this is through the process of meditation.

It is important that we *feel* the effect of practice. This can then be something we integrate into our life because it is transforming us. For this to happen we need to learn how to meditate in a way that will truly touch us. A way of practice that genuinely addresses our psychological issues and therefore enables our own personal transformation. Otherwise we may put a veneer of so called spiritual practice over deeper emotional problems that never get resolved. A central principal in what I am writing here is my belief that we cannot and must not separate the spiritual and psychological process.

In my work I sometimes encounter those with deep meditation experiences on one level and yet relatively serious psychological difficulties on another.

In the process of teaching and mentoring I have found that people respond to an approach to meditation that addresses our particular Western emotional and psychological nature. The guidance I received from Lama Yeshe has been my greatest inspiration in this. He seemed to really understand what makes the Westerner tick. What was crucial in his approach was that he held to the essence of the tradition of tantra, while seeing how meditation practice can be creatively shaped to suit our individual emotional and psychological makeup. In this he was also instrumental encouraging my own integration of Western psychology and Buddhism.

Since Lama Yeshe's death, I have been engaged in teaching Buddhist tantra to fellow Westerners and have found it of great value to have a bridge of understanding that meets our psychological nature. It has been the work of C.G.Jung and his exploration of the world of the archetypes and the unconscious that has provided this bridge. In my own relationship to the tantric tradition I have hugely benefited from his insight and understanding. By some coincidence at the age of 21 I simultaneously encountered the Tibetan tradition and the work of Jung. As a result, I have always seen my practice of tantra through two subtly different lenses. One through the profound teachings I have received from my Tibetan teachers, the other reflected in my studies of Jung's work. It is the combination of these two perspectives that is now integral to how I teach others some of the rich and beautiful practices within the tantric tradition.

In 1999 when *The Alchemical Buddha* was published (republished in 2006 as *The Psychology of Buddhist Tantra*) it was the culmination of many years exploring the psychological nature of tantric practice. Since that time, I have increasingly felt the need to take that work further and go more deeply into the way in which we meditate within tantric practice in the West. In this book, therefore, I wish to describe a way of meditation that Lama Yeshe initiated. A way of relating to the essential core within the process of tantra that helps bring about a real taste of its potential for transformation.

As the Tibetan tradition comes to the West it is clear that our psychological background is very different to the Tibetans. We grow up and live in a busy, over-stimulating, competitive, often insecure world where the level of impact upon our emotional and psychological health can be very great. If tantric practice is to be effective, this emotional or psychological wounding must be addressed. To facilitate this both in my own practice and with those I teach, it has been necessary to cultivate a deeper capacity for meditation both in relationship to emotional process and the body. As a psychotherapist this is a very natural way to work and is central to the principle of tantric process. Bringing the practice of tantra into the body is in my experience crucial for this process to be effective.

It is here, however, that our Western psychological nature can come up against difficulty in relation to the traditional way in which tantra has been practiced. Tibetan teachers have great reverence for the creation and recitation of often complicated and detailed visualisation practices called *sadhanas*. As tantra has evolved in Tibet, certain lamas have composed beautiful, poetic texts full of devotional prayers and detailed visualisations that suit large groups of monks or nuns that gather to chant together. Increasingly as Tibetan lamas introduce these practices to Westerners they see that their complexity does not always suit us. The recitation of detailed and often lengthy texts does not lend itself to a depth of meditation that really touches us and can exacerbate a tendency for many of us to be out of touch with our body. As a result, our practice remains disembodied and in the head.

The body is central to tantra, because a relationship to its subtle energetic nature, enables the gradual clearing of what obstructs the awakening of our innate 'wisdom energy'. In the process of this clearing, our emotional life, intimately tied to the energy-body, is also gradually healed. To facilitate this, we need to restore our relationship to the body. We need to develop a capacity of quiet stillness in meditation and perhaps more crucially to become aware of our felt-sense and its underlying energy. It is from this place that we can receive the depth of transformation that is possible with tantric practice.

I am indebted to Lama Yeshe for introducing this fact to me in how he taught, even though I may not have fully grasped the implications for some years. To create a good ground in which tantric practice can ripen, we need to quieten our conceptual mind to cultivate an awareness of our body and its energy. Otherwise when we become involved in the recitation of detailed sadhanas, the danger is that we perpetuate a busy mind and disembodied awareness. As Lama Yeshe would often say, at some point "we need to drop the concepts and just meditate". It was for this reason that he introduced the practice of *mahamudra*, meditation in the nature of mind, at an earlier stage in practice than might traditionally be taught. This then becomes integral to tantric practice rather than separate from it.

It is with this in mind that in Part One I will explore how we can embark upon deity practices that emphasise an embodied meditative process. For this I will look at how tantric practice can, from the beginning, be brought more specifically into the body and its energetic nature. I will also show how the practice of mahamudra provides a context or ground of meditation that helps us feel and digest the effect of deity practice. I will introduce a way of practice that is less complex, to enable a more spacious and more embodied, deeper settling in meditation. Following Lama Yeshe's lead, I will also look at how tantric practice can be shaped to be more directly relevant to our individual psychological and emotional needs, while holding to the essential principles of the tradition. I will explore the particular ingredients of practice that can truly touch and transform our Western psychological nature.

In Part Two I will look at the inner psychological journey of depth that can unfold within or perhaps beneath the path of practice. From my own journey and that of many I have taught and mentored, I have seen that tantric practice can bring out deep, sometimes painful psychological material, in a way that is often not explained in traditional teachings. I want to explore how our Western psychological understanding of what we call the unconscious can shed light on what is actually unfolding in tantric practice. This will clarify how tantric practise can be a valuable way of relating to our inner process and heal psychological difficulties, when practised skilfully.

In Part Three I look at one of the key elements of the way tantra is taught, namely the emphasis on the relationship between teacher and student. In this I wish to explore the significance of the role of the guide in practice, but also the way in which this role can be developed to orient towards what I am going to call a more person-centred approach. This is to emphasise that our individual process needs to be central to how we integrate tantra.

As Tibetan Buddhism arrives in the West increasingly there are people who make intensive study of the technicalities of deity practice, particularly exploring the traditional texts and commentaries. Today many of these commentaries have been translated and are available to Western practitioners. In this book, however, it is not my intention to approach the subject in this way. I am not a scholar and make no pretensions to be so. Rather I am a meditator and wish to write from a place of how meditation practice touches me and what enables a greater depth of experience in myself and my students. I am, however, also a psychotherapist and as such have wanted to emphasise what can be most relevant to our psychological nature and our inner process.

To do this I will refer to the tradition of oral teachings I have received from some of my teachers, in particular H.H. Dalai Lama, Song Rinpoche, Lama Thubten Yeshe, Lama Zopa Rinpoche and my retreat guide Ven. Gen Jhampa Wangdu. I also wish to draw upon my own relationship to practice developed particularly within the context of meditation retreat, where tantric practices really come alive. It is in the context of retreat that we begin to discover what many of our difficulties with practice as Westerners can be, but also how to resolve them. I will also draw on the conversations I have had with many of my older peers who have practised intensively for many years and have spoken of the extraordinary benefits of practice but also of their struggles and problems. Finally, I will turn to years of teaching and entering into a dialogue with those I teach around how they experience these practices; what helps and what does not. I hope in the course of this exploration that the reader will begin to gain a sense of what is possible as we approach the tantric tradition from a more embodied place of creativity and exploration. Through this we can gain a taste of the extraordinary quality of this rich and profound path. This hopefully will make it accessible to those who have an interest in developing their practice as well as those who, as long-term practitioners, have encountered obstacles in their practice.

What I am exploring here holds closely to the essential nature of the Vajrayana or tantric tradition as shown to me by my teachers and attempts to get to the heart of what this way of embodied meditation is about. I have a profound love for this path and feel that it is only through understanding the essence of tantra that we will genuinely integrate it into our experience and enable practice to come alive. This was at the heart of what I learned from Lama Thubten Yeshe and his extraordinary capacity to understand Westerners. Following his example, I have needed to explore what enables us to gain experience and recognise what may not be not helpful. This is not about cherry picking those things we like and getting rid of what we don't. This also does not mean we throw away the tradition. It is about exploring how we can be genuinely touched and transformed by this incredibly valuable resource. I suspect this is something that may have happened in Nepal, Tibet and China, perhaps it is now our turn in the West to take up the challenge. This is a time of discovery, of learning from our mistakes and gradually bringing out the gold from the alchemical process.

Part One

A Way of Meditation

1

Preparations for Practice

IN EXPLORING THIS JOURNEY into the practice of tantra it is
important to clarify something at the beginning, that was emphasised
to me in my early years as a practitioner. Someone who wishes to
practise tantra needs to have a ground of understanding of certain
very significant Buddhist principles. This is in part to ensure that
when we embark upon this path, we do so with the right intention.
It is also to ensure that we have a relatively sound psychological basis
upon which practice can grow. This path requires that we respect its
sacred nature and do not use it as some kind of materialistic
acquisition or merely intellectual pursuit. Historically tantra has
often been held as a secret practice not to be displayed or exhibited
to others. This is less the case today where it is more openly taught,
even so, we need to retain a respect for its sacredness and depth of
meaning.

Our underlying preparation for entering into the tantric path is
often described on three levels, known as the three principles of the
path. The first of these is the cultivation of what is sometimes called
renunciation or more accurately 'definite emergence' (Tibetan: *nge
jung*). The implication of this quality is that we need to recognise the
psychological habits that bind us in ways of being that are counter to

the process of awakening. Definite emergence is the willingness to begin to wake up and face where we have become caught in unconscious habits in our life. We often unconsciously take refuge in things that perpetuate a kind of anaesthetised way of being so that we do not have to look at ourselves. We can use many different aspects of our life to do this. We may be caught up in material possessions and sensory gratification in an attempt to satisfy ourselves. We may take refuge in food, alcohol, work, relationships, the television and many other things, so that we do not have to face ourselves, with our fears and insecurities. Renunciation in one sense is seeing that these things are not ultimately satisfactory and cannot bring true lasting happiness. It is not the things of our life that are the problem, however, but our relationship to them and the attachment that arises. Definite emergence is the willingness to wake up, face our habit patterns and live our lives consciously and courageously, taking responsibility for our journey. Renunciation tends to suggest giving up or avoiding attachment to things that pull us into more confusion and unconsciousness. Definite emergence on the other hand is to engage fully with life, but with an awareness that faces what we are doing.

The foundation of tantric practice is definite emergence, where we are willing to wake up to our habits and emotional motives. This leads us to the next level of intention, which is that we do not engage in this path with a view that is interested in just our own happiness or salvation. While the practice of tantra will undoubtedly bring a great sense of inner peace and happiness for oneself, we need to be broader in our intention than just our own personal interest. The second important quality of the tantric practitioner is therefore, the growing experience of what is called *bodhichitta* or the awakening mind. This could be described as the aspiration to awaken to our innate potential for the welfare of others.

We may embark upon the spiritual path for a variety of reasons. We may be seeking some sense of meaning in our life. We may be responding to a deep call to wake up and view life differently. We may be seeking a means to overcome our unhappiness and gain some peace of mind. We may also embark on this journey because we have a growing sense of concern for the welfare of others. When we open our hearts to the presence of others in our life, we see that they are no different to us in how they are also wishing to experience happiness and be free of suffering. Why should we consider our happiness alone, when our lives are so intimately bound up in the lives of others. What we have, what we do and what we experience and enjoy in our life is intimately related to the presence, the kindness, the efforts and often the hardship of others. We cannot ignore this inter-dependence. To make this life meaningful we begin to see how we can use it for the welfare of others and of the planet that supports us. From a place of compassion and loving kindness towards all those around us we can then consider what would be of greatest benefit.

In tantric practice we recognise that our innate nature is essentially pure, clear and spacious. When awakened, we see that the qualities this brings will be of great benefit in our relationship to others. If we can actualise some experience of this extraordinary inner potential then our lives and our ability to serve others will change radically. We can see this in the example of those who have awakened this innate potential like H.H. Dalai Lama. Bodhichitta, the awakening mind, is the willingness to dedicate our life to the service of others and to gradually awaken our innate buddha potential to do so.

Bodhichitta is often spoken of as the intention to attain the goal of buddhahood for the welfare of others. This is true, but there is the danger of becoming too goal orientated in a way that is more like a kind of ego ambition. We need to understand that bodhichitta is paradoxical; while we may aspire to become a Buddha, this has to be something grounded in the present. It is in the present we engage in opening to our innate nature so that we can manifest that quality in the world in every moment. When we practise tantra, bodhicitta takes on another level of meaning. Our relationship to a deity is a relationship to our innate buddha potential that can be awakened right now. We open to an expression of wholeness that is not just some distant aspiration to become a Buddha, it is immediate, in the present. Bodhichitta then becomes the awakening of this innate quality of wholeness in each moment as we live our life and the deity is embodied through us.

There is an expression in the *Heruka* tantra I have always found very profound, where it says "to benefit sentient beings I offer myself immediately to the Buddhas". This sense of surrender to the Buddhas is an opening in the present moment to be a vessel or vehicle to manifest in the world. Bodhichitta is like stepping into the flow of a river that is taking us to the ocean of enlightenment whether we will it or not. We do not have to keep checking to see if the river is still going there. We open to its natural flow and surrender to that process in each moment giving ourselves to the welfare of others. To do this our ego has to begin to get out of the way and not be goal oriented. Otherwise we will find ourselves striving to become a Buddha and this striving itself will become an obstacle.

To embark upon this awakening process, we can see that the ego has to gradually relinquish its dominant position. It is for this reason that we engage in the next level of preparation for the path of tantra, which is to recognise our innate emptiness. This is often described as an understanding of *shunyata* or the wisdom of emptiness.

Unless we understand that our sense of self or ego and the reality of the world around us lack any solid, enduring and inherent nature we obstruct or limit the transformative nature of tantra. We limit our potential for change. We can see this on a relatively ordinary level where we may hold onto a sense of ourselves and habitual ways of being that give us a feeling of security and control. We do this because it is familiar and safe whereas change is a challenge. Circumstances may require that we adapt and adjust, but something in us can resist it and does not want to let go. At some point, however, we may have no choice, even though this is very uncomfortable. Change is always possible if we are aware that everything is arising and passing moment to moment and only has the appearance of solidity and permanence. If we can rest in the natural fluidity of our being and see ourselves as a process unfolding, then change is completely natural and transformation occurs with greater ease. In the practice of tantra we begin to open ourselves to the natural flow of creative transformation that is possible because we have no enduring nature. Tantra rests in the essentially fluid empty nature of appearances as they manifest and dissolve within the sphere of clear awareness. This is particularly so with our sense of self.

Many people hear that in Buddhism we speak of 'no self' or 'emptiness of self', or that the ego has to be eliminated on the path. These ideas, while holding some truth, can be very confusing. When we speak of surrendering and giving ourselves to the service of others, as I have described before, a process begins that can go deeper and deeper. The ego, our ordinary sense of self, does indeed need to begin to let go so that it is not so dominant in our lives. Its dominant position may have served us through part of our life to cultivate the capacity to be in the world, to have work, relationships and so on.

We do need a relatively stable sense of identity to function in the world and the ego is a central focus to this.

The ego, therefore, is not something to be seen as all bad. We need to develop a healthy sense of self, but the way we contract and tighten around it can be very destructive and becomes the source of suffering. In Buddhism we call this 'ego-grasping' (Tibetan: *dag tsin*). Ego-grasping is the instinctual disposition to cling to the sense of 'me' as though it actually has a solid and enduring, inherent nature. This is something that *feels* to be true especially when someone upsets us or we are frightened or angry. We feel very solid and tight as we contract around an apparently substantial or 'true' sense of me. This tight feeling of me is the inherently existent me that is actually not real and cannot be found if we investigate more deeply. Although it can feel to be solid and truly existent it is in fact something we have created, albeit unconsciously, as we grew up.

This means that we have two aspects of the ego. One is a natural focus of identity that simply conveys a sense of orientation and the capacity to say I am sitting, eating and so on. This is the healthy sense of our relative identity needed to function in the world. The other is a contracted tight sense of me that is more emotionally charged. It is this latter *me* that has no basis of existence. It is merely created by contraction like the surface tension of a bubble. When we begin to recognise this contracted sense of me and see that it actually has no true existence then we can start to let go.

Letting go means that we begin to relax and allow our sense of self to be more fluid, more permeable and flexible. As the contraction softens and opens we will begin to feel more inner space. Life is less of a battle or struggle because we are not so tight and contracted. Our reactions to the world and events loosen and we will not suffer so much because we are not holding the core of suffering, the ego, so solidly. This does not mean we are getting rid of the ego. It was never there as a solid phenomenon in the first place, it was empty. Our sense of me is still needed as a relative functional identity that operates in the world and knows what I am doing, saying and so on. What goes is the solid sense of contraction at its core. There is inner space and movement because nothing is held and locked in time as a solid me.

We begin to see that we are merely a moment to moment unfolding process. Just as a river is a process of the flow of water it has no enduring substance. So too we are a momentarily changing process upon which a name been placed that we will answer to. This is the realisation needed as we embark upon the practice of tantra. Then there will be the fluidity in our awareness to enable creative transformation to unfold. Tantra is a way of being with the natural fluidity of reality as it unfolds moment to moment. Unless we have the capacity to let go of the contraction that freezes our experience into solid forms then there is no potential for change. With the awareness of our empty, insubstantial, fluid nature, change can occur and the practice of tantra will transform us.

I have described what Lama Tsongkapa called 'the three principle aspects of the path'. His view was that if we begin to cultivate these qualities then we will have a good basis upon which to practise tantra. That does not mean we have to have a perfect experience of them. This is something that grows with time. It does mean that they are important foundations upon which our spiritual life and tantric path in particular can grow with skill and clear intention. As we deepen our experience of these three guiding principles, we can feel confident that we are changing the tendencies that run counter to our spiritual path. If we continually come back to them they are a touch-stone for our journey forward.

2

Levels of Practice

It MAY BE HELPFUL to clarify what differentiates tantra from other aspects of Buddhism and to place it in the broader context of Buddhist understanding. This is not a simple thing to do but there is a way in which we can see an evolution of practice that changes as we move forward so that some of the apparent contradictions within the Buddhist path can make sense. To clarify this, it is useful to consider three levels of practice that build one upon the other. To describe this in its simplest form we could consider Figure 1.

If we begin with what I am calling the 'path of cultivation' we see an approach to practice that has a fundamental duality at its root. This is the duality that sees what leads to suffering and what leads to happiness in a very basic way. We are cultivating the discernment or discrimination which understands that what is unwholesome leads to suffering and what is wholesome leads to happiness. Positive states of mind are to be cultivated and negative and detrimental states are to be overcome or abandoned. This path gives us the basis of our ethical sense that we live with a moral code which abandons what is unwholesome and holds to actions of body, speech and mind that are beneficial to both self and others. With this level of practice often great emphasis is given to the intellectual study of Buddhist principles of psychology and philosophy as well to the cultivation or accumulation of what is called merit or positive virtuous actions.

Figure 1

The path of Cultivation	Sutra	Considering what is to be accepted and abandoned, wholesome and unwholesome, pure and impure. Basic dualism.
The path of Transformation	Tantra	Releasing the essential nature within whatever is present, revealed through a process of purification and transformation. Subtle dualism.
The path of Self-liberation	Mahamudra & Dzog chen	Recognising the innate primordial non-dual nature of whatever arises and allowing its natural liberation. The path of non-modification.

The value of this path in a very basic way is that we recognise we are responsible for the effect of our actions of body, speech and mind as they shape our life. If we wish to experience a happy, fulfilling and meaningful life then we need to overcome certain tendencies as deluded and unwholesome and cultivate those habits that lead to a beneficial effect. In our desire to be 'good' and 'wholesome' we are encouraged to tame, control or abandon what is not.

The hazard, however, with the notion of abandoning or overcoming what is unwholesome is that so called negative emotional habits potentially become repressed rather than transformed. This can lead us to 'split off' and suppress what is unacceptable leading towards the creation of an unconscious shadow. The basic duality of this path can cause us to become somewhat dogmatic or rigid about what is acceptable and what is not. In its extreme it can lead to a kind of rigorous fundamentalism that becomes caught up in superego ideals that are judgmental and lack openness and compassion. If we hold relative beliefs and doctrine as ultimate truths then our mind has solidified this duality in a detrimental way that no longer sees the truth that is beyond that duality.

It is interesting that the next path, the 'path of transformation', addresses this question of dualism in a way that does not lead us to split what is acceptable and what is not. At the heart of the path of transformation is the understanding that whatever arises and whatever is within us has an innate pure nature if we can reveal it or release it. This is the alchemical view that sees that whatever we bring to the process of transformation can be gradually brought to its innate potential, the gold or philosopher's stone that is the result of transformation.

This is the path of tantra that works with the knowledge that all of who we are is the essential material of transformation. If we place ourselves into the process of tantric transformation we do not need to say this is acceptable and this is not. Everything is seen as the raw material of transformation. This includes our inner emotional states and the energetic nature of our being in its raw and unrefined state as well as the body.

This inclusiveness means we do not try to shut away what is unacceptable because we can see it is part of the process. In this way we do not fall into the trap of creating a deepening shadow of repressed material. That side of our nature is invited into the process of transformation. There remains, however, a subtle duality because we are still saying that this needs to be refined and purified into its pure nature. Transformation still implies that something needs to be different and to change to become fully awakened. If there is a danger in this path it is in one respect the tendency to hold onto ideals of what we should become. There is also the potential to delude ourselves into thinking we are capable of transforming certain things when actually we are not. Sadly, I have worked with people who, having practised tantra for years, begin to realize they have not actually transformed very much on a deeper psychological level. An important requirement for this path is that we have a sound psychological ground to hold the transformation of deep often powerful psychological emotional and energetic processes.

In the third level of path there is an awareness that actually nothing needs to be different from what it is, because everything is in itself primordially pure and empty. Our problem is that we do not see it. This is the basic blindness (Tibetan: *ma rigpa*; ignorance, not seeing) that does not see that all appearances arising within our relative world are not other than the play of non-dual awareness, of emptiness. We hold relative things to have substantial enduring form in a way that does not see their fleeting empty nature. They are, however, merely reflections of the mind, clear-light mind, or primordial mind. Although we use the term mind this is the fleeting unfolding flow of awareness momentarily arising and empty of any innate enduring nature, it is the source of all the appearances that arise. When we recognize this, when we *see*, then we see the illusory nature of appearances as they are. We do not have to do something to them to change them, or to purify them and make them different, they are already essentially the nature of awareness and empty. This is the path of non-modification, we are not trying to transform anything.

This is a path that does not engage with ideals of transformation, it does not become interested in complex details and systems of practice. It goes beneath conceptual experience and touches directly into the root of our non-dual clear nature. When we totally open to this depth of awareness (Tibetan: *rigpa*) all appearances are liberated in their nature, they are self-liberated. This is the practice of mahamudra and dzogchen.

If there is a hazard to this last path, it can be that sustaining the subtlety of view it demands is a challenge. It is considered an advanced approach to practice, which is why it is usually considered the final stage or completion of practice. Due to the subtlety of the view held it is not difficult to fool ourselves into thinking we are able to liberate all of our experiences into emptiness and non-duality when in fact we aren't. Rather than going beyond the ego-grasping in our nature it is still well established and instead we are going into a kind of dissociated absorption that looks like rigpa. We are spiritually by-passing, to use Welwood's phrase.

These then are the three paths described in the diagram above. We could say that we need to begin with the first and proceed through to the last. There are those that see the potential for an instantaneous leap into the third of these paths, the 'path of self-liberation', which is how dzog chen is often considered. However, this is not an easy way to follow and as I have said before, we may delude ourselves. If we cannot automatically do this we need to come back to the earlier 'path of transformation'. This is true for many or perhaps most of us so that we prepare the ground for the shift into the third phase. The path of transformation, however, may also have its challenges so that we are not easily able to use the practices to bring about the results we may wish for. We may become caught in the belief that we can include everything that is raw and disturbed in our nature, thinking that we are transforming it when in fact we are just taken over by it. When this is the case we may need to come back again to the basic ground of practice in the 'path of cultivation', discerning what is wholesome and beneficial and what is not.

These three paths are not separate from one another and almost certainly we will need to move back and forth between them. There are times when it is important to make the discernment to abandon certain things that are not useful for our practice or our lives, and to uphold ethical principles. There are times when we can see that to include all of who we are in the process of transformation is the compassionate and real way to be with our practice so as not to avoid our shadow. There are times when we need to just open and allow what is arising to be as it is in its innate empty clear-light nature, liberated because we don't interfere with it.

In what we are exploring here within the practice of tantra we see how all these phases are there in the background. At the root of tantra is a skilful ethical ground upon which it is based. Tantra emphasises transformation and the recognition that however we are, has at its core our pristine buddha-nature. This can be revealed through the processes of both purification and transformation. The third phase of self-liberation is also crucially important in enabling us to deeply digest and integrate what is transformed so that it is rooted in the nature of mind and emptiness.

3

The Essence of Tantra

I AM OFTEN ASKED, "what is the essential principle of tantra?"
This is never an easy question to answer in a relatively brief way but
I feel it may be useful to attempt to do so. I am aware that there will
inevitably be different perspectives, so I do not want to imply that
this is some kind of definitive or correct view. I can only offer my
own opinion from my experience of practice. I am also aware that
there are many different aspects of tantra that have evolved over
time, so I wish to focus on what for me is the heart of tantra as it is
most likely to be practiced in the West. In order to clarify what I will
describe I have attempted to put this into a diagram in Figure 2.

Perhaps it could be said simply, that tantra involves the
transformation of our mind, emotions and body. It could equally be
described as the liberation of our innate primordially pure nature of
mind, emotion and body which are the three aspects of our buddha-
nature, known as *dharmakaya, sambhogakaya* and *nirmanakaya*. [1]
Dharmakaya is our pure mind, sambhogakaya is our pure energy-
body and nirmankaya our emanation body, the body within which
the former two manifest. These three components are there within
our nature right now in their ordinary aspect. Even though they may
not be developed at this time, our mind, emotions and physical body

Figure 2
The Essence of Tantra

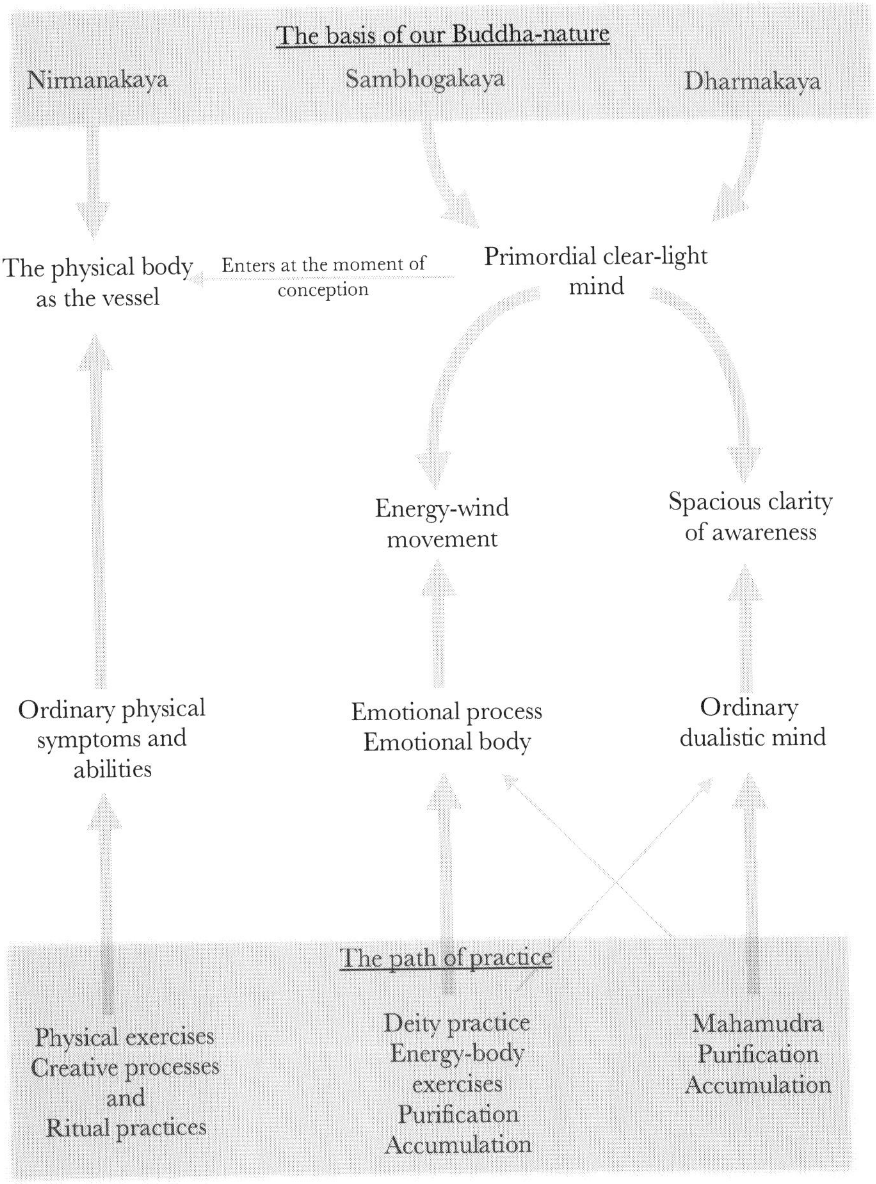

The basis of our Buddha-nature

Nirmanakaya   Sambhogakaya   Dharmakaya

The physical body   Enters at the moment of   Primordial clear-light
as the vessel   conception   mind

Energy-wind   Spacious clarity
movement   of awareness

Ordinary physical   Emotional process   Ordinary
symptoms and   Emotional body   dualistic mind
abilities

The path of practice

Physical exercises   Deity practice   Mahamudra
Creative processes   Energy-body   Purification
and   exercises   Accumulation
Ritual practices   Purification
                      Accumulation

are nevertheless the basis of the three bodies or *kayas* of a Buddha through the process of tantric transformation.

At the heart of tantra is the liberation of our innate wisdom nature through a dynamic process of creative transformation. The essential nature of our consciousness is clear and pure, our clear-light mind, sometimes called 'primordial mind'. It is 'primordially pure' in that it has never been defiled, but is obscured by ignorance, the confusion of our dualistic conceptual mind. The continuity of this consciousness enters the fertilised egg at the time of conception bringing with it the accumulation of lifetimes of confusion and emotional habit patterns. The practice of tantra is intended to purify our mind of these obscurations and awaken its innate nature.

Our primordial clear-light mind has two significant attributes. These are inseparably connected as two dimensions of the same unified phenomenon. One attribute is a quality of spacious awareness, clarity and brightness, the nature of the mind itself. The other is a quality of energy, movement and luminosity. This second quality is known as the energy-body or energy-wind upon which the mind rests like a rider on a horse. When I said that tantra involves the transformation of our emotions, what I am referring to is this energy-body, in Tibetan *lung ku*, that is sometimes known as the 'emotional body'.

In the practice of tantra, therefore, these two inseparable attributes of mind and energy-wind (Tib: *lung*[2]) are liberated from their obscuring veils through methods that awaken, activate and transform their nature. When liberated, our mind then becomes what is called the truth body or dharmakaya, our energy-body or emotional body becomes the blissful, indestructible 'vajra' body known as sambhogakaya. Because these two aspects are contained within the vessel of the physical body, this then becomes known as the emanation body or nirmanakaya.

Tantra therefore contains ways of meditation that are partly oriented to the transformation of the mind and others that are oriented to the transformation of the energy-wind that pervades the whole of our emotional, psychological and physical life. Since our mind and its energy are intimately connected, we can say that what transforms one will also have an effect on the other. They are never completely separate. These two in turn promote the health of our physical body and our capacity for embodiment.

The transformation of our mind is done both directly as well as indirectly. Directly because of powerful methods that clarify awareness and clear the mind of its confusion and ignorance. Indirectly because within tantric practice great emphasis is placed upon the purification and transformation of the energy-wind upon which the mind rests. If you purify and transform one you affect the other. There are those within the tantric tradition who have asserted the view that our relationship to the body and its subtle energy-body or vajra-body is even more important than the mind. This may be controversial but has a very sound basis from the point of certain tantras such as the *Heruka* tantra going back to the time of the early *mahasiddhas* of India.[3]

At present our energy-body can be in varying degrees of health or ill health, which is reflected in both our emotional and physical life. When we awaken this energy and transform it within tantric practice it moves from being disturbed, blocked and unhealthy to becoming the source of immense vitality, luminosity and bliss. This in turn becomes the basis of health, creativity and 'wisdom energy'. It is a distinctive attribute of tantra that as this energy awakens, it is given a channel through which it can be transformed. When we understand how tantra works to transform our energy-body, we could say that many of our creative activities could become a means for doing so, not just sitting on the cushion and not just the visualisation of deities. This is partly why within tantra there are many different kinds of practice such as creative processes, body-oriented exercises and rituals, all of which can act as a means of transformation.

However, the primary way of transformation in traditional tantric practice, is through a relationship to a deity which is a manifestation of our innate nature. This relationship to a deity acts as a natural channel for our vitality to be awakened and transformed. The deity brings us into relationship with the source of our innate buddha potential and therefore the source of our intrinsic health. It also opens us to that same awakened quality possessed by all the Buddhas as a source of blessings and inspiration.

Central to tantra, therefore, is a process of deity visualisation. In some ways tantra has mastered the art of visualisation, which is a natural capacity of the mind used in many spiritual and psychological traditions. Our mind readily fantasises and imagines. This is something we find very natural as children but sometimes closes down as we become adults because we have a somewhat ambivalent relationship to fantasy. Jung once said that in the East they disregard fantasy not because they think it is childish as we often do in the West, but because it has been turned into a spiritual practice.

Visualisation is a powerful capacity of the mind that is intimately connected to the energy-wind. Visualisation is not just imagining things with no effect, it has an effect: it changes the mind and our energy and importantly we *feel* it. If I visualise I am a useless piece of garbage then that affects my whole constitution and is what I will become. If I visualise I have good qualities and am capable, then that is what I can become. We do this all the time, in both a positive and negative way, in relatively ordinary contexts. Tennis players, for example, are often taught to visualise their strokes in such a way that when they actually come to play, their body naturally follows this visualised pattern.

The power of bringing visualised forms of deities into our awareness is that it opens up a relationship to our innate nature and its qualities. This process is like tuning a radio to a particular frequency, it connects us to the source. We also attune to that same quality, possessed by all the Buddhas, that dwells within the dimension of sambhogakaya. The deity is not just an *image* of buddha-nature, it is an emanation of it and embodies particular archetypal qualities. When we bring this vision into our awareness we open up a relationship and can begin to activate this quality in our nature. Once this relationship is awake, the intention is to begin to embody this quality rather than just let it remain a mental image. In deity practice the process of visualisation brings a deeper and deeper taste of our true nature and our potential wholeness, our buddha-nature. Our practice then becomes integrated and more real as we increasingly bring the deity into an embodied, felt experience.

Tantra is sometimes known as the resultant path because it enables us to directly access an experience of our buddha potential, by bringing the result of the path into the present. Often, we are taught to consider the Buddhist path as one that gradually unfolds towards a state of enlightenment. On one level this is true. But we should remember that our pure buddha-nature has always been present within us. Tantra works with the paradox, that there is an unfolding path with a goal and yet it is in the present that we can open directly to our enlightened nature. This is specifically through the activation of the deity as the personification of this potential brought into the present.

We could say this requires that we have great faith in the presence of our innate nature as the root of wisdom, meaning and wholeness. We *do* need this faith, but with tantra this faith can be turned into a profound sense of knowing, that enables us to rest more and more deeply in the presence of that nature. Perhaps to illustrate this we could take the metaphor of fog. On a very foggy morning we may see a figure walking towards us that is just a grey blur. As the fog begins to clear or we walk closer, the outline of the form begins to become more solid and then details start to emerge. Eventually we have a clear recognition of who is there before us. Lama Yeshe used to say that we have foggy minds and that with meditation and purification we can clear that fog, then our innate nature shines through like the sun shining through clouds.

In tantra therefore, there are two ways in which this awakening happens. One is, as I have described, through a relationship to a deity that brings a special quality of meaning, within a particular form. The other is with meditation known as mahamudra, where we are not considering a deity form, but rather the natural quality of spacious awareness itself. This meditation on spacious awareness gradually brings us into a direct experience of our primordial nature of mind. Deity practice purifies, heals and transforms the nature of the energy-winds upon which the mind is said to 'ride'. This also effects our capacity to awaken the nature of the mind. Mahamudra practice goes directly to the clear awareness of that primordial mind. In tantric practice, therefore, we can move back and forth between these two ways of practice, one on the form of the deity and the other on the spacious nature of awareness. They support and deepen each other.

In the process of practice, therefore, we gradually purify and transform the subtle energy-wind and the mind both of which abide within our body. We can do this in ways that are often described as either peaceful, increasing, powerful or wrathful. Peaceful ways are used to pacify and heal our mind/energy to make it more refined and healthy. This process clears blocked, unhealthy, depressed energy and brings a natural quality of health and contentment that is then able to settle and open. Increasing means to re-vitalise and enrich our mind/energy so that it is full of inspiration, vitality, bliss and joy. This inspiration brings a quality of interest and enthusiasm that is deeply satisfying and nourishing. It makes our lives fruitful and our actions of body, speech and mind successful and effective in the process of transformation. Powerful methods relate to our capacity to channel and harness the natural potency of our mind/energy and use it for the purpose of transformation. Again, we can see this expressed in ways that can make us more effective in what we do as any blocked energy is released and made accessible to us. Powerful transformation leads us to awaken to the power of our intrinsic clear nature, and as we awaken we see how this can affect reality. Finally, wrathful method implies that we utilise a kind of forceful intention to overcome and harness aspects of our nature that are potentially shadowy and demonic. Wrathful methods bring us into an archetypal domain where we treat like with like. We channel forces in ourselves that are wild, passionate and aggressive through a process that has a similar nature to what is to be transformed.

When we consider these four ways of transformation in the tantric tradition we may think that this is exclusively within the context of deity practice. It is true that the deities of tantra tend to utilise one or other of these ways of transformation. It is useful to consider, however, that if we understand the principle at work in these ways of transforming our energy, we can apply them in many different contexts. Peaceful ways can for example be experienced through the body with subtle processes of healing and movement. Increasing and enriching ways can be through many different creative activities such as ritual or art. Powerful may mean using more energetic activities, some of which may be very physical, that help to channel and transform our energy. Wrathful may mean bringing destructive energy into some process that magnetises the forces of our physical passion or aggression to transform it, again, often through physical practices or rituals.

Tantra is a way of liberating our mind and our energetic nature from its present relatively limited state to its fully awakened potential. As I have said earlier, when our mind is freed of its obscuring defilements its true clear-light nature shines through as our innate dharmakaya or truth body. When the energy-body, or emotional body, that is currently disturbed and blocked by emotional patterns, is purified, it becomes our natural indestructible energy-body of bliss, known as our sambhogakaya or enjoyment body. We need to remember that both of these aspects of our nature are present even now within the physical body and so it is our relationship to the body that is a primary resource in the process of transformation. When we are aware of this, it means that our relationship to the body as the vessel of tantric practice is where we must begin.

Having given this brief synopsis of how we might understand the process of tantra, I will begin to look at the way we might enter into actual practice. In this I will not discuss the intricacies of particular deity practices; these are to be found in the countless commentaries taught about deity practice. It is not the specific complex symbolism of each tantra that I want to explore. Rather I want to look at the inner process of meditation practice that we need to embark upon if we are to make this complexity and symbolism touch our inner reality as a felt experience.

4

The Challenge of Our Time

THE TANTRIC TRADITION has come to the West and many
of us are fascinated by this extraordinary path. We could attribute
this attraction to a number of things. In the late 60s and early 70s
many Westerners, of whom I was one, were part of an adventure to
the East to find spiritual depth that seemed absent in the West.
Tibetan Buddhism appeared to respond to a need for understanding
and wisdom many of us hungered for. The tantric tradition was part
of this package and while we may not have always understood what
we were getting ourselves involved in, there was something exotic
and exciting about the magic and mystery it seemed to be imbued
with. Meeting Tibetan lamas was also something that offered an
irresistible source of guides, teachers and gurus that we were
magnetically drawn to. It was inevitable with this collection of
circumstances that many of us dived headlong into Tibetan
Buddhism and as part of that process were given tantric
empowerments and practices that we then tried to integrate into our
lives.

From my own experience back in 1973, I felt a level of wonder and excitement at being given this opportunity while I was in Nepal and India. On one level it felt very natural to dive in and immerse myself in the teachings and practices I was given. I was in awe of what I was seeing and hearing. Very quickly I felt a sense of enthusiasm and commitment to this path and wanted to devote myself to practice. There was a great deal of idealism in this, and I don't think that in those early days I was aware of what this path might entail, but I genuinely wanted to try. At that time there wasn't a great deal translated into English, and the teachings we received were in their raw undiluted Tibetan form. This often meant we were having to take in something relatively obscure and gradually try to digest it. Our enthusiasm and thirst for the teachings, however, meant we would endure a lot of hardship for the sake of what we were learning. Some of us were also very keen to try and emulate the Tibetans' cultural way and would buy all the ritual equipment and even begin to dress like Tibetans. When I think of this in retrospect I can see that many of us were rather lost and our identity somewhat confused, but then we were hippies in our twenties often dislodged and alienated from our own Western culture.

Times have moved forward and it is now a familiar thing for Tibetan teachers to come and live in the West, particularly in the USA. Here they have established a powerful culture of revered lamas, principally *tulkus*, or reincarnated lamas, giving some of the most extraordinary and profound empowerments and teachings. Today there are also a vast number of translated texts, commentaries and teachings in English, Spanish, German, French, Dutch and Italian, so that it is possible to study and acquire a huge amount of knowledge about Tibetan Buddhism and tantra in particular. Our Tibetan teachers have been very skilful at creating the conditions to preserve, maintain and transmit the tantric tradition so that it does not become lost since they were evicted from their homeland. Many of them have been very generous in giving empowerments into their cherished practices as well as extensive and detailed commentaries.

Having been a practitioner of Tibetan Buddhism for over 45 years and teaching and mentoring Westerners for the last 30 years, I feel increasingly there is value in looking at the efficacy of tantric practice in the West. There are many dedicated practitioners who have devoted years to practice and have gradually deepened their experience under the guidance of traditional teachers and teachings.

We have given great care and attention to establishing centres of learning and practice in the West. We have supported the Tibetans in their aspiration to preserve the Tibetan tradition and its culture in all its rich diversity. I personally devoted many of my early years as a Tibetan Buddhist to building a Buddhist centre and then receiving extensive teachings of some of the key texts and commentaries of both sutra and tantra traditions from eminent Tibetan lamas. People meeting Tibetan Buddhism today are extremely fortunate to have all the conditions to study the tantric tradition in great depth without many of the hardships we encountered in those early years.

As the years pass it is, I feel, worth considering how this transmission of Tibetan Buddhism and especially tantra has impacted upon us as Westerners. I feel it's useful to begin to ask ourselves a number of questions: how is the practice of tantra really being integrated into our Western experience? Are we practising in a way that is truly enabling us to attain a depth of realisation? Further, we might ask: is the practice we are doing genuinely touching us and healing and transforming our psychological and emotional life? There are no simple answers to these questions particularly because we are all very individual in our capacity to practise as well as in the nature of our psychological makeup. There are also so many styles and variations in the way tantra is taught by Tibetan and Western teachers in the West.

Increasingly, in my role as a mentor and teacher, I speak with people who are clearly not finding this process easy, but then whoever said it would be? From what I have seen, it is evident that translating the tantric tradition into real experience is not straightforward. It is not that practitioners lack commitment and a genuine desire to practice. Neither is it that there is something wrong with us as Westerners that makes us somehow spiritually inept or less capable. Nor that the essence of tantra is inappropriate for us. We can see by the way many Tibetans manifest extraordinary qualities, that the tantric tradition has all the ingredients necessary to enable transformation.

The number of Westerners who begin to practice tantra and then lose faith or confidence in practice, however, is significant. This can often be because it is not easy to fully understand how tantra works and its psychological relevance. While we may have great expectations as to the effect of practice, these are not always met. For a long time I looked towards Tibetan Buddhism as a way of resolving some of my core psychological problems and this was not necessarily what happened. It is also increasingly apparent that some people do gain notable experiences from practice but this does not necessarily change, heal or transform deeper psychological problems. I mentor many people who feel they are very dedicated to practice but don't find a way to bring this into relationship with their psychological issues and sometimes deeper emotional trauma. This can lead to placing a veneer of practice over deep unresolved psychological issues.

To repeat something I said in my introduction, in my own journey and my work teaching and mentoring, I have seen that we cannot separate the spiritual and psychological processes. When we do we are in grave danger of what John Welwood called spiritual bypassing, or simply coming up against psychological obstacles in our path that are not being resolved. With many I have mentored these psychological issues are only addressed either when we bring them into relationship with our practice in a skilful way, or when they are explored through some kind of parallel therapeutic process. Either way we cannot assume that a spiritual practice alone will resolve them.

For a growing new generation of Western practitioners, one message comes through clearly; they wish for an approach to practice that really touches them psychologically and is emotionally healing and transformational. This cannot always be found in the traditional form of practice. It is here that we need to consider how we might bring together aspects of Western psychological understanding alongside or within our Buddhist practice. This need not change the essential way tantric practice works, but it will mean that how we apply it becomes more directly appropriate to our Western psychological needs.

There are those who find the traditional form of practice relatively straightforward and seem to settle very naturally into the entire process. This may well be the result of previous life experience although we cannot clearly know this. However, with those who do not find this easy a number of key issues seem to arise. One difficulty many encounter when they first become involved in Tibetan Buddhism, is that the complexity of certain aspects of tantric practice can be hard to relate to and that reciting long rituals is simply too much. Even those who are dedicated to doing complex *sadhana* recitations (the texts that describe the process of deity visualisation), after a while can begin to feel they become dry and mechanical; the sense of connection weakens. Having a lama close to hand can help sustain this, but people practicing on their own can easily lose the inspiration that is so necessary for practice to feel alive.

The difficulty voiced by older hands at practice is often that they have received many empowerments into different practices with commitments they are not able to maintain. I have heard certain Tibetan lamas, such as Gelek Rinpoche, express that we are vulnerable to receiving empowerments into too many different deities and then not really benefiting. Some people I know have said that after many years they simply stopped their practice because they felt the connection had gone and they were just doing things mechanically. Those who have gone through this, often feel considerable inner conflict and feelings of guilt. This is made worse by the view that a breach of commitment is often seen as the cause of terrible consequences, principally birth in some awful state. If we take this view very literally, we are likely to suffer horrible inner conflict because we have become involved in something that we are not able to fulfil. While I was in India I became aware that I was in danger of exactly this kind of problem. I decided that I was not going to receive any more empowerments because I simply had enough. I did not wish to get myself into deeper water with practices I might never use and more commitments.

The question of the complexity of tantric practice is not simple to resolve. Complex detailed sadhanas are very familiar to Tibetans but may well not suit Westerners. There are people I encounter who have a strong intuitive resonance with what tantra touches in us and yet do not find a way of practice that suits them because of the complexity of a traditional approach. How, then, do we discover a simpler way to practise that still retains the essential heart of the practice? This is where the value of tantra is not about complexity, or accumulating empowerments and reciting long texts, nor about gaining intellectual knowledge. It is how practice really touches us and affects us on a felt level and then changes our mind. This may mean, in part, that we need to have a different attitude towards the way we step into the tantric process. We may need to stop having what we might call an ambition to receive more and more advanced practices and more and more knowledge. Instead, we need to recognise the value of foundation practices that can also take us into deep experiences. We can be in a hurry to receive initiations into higher tantras like Yamantaka or Chakrasamvara because they are the 'real business' and fail to see the profound experiences that can come from simple practices practised well, such as Chenrezig or Tara.

Perhaps the most significant thing I have encountered with practitioners both new and old, is that many say that as a result of the demand of lots of recitation commitments, they have not really learned to meditate. They feel they have not gained a deeper sense of quiet stillness in meditation. I found in my early years of practice that I was also so busy doing sadhana recitations I did not easily drop beneath my conceptual mind and gain any depth of stillness in meditation. As a result, deity practice did not touch me very deeply and I did not really feel its transformational nature. In my own practice, particularly during and since a period of long retreats in India, my need to develop the capacity for deeper meditation has been crucial. To simplify my tantric practice and open up meditation space within it was, however, something that needed the guidance of particular teachers. Ones who had long retreat experience. Once I received this guidance, my practice changed. I began to have a deeper felt sense of transformation that gave more confidence in how tantra works. When subsequently I began to teach in this way the feedback I received from those I taught confirmed its effectiveness. I was very happy when a number of people in Prague, where I have taught for many years, came to me and said, "Rob this really works."

This brings me to want to clarify what I feel are perhaps the two greatest challenges in the integration of tantra into Western experience. Firstly, most of us in the West have a disposition to be bound by the intellect and the conceptual mind. We are largely in our heads and our education system and culture supports and reinforces this. Unfortunately, many of us have embarked upon our exploration of Buddhism also in a very intellectual way, seeing study and intellectual knowledge as some kind of mark of our experience. Intellectual understanding has its place. It has meant that traditional teachings have been sustained in the process of Tibetan Buddhism coming to the West. But when over emphasised it can block the potential for direct experience and realisation. This will be particularly so with the meditation necessary to gain a genuine experience of the effects of tantric practice. As Lama Yeshe would repeatedly emphasise, to gain experiences of tantra we must go deeper than the intellect. Intellectual study alone and conceptual practice will not do this. Once we begin to drop beneath our conceptual mind we will come into relationship with the aspects of our inner life that are the basis of transformation. To do this we need to learn to meditate with a non-conceptual awareness that is present within our inner processes.

This leads to the second challenge which is that we also need to develop a relationship to the body if we are to truly experience the transformational effects of tantra. It is within the body that the essential ingredient of transformation lives, which, from a tantric point of view, is the energy-body. It is here also, that we will begin to encounter the roots of our emotional and psychological wounds. They are present within the energy-body. Unfortunately, our Western culture has for centuries led to an increasingly disembodied and disconnected way of life. The emphasis on mind and intellect has brought an accompanying level of disconnection from the body, which is one of the most detrimental obstacles in our attempts to practise tantra and gain a deeper experience. Many of us have an ambivalent relationship towards the body, ranging from denial or dissociation on one hand to an unhealthy obsession on the other. We can also be abusive towards the body in how we treat it. Our ambivalence often stems from an awareness that within the body we will re-discover painful feelings and emotions we would rather not feel.

An orientation to the intellect and a disembodied way of life can mean that meditation with depth is difficult. I am aware that this is not a new insight and that there are other Western teachers who are increasingly recognising this fact. I point to the significant work of teachers such as Reggie Ray, who brings considerable insight into a way of practice that addresses this problem.[4] Essentially, the greater our capacity to bring meditation into an embodied experience the more we will be able to absorb into the process of practice and actually feel its effect. We cannot avoid the reality that it is the felt experience of practice that is very significant. Without this felt change we may then be very disappointed by our lack of real depth and transformation within our practice, it will just remain what we might call 'head stuff'.

If we in the West are genuinely going to experience the value of tantra, I feel we must find a simpler, psychologically relevant, embodied and meditative way to practice. There will be those who prefer to practise in the traditional way and continue to find this rich and inspirational. From my own experience, however, I feel much is to be gained from bringing together the Eastern tradition with our Western psychological understanding to address our particular need. Then we can begin to practise in a way that holds to the essence of tantra while being able to transform and heal our psychological life. In this process we cannot assume that all of our Tibetan teachers will be able to guide us. They do not have our cultural and psychological background and do not seem to suffer the same kind of problems we do. There are some Tibetans who are increasingly learning what will truly help us and are willing to develop and change the way they teach accordingly. What Lama Yeshe wanted us to do was to also listen to our own inner wisdom and trust in our growing sense of what is and is not working. He once said that he felt ultimately it had to be Westerners who brought Buddhism to the West, because we are not Tibetans and must find our own way of practice. I recall him once joking that perhaps there will be Italian Buddhism, German Buddhism, American Buddhism….. He appreciated our cultural and psychological diversity.

Our Tibetan lamas, particularly those tulkus who are considered the holders of tantric lineages, are a vital link to the transmission of the tradition. Their role is unique in this, and they embody the experience of an extraordinary path. It is, however, for us as Western practitioners to take some responsibility for how we integrate this into our life. These powerful initiating lamas are often thousands of miles away, and we have little or no chance to have any relationship to them. It is those who have experience as Western meditators to then find a way to bridge these worlds and bring tantric practice into our experience. This requires that we learn from our own mistakes and experiences how best to practise. It is clear that we have a long way to go in this journey, but this is perhaps the challenge we must take on if we are to experience the fruits of tantric practice.

5

A Bridge to the West

IN 1984 SADLY LAMA THUBTEN YESHE DIED in California and his body was cremated at Vajrapani Institute near Boulder Creek. His death marked for many of us the end of an extraordinary life that was the source of incomparable wisdom and inspiration. He was one of a number of inspired, innovative and often unorthodox lamas such as Chogyam Trungpa Rinpoche, that emerged at the beginning of the 70s and who are unfortunately no longer with us. These lamas played a role of initiating the introduction of the Tibetan tradition to the West before the major organisations now present began to form. While Lama Yeshe was alive I felt extremely fortunate to receive instructions from him on many different practices and aspects of Tibetan Buddhism. Something that inspired me was that he rarely taught from a text but simply from his own experience. Whenever he spoke I felt his style of language and way of communicating had a particular intuitive quality that did not seem to follow traditional lines. He seemed to me to speak directly to my own intuition, bringing it alive and instilling a kind of inner confidence that we already had wisdom, we simply needed to begin to listen to it. "You check up," he would say, and "trust your inner knowledge wisdom" was a familiar phrase in his teaching.

What Lama Yeshe seemed able to do was to speak directly to Western mind with remarkable psychological insight. Very recently an old friend mentioned that he had some audio tapes I had given him to listen to some 25 to 30 years ago. They were of Lama Yeshe teaching mahamudra at a Buddhist centre in Australia. He returned the tapes to me and I was delighted to once again hear Lama's voice after all these years. What still continues to amaze me today is the way he taught. Even though his English was not brilliant he had the capacity to explain important aspects of Buddhism in a way that could be so accessible to Westerners. He also had a willingness to really challenge some of the orthodoxy of the tradition and was not one to see the Tibetan style and culture as something we needed to emulate. He was an extraordinary mixture of someone with a profound knowledge of the tradition yet with a willingness to bring it alive in a radically new way. Perhaps the most important thing he seemed able to do was to empower his students into a sense that this path was really possible for us and that we all had some innate capacity that simply needed to be brought out. He was someone who was not interested in intellectual knowledge of the dharma for its own sake. He wanted us to experience the benefits of meditation and have a taste of tantric practice. To do so he was prepared to make it something we could engage with in our own way, rather than become caught up in tradition for tradition's sake. An amusing example of this was when he was giving a *Mahakala* protector empowerment and realised he did not have a *torma*, a traditional offering to Mahakala. He whispered to one of the monks to fetch something. The monk returned with a loaf of bread standing on a plate. Lama laughed, saying, "this is *ingie torma*" (English *torma*).

I feel we are extremely fortunate if we can find an Eastern teacher with a good understanding of Western mind, and Lama Yeshe seemed particularly gifted in this way. Not all Tibetans who come to the West are able to teach outside of the form of the tradition. We cannot expect or assume they can understand the kind of influences Western life has upon our psychological makeup. This is neither their direct experience nor their training so there is no blame. It is in this respect significant that Lama Yeshe really tried to enter our world and bridge East and West with his way of teaching. He was often known to have sat watching the television because he was fascinated by the things that 'made us tick'. When I was in the process of writing my first book, *The Psychology of Buddhist Tantra*, I was responding in part to my own need to bridge Eastern and Western understanding, but also to something Lama Yeshe had always encouraged, which was my desire to bring the work of C.G.Jung and Buddhism together.

In 1976 many of us were both amazed and intrigued by the invitation Lama Yeshe had made to bring a Jungian sand-play therapist named Dora Kalff from Switzerland to teach alongside him in the UK. He would come to all of Dora Kalff's talks and later, when he was teaching the *Manjushri* tantra, he would make reference to things she had said. He particularly seemed to respond to her views about the nature of the archetypes and the unconscious. He was clearly very interested and attuned to her views of the psyche and Western psychological needs. I remember one comment he made in relation to the group of young men who were building the centre, myself included. He said 'without a relationship to the feminine sometimes men go a little crazy'. His interest in Jung's work on the masculine and feminine was clearly apparent. Whenever I subsequently spoke to him about this, I could see that his interest in Jung and Western psychology was a genuine attempt to make sense of aspects of tantric practice in a more Western way. His encouragement to make this bridge has continued to inspire my own practice, teaching and writing ever since.

Some years later during my period of retreat above McCleod Gange in India, I was fortunate enough to have several of Jung's collected works with me. This gave me the opportunity to study both my tantric practice and the work of Jung side by side. The masses of notes I made over those five years led eventually to the writing of what became *The Psychology of Buddhist Tantra*.

Many years have passed since that early foray into bridging Buddhist and Jungian perspectives. Over that time, I have found myself leading retreats and supporting many people in their Tibetan Buddhist practice. This had led me to see more and more clearly the way in which the Tibetan tradition, and tantra in particular, often needs to be reshaped to suit Western psychological needs. It has also clarified for me the skill with which Lama Yeshe taught. He was willing to move away from the orthodox approach and respond to what he saw would benefit us. In this he did not lose the essence of tantric practice. Rather he recognised that Western psyche is different to the Tibetans and needs a different approach to gain a taste of the practice, to 'taste the chocolate' as he put it.

I find myself continually referring back to what I experienced of Lama Yeshe's approach. It leads me to reflect on how tantra can evolve to suit our Western psychological nature without losing the essence of practice. Over the years I have worked with many people who have dedicated themselves to practice and learned from their experiences what seems to work with Western mind. Many of my older peers have now been practicing for 40 years or more and also have a much clearer sense of what works and what does not.

Perhaps it is time to look more closely at tantric practice and how Western psychological nature responds to it. What I have needed to do is to explore fresh ways of looking at this practice, that feel to be more appropriate for our psychological and cultural needs. I am very aware that in this attempt, there will be those who may respond with the belief that this is going to dilute and undermine the nature of tantra. To these I can only say that, rather than dilute, if this path is going to continue as a living tradition, it will only be by practitioners truly experiencing the essence of practice.

I feel incredibly fortunate to have been able to study with some eminent Tibetan lamas and learn this tradition from them. They have carried a transmission through the centuries and sustained a living lineage that is priceless. Inevitably in this process they have also reshaped it as it came from India into Tibet. They have made it a reflection of their own extraordinary culture and their own particular psychological make-up. They have generated complex elaborate practices and vast collections of commentaries based on profound experiences, and the value of their work is beyond measure. Today there are also significant Tibetan teachers who are embarking upon a gradual change in how they bring the dharma to the West. In this I feel H.H.Dalai Lama is perhaps one of the most significant. I have no wish to pretend that I have even a fraction of their insights. What I have, however, is the experience of trying to integrate what I have been taught into Western life and Western psyche. My struggles and occasional discoveries or even realisations have been born out of desire to continue Lama Yeshe's extraordinary example and find a way to make this path accessible to fellow Westerners as a way of meditation.

6

Discovering the Body as the Vessel

As I BEGAN MY JOURNEY within the Tibetan tradition I found myself in a contradictory relationship to the body. On one hand I was given the message in the writing of, for example, Shantideva,[5] that the body was a problem. My attachment to it would be a cause of suffering and that I needed to renounce it. On the other hand, within the practice of tantra, I received a different message: the body is of huge importance and actually to be taken care of because it is the vessel for awakening. These conflicting messages came to meet my own somewhat ambivalent relationship to my body and relatively superficial awareness of what was arising within it. I was someone who, when I was young, could easily be caught in my head and oriented to intellectual knowledge rather than felt experience, partly because this was how I was educated. Like many Westerners, my body was something I was either attached to, or felt aversion towards. At the same time, I often treated it like a machine that had to perform or look a certain way. In addition, I had the usual anxieties and concerns about my sexuality. I did not have any understanding of the significance of the body as a vehicle for awakening, partly because, growing up in a Christian culture, I saw spirituality as something antithetical to the 'sins of the flesh'.

While it became clear to me over years of practice that the body is central to the tantric path, I could not, in retrospect, understand why this message was not given more emphasis early on. There were perhaps a number of reasons for this. One could be that the Tibetans are by nature much more embodied and don't immediately recognise the degree of disembodiment and confusion we suffer. A second reason is that the Tibetan school within which I studied, has a great emphasis on the intellect as the foundation of Buddhist practice. A third reason is that in the tantric tradition, the body and its internal processes are often seen as more significant in the latter stages of practice rather than at the beginning.

When traditional teachings of tantra are given there is an evolution which has a somewhat linear sense to it. In the practice of higher tantra, for example, the path begins with an initiation into the practice of a deity, which is then followed by what is usually called the *generation* or *creation stage* (Tib: *kye rim*). This is the process whereby we are taught to recite a *sadhana*, which contains descriptions of visualisations, prayers, praises and offerings to the deity, followed by the recitation of the deity's mantra. When this has been followed, often for many years, to stabilise a certain depth of experience, a meditator may proceed to what is then known as the *completion* or *fruition stage* (Tib: *dzog rim*). Here the emphasis begins to be on the body, and the subtle-energy nervous system it contains is more explicitly described. At this time the various practices and exercises associated with it begin to be taught. It is often said that within the generation stage we visualise ourselves as the deity and within the completion stage this begins to be actually embodied through the energy-body, or in Tibetan *lung ku*.

When meeting tantra in the West it is very common for us to be introduced first to the practices of deity visualisation. This is consistent with a traditional approach to practice. We may spend a great amount of time studying the technicalities of a practice and learning to recite its sadhana. We may not realise, however, that everything that is to be transformed within deity practice is held within the body. If a deity visualisation process is just in the mind but has no relationship to the body and its energy, then there may be little real transformation. In my own experience, what this has led to is the recognition that for many or most of us as we embark upon deity practice it is also important that we are introduced to the nature of the body and its inner life. Of particular significance in this, is our relationship to our feeling and emotional process and its close connection to the energy-body. From an Eastern point of view what underlies the entire process of our feeling and emotional life and its relationship to the physical body is the energy-body. It is for this reason the energy-body is sometimes called the emotional-body. Furthermore, just as we cannot separate our body from our inner energy, neither can we separate ourselves from the subtle energy in the environment.

When I first began to practice tantra I was taught the technicalities of the energy-body on an intellectual level. I amassed considerable knowledge but my practice was primarily to recite sadhana texts. I was not instructed how to meditate in the body with an awareness of its energy. As I embarked upon deity practice in retreat I began to feel increasingly dissatisfied and frustrated with a sense of disconnection I experienced. My practice clearly affected how I felt but I tended to see this as secondary to what should be happening in my mind. My visualisations were primarily in my head and not really embodied. How then was I to make the shift to actually begin to feel the effect of practice within my body?

It became clear that rather than continually doing recitation of sadhana texts (something I will explore in Chapter 12), I also needed to take time to slow the process of practice down and begin to meditate. I needed to get out of my conceptual mind and open up space within my deity practice that allowed me to settle into my body and digest what was happening. Once I began to be more present with the felt-sense in my body, I also began to be more aware of the subtle vitality that lay within. When I then brought my deity practice into relationship to this felt-sense, I could feel that my energy-body and the deity were intimately connected. Slowly my practice came alive and my awareness of its energetic effect began to wake up. Gradually I was changing the way I engaged in the processes of practice, giving much more space and time to meditate and settle directly into its effect. It may be true to say that my energy-body was not yet 'becoming the deity', but it was deeply affected by it and at least the two were not separate. I could directly feel the sense of transformation as it was happening in my energy.

What I also began to recognise, was that in the process of sitting over long periods, the energy in my body would sometimes become stuck and lead to pain, tension or a sense of stagnation that needed to be released. I saw that I needed to include some kind of movement practice such as yoga, *kum nye* or *qigong* alongside my meditation to aid this process. Ironically, in teaching Westerners, it is almost always those who are experienced in yoga, qigong or a similar practice that find this relationship to the energy in the body more natural. Many of them say that they make an immediate connection with tantric practice that takes their yoga in a direction they have wanted to go but not previously found. This makes me consider that when tantra was emerging in India after the time of the Buddha, practitioners were almost certainly practising forms of yogic exercises alongside their deity practice. Tibetan teachers coming to the west have shown some reluctance to introduce these practices until relatively recently. Thankfully, increasingly there are Tibetan and Western teachers of the tantric tradition who have recognised the need and so are beginning to bring these energy-body exercises in much earlier.

When we begin to restore our relationship to the processes within the body we may see this as primarily so that we can awaken the energy-body, but there is another significant reason. It can also facilitate a means of psychological healing. When tantric practice is not in relation to the body we are less able to address the underlying psychological or emotional wounding most of us carry. From a Western psychotherapeutic understanding we can say that our psychological and emotional life is intimately associated with the body, even though this may be largely unconscious. When we begin to look at the underlying emotional wounding or trauma in our experience this is always held within the body. When we do not address our emotional life and instead block or suppress it, it will bury itself in the body. There it may remain out of conscious awareness and yet is the basis of all manner of disturbances that effect our daily life when activated. It may also potentially become the cause of future physical illness.

This mind/energy/body bridge has been understood in the East for hundreds if not thousands of years. It clarifies what in the West we consider as the psycho-somatic relationship, which is still not fully understood in Western psychology, partly because it is not easily measured or quantified in scientific terms. Within certain styles of Western psychotherapy, however, this mind/energy/body connection is well explored. The psychotherapy world has become increasingly sophisticated in its potential to work with the psychological, emotional and energetic subtleties within the body in a therapeutic healing way. From a psychotherapeutic as well as tantric perspective, our relationship to the emotional energy within the body is central to transformation and healing. It is therefore helpful, to bring this awareness into our practice from the very beginning and for it not be left as something that is introduced way down the road. It is our relationship to the body and the energy-body that gives tantra its raison d'etre, and for Westerners who enter into the Tibetan tradition this is significant.

Tantra has the potential to heal and transform psychological and emotional difficulties if it is practised skilfully in a more embodied way with suitable guidance. It is unfortunate that a split between formal meditation practice and our relationship to the body contributes greatly to some of us practising for years but not really changing our psychological problems. Having spent a considerable amount of time working with Buddhist practitioners in a therapeutic context I have seen that usually the reason tantric practice does not touch and transform their emotional life is because they are out of relationship to the body. The process of becoming more embodied, however, takes time. It is not going to happen overnight. We need to allow for the fact that our relative dissociation from the body happened for a reason and we should not judge ourselves harshly for this. As we begin the process of re-connection we may re-awaken those experiences of emotional wounding that caused us to become disconnected in the first place. Again, we should not see this as a problem or a bad thing. This is not something to fear even though that may be our first response. For most of us this exploration can open us to aspects of our inner life that will gradually heal with care and patience. We learn from the therapeutic understanding of how we begin to heal what is held in the body, that the process of reconnection I am speaking of within tantric practice needs to be approached carefully. As we restore an awareness of more subtle processes within the body we can potentially re-awaken aspects of our personal wounding or trauma that may be disturbing. We cannot then assume that our meditation practice alone will be able to hold and heal this as it arises. We will, as I describe in the next chapter, sometimes require more experienced support if this trauma is to begin to be healed. If we approach re-embodiment with kindness and compassion allowing ourselves time, then we can gradually re-awaken a deep felt-sense relationship to our body's inner life. Our body's re-awakening brings us back to our emotional processes and also to the natural joy and bliss that is there in our being.

As we re-established a relationship to the felt-sense in the body, we will also be able to gradually connect to its underlying subtle energy. If we can do this we will have a much more immediate resonance with the felt presence of a deity within the context of meditation practices. In many ways this felt experience can become more important than the visualisation of the deity, especially for those who are not so able to visualise well. I have encountered many people who find visualisation difficult and can easily become disheartened. If, however, it is possible to develop a deeper relationship to the felt experience of the energy in the body then the relationship to the deity can be equally profound.

It is with this in mind that we will find it very beneficial to prepare the ground for deity practice by meditations that bring us back into relationship to the feeling life of the body. In retreats that I lead with my wife, Anna, who is a healing movement[6] therapist, we have found that the combination of a movement process alongside body awareness meditation enables people to sit more deeply and feel a much deeper connection to deity practice. Being guided to meditate within the body is therefore, I feel, a fundamental beginning to tantric practice.

Body Awareness Meditation

Within the retreats I have led over the past 25 years I have developed many approaches to meditating within the body which are intended to gradually deepen body feeling awareness. There are too many to describe here but they fall into three basic approaches. The first of these is a relatively simple body-sweep meditation (Appendix 1), where we progressively take our awareness through the felt experience of the body. The purpose of this is to gradually wake up areas of the body that may be 'asleep' and begin to recognise where we hold tension or contract around discomfort. The intention is to eventually come to a restful awareness of the whole body that is increasingly relaxed and open, free of discursive chatter.

From this I move on to meditations that facilitate restful spacious awareness in the body, developing at first the capacity to rest in a sense of ground (Appendix 2). By this I mean enabling the whole body to begin to settle into an awareness of the weight of the body upon the cushion and of the pelvic floor. I call this the root or ground of the body. This also means an awareness of sensation and feeling in the legs, the hips, the base of the spine and the region of the perineum. We can then open to the feeling of a deepening connection to the earth beneath us and the support of the ground.

I emphasise this because for many of us our relationship to a sense of ground in the body is very poor. This often arises from very early in our life, where we may not feel safely held and therefore unable to rest in an ease of being essentially ok. Instead we contract and lift up, into a state that can become increasingly ungrounded and disembodied. As we then grow up, the intellectual orientation of our culture can exacerbate that disembodiment even more. Adding to this the potential that many of us have experienced some form of emotional trauma, then our capacity to feel grounded in the body becomes very problematic. It is this disembodied state in particular that we are trying to counter within body awareness practices, and to do this we need to learn to feel safe and grounded in the body to restore our capacity to rest, relax and open.

Following this grounding process, we then begin to open into an awareness of sensation and feeling throughout the entire body (Appendix 3). This time we are not scanning but just opening to a more spacious awareness of whatever arises. Within the world of mindfulness this may be very familiar, but perhaps a difference here is that I am encouraging a more spacious natural awareness rather than being too focused. This is to cultivate a quality of attention that is relaxed and open in relation to feelings and sensations. We begin to recognise more subtly how we respond to what arises often by contracting or pushing away rather than allowing a natural flow. We learn instead to cultivate what I sometimes call a 'non-stick' awareness that allows space around feeling and sensation. We let whatever is there to be there without judgement and with equanimity. As this becomes more established we can learn to witness the arising of feeling and sensation with quiet, present, spacious awareness, imbued with a sense of acceptance and compassion. This is a theme I go into in some length in *Feeling Wisdom*[7].

The capacity to be present in the body and its feeling/sensation nature has an extremely important side-effect which is that we are also learning to be with our emotional processes in a different way. When we are able to rest with present awareness in body feeling and sensation, we learn to allow feelings to be as they are. We learn not to react to them and contract into them or push them away, but to create a sense of spaciousness that allows them to simply move through. In this way we learn to allow the energy of the emotions and feelings to go where it needs to go without interfering with it. This is very liberating and enables us to be with our emotional life in a much more healthy way. It begins to counter the habit that is often in our body of tightening and contracting around our emotional experiences, making them much more solid and fixed. At the heart of Buddhist understanding is the recognition that the basic cause of our suffering is this reactive contraction that blocks the natural unfolding of our inner processes.

When I wrote *The Psychology of Buddhist Tantra* some years ago I included a chapter titled *Becoming a Stable Vessel* [8]. I wrote this because I felt very strongly that one of the most important preparations for entering into the process of tantra was to have a stable sense of identity. This is gained primarily through our capacity to be with our emotional processes in a way that neither overwhelms us nor requires that we split off or suppress them. They are the stuff of transformation and will arise as a result of practice such that we need to be able to 'handle' them skilfully and with awareness. We could say that if there is not the emergence and arising of emotional material it is questionable how much transformation is actually happening. To be able to be with this skilfully is therefore crucial. If I return to a comment I made earlier, we also need to recognise that there may be times when some emotional trauma emerges that is too much to work with on our own. When this happens, our meditation can be of great value, but we may also need therapeutic support as well.

In a further progression of the meditations I have begun to describe, there are many ways in which we can subtly affect how our mind rests within the body and the kind of insights we may explore. One example of this is a way in which we can increasingly enable a more subtle and fluid awareness of the arising of what is in the body (Appendix 4). In this we can gradually soften the sense of contraction and holding as we breathe, allowing an awareness of the continual changing insubstantial nature of what is arising in the body. Tantric practice rests in the continual shifting fluid nature of our experience of our form as it changes moment to moment. Once we are back in the body and able to rest with the awareness of what is there we can slowly open to this fluid, changing nature, where nothing holds any enduring or substantial form, it is empty. This is the reality of the body and all that arises within it. When we see this, we can respond more immediately to the transformational nature of tantric practice.

When we have a deeper relationship to our body we can begin to open to the underlying vitality within feeling and sensation. We begin to be aware of its intrinsic energetic nature. Our practice is then naturally more embodied, more grounded and less subject to problems with the energy-body. The potential for psychological and emotional transformation will also be greater. In tantric practice it is usually considered that we need to prepare the ground for practice so that experience can arise more naturally. To do this there are often what are called preliminary practices, or *ngon dro*, which I have explained at great length in *Preparing for Tantra*. One of the main intentions of these practices is to heal and clear the energy-body, which again we will do more effectively if we are able to meditate deeply in the body.

If the aim of tantric practice is to be able to embody the deity in our life then our relationship to the body is an important starting point. When I first became involved in the tantric tradition it was explained that we would not be able to practise without this human body and its subtle energy-body. Within the context of higher tantra and the vows we take, we are expected to not harm the body because of its precious nature. The body is the vessel within which tantric transformation takes place and it is said that even the devas pray to be born into a human form for this purpose. Essentially tantric practice needs to be embodied and when it isn't there is a question as to what is really being transformed.

Becoming embodied therefore brings a far more grounded way of practicing for us as Westerners rather than being stuck in the head. Slowing the process down and returning to awareness in the body gives a more stable base to deal with the emotional material that can and will arise in our practice. It enables the awareness of felt experience that is vital for digesting the effects of practice as they arise. This means we may truly begin to feel the quality of the deity and the nature of transformation possible within our practice.

Lastly but most significantly returning to the body brings us directly into relationship with the raw material of tantric transformation namely, our emotional or energy-body. This leads us to a shift of perception that recognises the underlying vitality of the energy-body. It is the cultivation of more subtle awareness within the felt experience of the energy-body that will enable us to meditate very effectively upon a deity. We will find that we are more attuned to the presence of a deity and the effect of visualisations and mantra recitation. It will mean that during the process of deity practice we can slow the process down and deepen meditation, going beyond conceptual experience, digesting and assimilating the effect of practice.

7

Working with Subtle Energy

EARLY IN MY OWN EXPLORATION of the tantric path it was helpful to have a good understanding of the nature of the energy-body. It gave me a clear sense of how and why deity practice actually worked. In my own practice and over the years I have been teaching, it has become very clear that intellectual knowledge alone is of limited value. We need to be guided into a direct experience of the nature of the energy-body through meditation or some form of exercise. Many Westerners are already familiar with this through practices such as yoga, qigong, the martial arts and healing traditions such as acupuncture and shiatsu. I often find myself working with qigong and yoga practitioners who have a strong relationship to the energy-body. I have seen how, as a result, they are able to move towards the process of tantric practice, deeply feeling its effects within the body without much difficulty. For those of us who do not have this experience, we need to begin to meditate in the body, as I have described in the previous chapter, so that we can develop an awareness of the energy-body.

As I have said, the energy-body is a central aspect of tantric practice. In *The Psychology of Buddhist Tantra* I began to map the many different aspects of our nature that could be seen as reflections of its presence (Figure 3). What is significant in these expressions of the energy-body is the view, often emphasised in tantra, that the transformation of the energy-body is actually more important than the mind. This stems from the fact that the energy-winds are considered the primary 'motor' affecting our experience of states of mind and emotional processes in our daily life.

Figure 3

Energy-Wind Diagram

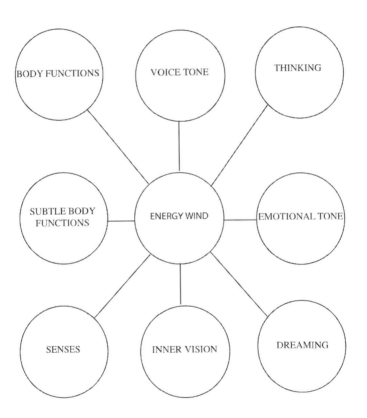

The energy-body is the name given to the combination of energy-wind or *lung*, the channels or meridians (Tib: *tsa)*, and what are known as drops (Tib: *tig le*). For now, I will focus specifically on the energy-wind. Energy-wind is intimately related to a range of experiences, many of which I have charted in *The Psychology of Buddhist Tantra,* but here I want to describe some of the ways in which this will be specifically experienced in meditation. Our mental and emotional states are directly related to the energy-winds, such that agitated energy generates agitated mind and emotions. A disturbed mind with strong emotional undercurrents will be a reflection of disturbed energy-winds. Peaceful states of mind such as compassion will have concomitant peaceful energy-wind.

As we begin to settle into the process of meditation, our first experience of the energy-winds will be through and within our emotional and feeling processes. This energetic movement will also stimulate the conceptual mind in ways that are often hard to settle. We need to shift our attention away from the stories and fantasies our mind generates to begin to connect to the feeling nature in our body in its more 'raw' and natural state. Once we can quieten the mental process, 'bare awareness' capable of witnessing feeling states becomes more natural and available to us. As we settle more into the felt-sense within the body it is not a great shift then to start to be aware of its underlying energy vitality. It is this shift that means we start to recognise the energetic nature within all of our emotional and feeling experiences in the body.

It is often said that where our mind goes the energy goes. It might equally be said that when the energy moves it draws our attention. To experience this process, we need to gradually relax our awareness deeper into the body and begin to open to its presence (Appendix 5). When we do, we become more able to 'feel into' the energetic quality that inhabits our body. This can be a more diffused awareness of the general tone of the vitality through the body as an underlying energetic flavour. It could also be stronger currents flowing through. It could be smooth and soft but equally coarse and agitated. It may be pleasant or equally unpleasant. I have, for example, often noticed at the beginning of retreats that the busyness of my life and work has left a kind of toxicity in my energy-body that can feel quite unpleasant, a bit like having the flu. One could see this as the effect of stress or the impact of relatively unhealthy situations that we have to live with. This may be things such as working in a busy office, going into a large shopping centre or perhaps more significantly being in emotionally charged and stressful relationships. I find it fascinating to feel this and then see how, in the space of a few days of more intense practice, it begins to clear. Then a far deeper, more pleasant level of energy begins to be present.

We can then begin to experience the 'condition' of the energy-body and its varied feeling tones when we specifically bring our awareness to certain parts of the physical body. One very beneficial way to approach this is to settle deeply into what in the previous chapter I have called the ground or root of the body and then gradually bring awareness up through the centre of the body. By ground of the body I refer specifically to a capacity to rest with a settled awareness in the base, in the region of the pelvic floor and the perineum. Resting and relaxing into this ground we begin to open to the felt experience. We need to give ourselves time to feel into the quality of energy that lives there. We don't have to do anything to it, simply rest and open awareness. From this place we can gradually bring awareness up through the trunk of the body, coming first to the region of the navel, then heart, then throat and then crown. This brings us to slowly discover the energetic nature of our emotional life found through the central core in the region of the chakras. I am not suggesting in this we go into the chakras, but to feel the quality of the energy that lives around them through the core of the body (Appendix 6). We need to recognise that the chakras are 'restricted' by the emotional energy that constellates around them. When we rest in this area with a spacious quality of awareness that restriction can begin to open.

Once we have this awareness of the emotional core and its energetic tones, we can then open to the rest of the body, spreading our attention gradually to the legs and arms and the head. Eventually our awareness can move out to the surface of the skin. In this gradual process we settle into the felt sense of the entire body. We become aware of the nuances of feeling and energy that are there with bare awareness. This is an awareness that is free of judgement and that does not contract into or push away feelings as they arise and move through.

As our sensitivity to the felt-sense of energy in the body increases, we need to learn how to be with the energetic processes that move within us. For some of us these may be noticeably very strong, for others they may be relatively quiet or less easy to sense. In the practice of tantra, our energy is going to be stimulated or activated and so how we work with it is important. As I have said earlier, to begin with it is good not to become caught in the story, the conceptual chatter that can be stimulated by energy moving. Then it is important to understand that much of what we experience is simply energy moving through. Our energy-body is trying to release and balance. It is trying to find a natural expression and movement of the energy as it seeks healing and health. It is helpful if we can trust in this process and respond to it in a kind and caring way. In a way that allows space for what arises to go where it needs to go. A key principle within this kind of work is to allow a natural unfolding of the energy. It is seldom beneficial to push and squeeze ourselves in meditation as this does not respect the nature of the energy and what it needs. It is not helpful to try and force processes to happen. Forcing doesn't heal, it will often re-traumatise us or lead to what in the Tibetan tradition is called *lung*, a disorder of the energy-winds.

One of the main difficulties with our energetic nature is the tendency to be tight, held and controlled. The more we open and relax our awareness within the body, the more this contracted tendency begins to release. It is as though our energy-body needs to feel safe to be able to open. To facilitate this, it is helpful to gradually allow our awareness to open and become more spacious within the space of the body. Relaxing and opening into the body, using the quality of the breath to allow every cell in the body to breathe, facilitates this more spacious, less contracted awareness (Appendix 5). This in turn gives the energy in the body the space within which it can begin to move more freely and healthily. We could say that the energy will find its natural place of health and balance, our problem is that we are not letting this happen because of a habit of contracting and holding.

It is significant that in the heart of Buddhist thinking is the view that all suffering arises from grasping and attachment. These could be understood as states of mind, but here we bring that into the body. If we consider an embodied direct *feeling* of what this is like, we can recognise it as an experience of *contraction*. This is so within the emotional processes that arise within the body, as well as their underlying energetic nature. A holding contraction around energetic processes locks them or freezes them into a painful suffering state that prevents their natural movement through the body and, therefore, release.

As energy in the body is released it may bring with it experiences that are not always comfortable. They may be painful emotionally because we hold pain and trauma in the energy-body. As it releases, we then need to be skilful and careful in how we respond. We could say that our energy-body is unfreezing, releasing and healing. It is finding the natural way to release and the practice of meditation can facilitate this. From my own experience and the experience of leading meditation retreats over many years, there are certain things that truly help. First, we need to be gentle and not try to force anything to happen. We need to sustain the quality I have called 'non-stick' awareness that is spacious and open, that does not judge or fear what is happening and that can 'trust in its process'. Often the movement of energy in the body can lead us to contract around it rather than giving it space to go where it needs to go. When we do this we once again block the natural flow of the energy. If we can remain open and allow the energy to spread and expand through the body it helps the sense of release.

When we are working in this way it is important to be aware of our resources, especially when stronger energy begins to move, so that we do not become overwhelmed. Within the therapeutic world these days, there is a great deal of experience and understanding in relation to trauma in the body.[9] If you are someone who begins to experience the awakening of some deeper level of trauma that is hard to cope with, it may be important to find professional support. Someone who was, for example, abused as a child may not have been aware of this experience until they return to this more subtle body awareness. If this is the case do not expect that this can be worked with on your own and solely in meditation. You will probably need some form of therapeutic support. For many of us hopefully this will not be the case, but some forms of trauma and emotional wounding can be hard to work with and so will benefit from support.

When leading retreats, there have been a number of occasions where it has become obvious that someone is experiencing the stimulation or triggering of strong trauma in the body. This has meant that to process this trauma and enable it to work through, required very careful guidance and support. In a retreat setting, because both Anna and myself have therapeutic experience, we have usually been able to create a safe holding environment for this to be worked with. Even so, we have often recommended that if someone wishes to go further in retreat in future, it would be beneficial and sometimes essential to first do some kind of therapeutic work to assist the healing process.

When I was in long retreat in India, I became very aware that there were areas of my psychological background that I needed to resolve before aspects of my practice could go deeper. I was very glad when I returned to the West to have the opportunity to do this in a therapeutic setting.

If we are fortunate enough to not have deep levels of trauma within the energy-body then the primary effect of our practice will be the release of relatively manageable emotional patterning. This is something we all have in varying degrees. This understanding is important if we are to benefit from tantric practices that are specifically aimed at 'purification'. Although the term purification is frequently used, perhaps in relation to the energy-body the term healing is more useful. It has a more kind, compassionate feel to it, understanding that much of what we suffer, in this life at least, we did not cause. We need to hold an attitude of care around the healing process that does not judge it or feel we are somehow bad or to blame for our wounding. This is not therapeutically helpful. This is not to overlook that we may also hold a lot of pain and remorse around detrimental actions for which we have indeed been responsible. In which case the notion of purification can still be appropriate.

Working with the energy-body is one of the most extraordinary aspects of our tantric path and does not necessarily need to be seen as an 'advanced practice'. What I am describing here is not the practice of specific yogic techniques that are intended to move the energy more directly. Practices such as the exercises within the *trul kor* system of the *Six Yogas of Naropa*[10] are extremely powerful but not always appropriate for us in the early stages of this path. Energy awareness processes of the kind I have described above are, however, extremely beneficial and, I feel, a necessity if our practice is to be stable and transformational. Once we are more stable in our awareness within the energy-body, some of these yogic exercises can be very helpful to free and clear energy blocks in the body. It is, however, important to have guidance so that we can navigate the processes going on.

In tantric practice we need to take care of our energy-body and that means our physical body as well. This can sometimes be overlooked in relation to Buddhist practice, especially if we are given the message that too much attachment to the body is detrimental. This care is not about attachment, it is about respecting the extraordinary gift we have been given of the human physical form with its energy system. It is the energy-body that will be a primary vehicle for our awakening and if we damage it, or neglect it, we are damaging our capacity to awaken and be of benefit to others. In higher tantra, *maha anutara yoga tantra*, vows are taken against abusing our body and these vows need to be taken very seriously. Pushing the body to extremes that harm it, or feeding it rubbish food all the time, can both be seen as abusing the body.

How we take care of this body and its energetic process is important. This can include diet and exercise. It can include using healing approaches that are supportive of the energy-body itself. There have been many occasions when I have found it very helpful to receive acupuncture, shiatsu or craniosacral therapy to help clear energy blocks that are giving rise to health problems where meditation alone cannot help.

As we become increasingly attuned to the nature of the energy in our body it opens up a sensitivity to a wider field of experience. We can become more sensitive to what we do with our energy, what we put into our body and also to the environment within which we live. This sensitivity is a great resource for us and can also at times be problematic. Learning to take care of our energy-system is part of the journey and this we learn in part through experience. We will become more open but also need to learn how to close and protect when necessary. We also need to learn how to clear and clean the impact of unhealthy energy that can invade our energy-body. This is understood within tantric teachings but not always made explicit. It is in this respect helpful to have guidance and support so that we can work with that sensitivity in a skilful way.

This support, however, is not always easy to find. It can be relatively easy to receive traditional teachings on the nature of the energy-body and the practices associated with its purification and transformation. What is not always so easily found is a more personal guidance from someone who has meditation experience. In long retreat during the monsoon I would often go into a relatively deep depression for several weeks. I could not understand why this was happening until by some stroke of good fortune I had the opportunity to speak privately with H.H.Dalai Lama. I asked him why this might be happening and his answer was immediate. "Because you are loosing heat energy from the navel" he said. "Wrap a scarf around your waste to protect it." Such an obvious answer, but it needed someone with that insight and experience to recognise it. I tried it and was pleasantly surprised by the result.

We are not always able to speak with Tibetan lamas about these things, often because they have many students or are thousands of miles away. Even so getting personal guidance around what is happening to our energy-body as we practice is very important. Hopefully, some of the suggestions I have made here will also be a helpful guide to begin to work with the energy in a skilful way.

Once we have a growing capacity be aware of and respond skilfully to energetic processes, then we are more able to work with some of the specific practices that affect the energy-body. These could be loosely divided into three groups. The first of these is within the actual meditation practices associated with each deity. This includes visualisation process as well as the recitation of mantras, all of which are intended to affect the energy-winds in various ways. The second group relates to the specific visualisations associated with the energy channels, chakras and subtle drops within the body. The third group relates to methods associated with the breath as well as more physical yogic exercises that are designed to activate and move the energy through the body.

With all of these practices we need to be able to relate skilfully to what is waking up in the energy-body so that it can be assimilated. We will also need to learn to gauge how much it is healthy to activate in the process of practice. Sometimes I have worked with people who have pushed too hard with certain practices and experienced detrimental side effects. If we have prior understanding of how to be with the energy-body, what it needs to move towards a healthy state, and how to recognise the signs of something being problematic, then we can relax and allow things to unfold. It is when this understanding is not there and practitioners are left in the dark about such things that problems can arise. We can potentially over activate the energy-body and precipitate what might be described as a 'spiritual emergency'.

It is important to recognise that many of the more technical practices associated with the tantric tradition are there to aid what is potentially a natural experience in all of us. It is also not just within the Buddhist tantras that people awaken energy in the body. In the shamanic world, as well as within some of the mystical traditions such as in Sufism and Christianity, the energy-body is awakened. Equally, many people experience very spontaneous awakening of the energy as a natural course of their emotional life, although sometimes as a result of some traumatic experience. We should not think that as tantric practitioners we have some sort of exclusive means of awakening. It is a natural potential within the body and many people awaken this who are not practitioners of a tradition such as tantra. Perhaps the advantage with the tantric tradition is that there is a sound understanding of the conditions that help integrate such experiences. There is also a clear sense of what can help and what can hinder such a process.

Increasingly in the west people experience what is called 'spiritual emergency' where the activation of the energy-body arises spontaneously and in a way that can be very disturbing. The most familiar way this is described is a 'Kundalini awakening'. Perhaps we can say that what distinguishes *spiritual emergence* from *spiritual emergency*, is the capacity to integrate the experience into our normal way of life without the problem of becoming unstable. With spiritual emergency there is an overwhelming activation of the energy system. This can bring intense energy through the body in a way that is sometimes extremely blissful but also sometimes very painful. It is often accompanied by shaking of the body and disturbance to the sense of 'reality' where hallucinations, visions and sudden expansions of awareness are extremely disorienting. In the event of this kind of spiritual emergency it is important to find the resources that can support integration. A process that may take time.

Spiritual emergence as a gradual awakening of the energy-body will not be so dramatic and will be a more tempered experience. It may also lead to the similar symptoms of energy rushes through the body, shaking, sudden bursts of strong emotional affect and dramatic expansion of awareness, but in a way that is more able to be integrated and digested. It can still be challenging and is sometimes a tough journey, but the crucial thing is we are able to integrate and process what arises. When we cannot maintain the stability of our normal sense of self and instead become overwhelmed and unable to cope with our ordinary life then this could be seen as an emergency and will need more experienced support. It is sometimes the desire for dramatic energetic effects that can lead us to seek out the more forceful practices found within the tantric tradition, but this is not always the most skilful way to go.

My own practice has tended towards the less dramatic slow process which has sometimes meant barely perceptible changes.

While this may have been less exciting than accounts of earth-shaking experiences, I am glad it has been this way, with opening and stabilising as a natural way of practice. Having said this, the process it has taken me through both energetically and emotionally has not always been easy. In this respect no awakening is without its challenges and its pain. We all have residual emotional wounds to some degree, held within the energy-body. Releasing and healing this takes time, care and patience. It is not always a comfortable process but can bring great joy and peace as our energy system becomes healthier. Probably the most important thing I have learned within my own tantric practice has been to continually come back to a grounded, steady clear open awareness that would allow me to digest and integrate whatever arose. It is here that the practice of mahamudra has been such a valuable resource, as I will explain in the next chapter. When we rush our practice we often do not do this digestion and so do not return to a natural place of health, especially if we are putting ourselves under pressure to complete mantra counts or trying to attain realisations. Personally, I have found whatever realisations come, they come through a slower opening and digestion rather than the pressure to achieve something.

8

Meditation in the Nature of Mind

AT THE BEGINNING of Chapter 3, I described the nature of *primordial mind* as having two dimensions or two aspects. Of these two in the previous chapter I looked at the importance of our relationship to the energy-winds and the energy-body, our basis of sambhogakaya. I also emphasised that to access this aspect of our nature we need to come back into relationship with the physical body as the vessel within which it transforms. The second dimension of primordial mind is its cognitive nature, its quality of clear, spacious, radiant awareness. This understanding of, and awakening to, the nature of mind I feel is equally important to entry into the practice of tantra for us in the West. This can be found through the practice of mahamudra. Just as with the energy-body, mahamudra is often only introduced within the *completion stage* of tantra rather than at the beginning. What I learned from Lama Yeshe, however, was that it is beneficial to introduce this meditation much earlier in the journey, not just in the completion stage. This has been very important in my own experience, and I have often felt that without it, deity practice would be like having a wonderful yacht but with no water to sail upon. Mahamudra meditation is like the water, the ocean upon which the boat of the deity can sail.

The various schools of Tibetan Buddhism consider that there are two principle approaches to developing the wisdom aspect of

Buddhist teachings. The first of these is where the emphasis is upon studying the philosophical teachings on emptiness. One then meditates upon the realisation that emerges, attempting to transfer a conceptual understanding of emptiness into a direct experience. The second approach is where one first develops the capacity of non-conceptual meditation on the mind itself. From this there naturally emerges the realisation of the empty nature of phenomenon within the state of non-duality. So, in the former there is first conceptual understanding and then meditation, in the latter there is meditation and then the awakening of insight.

In my own study of this process, I grew up in a Tibetan school that emphasised the first of these approaches. I spent many early years studying Buddhist philosophy with different lamas and the teachings of *madhyamaka* philosophy in particular. I found this approach incredibly helpful in giving me a conceptual understanding of the nature of emptiness. What I personally found very difficult, however, was translating that understanding into a meditation experience that was effective. I recall my retreat guide, Gen Jhampa Wangdu, saying to me that it is not difficult to understand emptiness intellectually; it is, however, less easy to cultivate a quality of meditative stability that can directly experience it. The metaphor he gave was that we may use a hammer to hit a nail into a piece of wood, but if we are unable to consistently hit the nail it is of little use. The shift from intellectual to a non-conceptual awareness that was in any way stable, was for me extremely hard. Unfortunately, within the school of Tibetan Buddhism I was studying there seemed to be less emphasis on learning non-conceptual meditation than one might find within other mahamudra and dzogchen traditions. Meditation tended to be either conceptual reflection on the teachings, the *Lam Rim,* or the conceptual liturgy of the tantric sadhana. It was only when Lama Yeshe began to give more specific instructions on non-conceptual awareness within the practice of mahamudra that, for me, this began to change.

Lama Yeshe's guidance was a missing link that enabled me to begin to sit and meditate in a way that many of the people I met from the Theravada tradition seemed able to do. It was when he began to teach about resting in what he would call the "clean clear" nature of the mind itself that I experienced a sudden shift in my awareness. He was a great advocate of going beyond mere intellectual knowledge, seeing it as something of a block to genuine realisation. Having conceptual knowledge, he felt was useful in the background but we needed to begin to meditate and still the mind into a non-conceptual state. Then we gain a direct experience of clear, spacious, empty awareness. When he began to introduce meditations on the mind itself I became aware that this approach was very different and seldom taught by the geshes that were teaching me. They were all extremely gifted and knowledgeable exponents of madhyamaka philosophy but direct meditation on the nature of the mind did not seem to be an aspect of their training. What I began to realise was that Lama Yeshe was unusual within that tradition in his experience of mahamudra and that he had received teachings from other schools which made this possible. Following his death in 1984 it became clear that for those teachings I would probably need to visit other schools of Tibetan Buddhism which gave greater emphasis to this approach.

When I heard H.H. Dalai Lama teach a text called *Mahamudra within the Gelug/Kagyu Tradition,* in Dharamsala in 1983, I understood an historical conflict that had gone on in Tibet for hundreds of years. What I learned was that these two approaches had been adopted by different schools that had then sometimes come into conflict as to which was the 'correct view'. Followers of madhyamaka, also known as the proponents of the *rang tong*, or self-empty view, go into great philosophical depth intellectually. Those who follow the nature of mind tradition, also called *shen tong* or other-empty, are often great adepts at meditation. They are yogis rather than scholars who spend much time in retreat to master a depth of stability of meditation within which insight grows in a non-conceptual and direct way. Historically these two approaches have caused surprisingly acrimonious disputes amongst the Tibetan schools around something that has at its root a paradox. H.H.Dalai Lama, however, during these teachings made it clear that these approaches can lead to the same experience[11], and that the polarisation of views is an unnecessary and unhelpful polemic when it is beneficial to actually have experience of both. In practice, these two views complement and aid each other. As H.H.Dalai Lama put it[12] in one approach the mind meditates upon emptiness in the other one meditates upon the mind whose nature is empty.

While I value the teachings I received on madhyamaka philosophy's intellectual understanding of emptiness, I was greatly inspired when I was guided to meditate on the nature of mind.

Initially this was by Lama Yeshe, then the Dalai Lama and later from Dudjom Rinpoche, the then head of the Nyingma school. What I subsequently realised is that Lama Yeshe was more often teaching a view that was aligned with mahamudra and dzog chen. It was in 1984 when I did a long mahamudra retreat in the mountains above Dharamsala, I found that for the first time I began to experience meditation that was free of conceptual disturbances and my mind would actually settle. Something this practice also enabled me to do as an incredibly valuable by-product, was to relate to my feeling and emotional life in a fresh and beneficial way. I found that as I rested in present awareness, free of constant conceptual chatter, I could then allow my emotional life more space to move through in a helpful way. What I also began to feel was that resting in clear present awareness gave a far deeper sense of ease and spaciousness within. My sense of self naturally became more open and less contracted, meaning that the ego-grasping at the centre of so much suffering began to loosen.

At the heart of our understanding of the nature of mind is basic awareness, in Tibetan *rig pa*. I find this subtle distinction important in my own meditation where I can directly recognise *awareness* as a subjective process rather than *mind*, an object. I sometimes reflect that I don't know what mind is, it is an abstract concept, but I can immediately experience awareness. In meditation it is not mind that I find myself 'witnessing' but awareness itself as an unfolding momentarily passing process. Clear awareness is an ever-changing direct present experience that has a number of qualities. It may be a focused attention that hones in on a particular object or feeling, but in mahamudra we are beginning to open to its natural, expansive, spacious quality that has clarity, brightness and presence. As we recognise the natural unfolding flow of this experience we see it is "free from arising, abiding, and going away,"[13] it cannot be found as a 'substantial' phenomenon and therefore is naturally empty. In *An Ocean of the Ultimate Meaning*, Thrangu Rinpoche uses the Tibetan term *rig tong*[14] to describe the nature of mind, where *tong* means empty and *rig* is awareness. The nature of mind is this union of awareness and emptiness.

From one perspective we may think we need to analyse the mind to recognise its empty nature. But when we meditate with the unfolding of awareness its empty nature becomes apparent. Just as H.H. Dalai Lama describes meditation on an awareness that has emptiness as its nature, this is something that reveals itself in the deepening of meditation. Furthermore, in meditation we gradually open to a quality of awareness that is not bound by the duality of subjective witness and object awareness. This space of non-duality does not discern awareness as an objective phenomenon with either conventional or ultimate nature. It is merely the space of non-duality. Many times, I recall Lama Yeshe saying in his somewhat enigmatic way, "Don't conceptualise, just let go into emptiness non-duality." He was constantly affirming that because the mind is by nature empty, that emptiness will reveal itself, we do not need to do a lot of analysis.

In my own practice, having struggled to convert my intellectual understanding of emptiness into direct meditation, I began to find a new way of integrating that insight. Within the clarity of a more settled spacious, present awareness I began to see that when I did wish to introduce the kind of understanding that comes with the philosophical view of emptiness, I was able to rest in a non-conceptual experience with greater ease. I did not need to reflect endlessly in a way that deconstructed everything with long analysis. Instead it was possible simply to look at the experience of something as it arose in awareness and see its insubstantial empty nature. This kind of subtle investigation the Dalai Lama described as like a fish that swims through water, it does not disturb the water, so too it does not disturb the nature of clear awareness.[15] In mahamudra the way we sustain our experience of meditation on spacious awareness is also the practice of insight or *vipassana*. When a thought, image or feeling arises, by giving it a subtle attention that does not interfere, then naturally it will evaporate back into awareness itself. This is because the thought or feeling is empty and not other than the nature of awareness itself. This process of practice is sometimes called non-modification, where we do not do anything to what is arising, trying to make it different or go away. Instead we simply look into its nature. It means that in practice the arising of thoughts and images is not considered a problem, they simply arise and pass through.

Today there are many detailed books written on the nature of mahamudra and so, for the sake of simplicity, I would like to refer the reader to some of these. I particularly recommend the work of Thrangu Rinpoche and his many commentaries on mahamudra. I also recommend the work of Sok Nyi Rinpoche whose teaching on dzog chen I found extremely helpful in my own practice.

Meditation Practice

To begin the process of mahamudra I want to emphasise something not always explicit in the teachings, that relates to our particular Western disposition. Having studied and practiced both mahamudra and dzog chen I have feel it is important and necessary to begin with our relationship to the body. If we do not, there is the potential for our practice to be disembodied and just a mental process in the head. It is also clear from teachings I have received that we need to increasingly relax the body. Tilopa says in the *Ganges Mahamudra*, "Like a hollow bamboo, rest at ease your body."[16] He emphasises that we need to remain "loose and natural" so that our awareness can quieten and open. The more we are relaxed and have the capacity to rest in a sense of ground in the body, the more our mind will become still and spacious. It will also help us to cultivate a deeper stillness of tranquil abiding or *samatha*. Because of this I want to come back to what I was describing in Chapter 6, where we learn to meditate first within sensation and feeling in the body. Here I was emphasising the need to settle into the ground of the body and let it relax deeply. Once we have developed this capacity we then start to open into feeling and sensation within the body. We remain with a quality of awareness that is open and present, allowing whatever is arising to come and go without becoming identified with it (See Appendix 3 & 4). This quality of quiet present awareness within the body and its sensation and feeling is then a good basis from which to move into the practice of mahamudra.

To describe briefly the way in which this experience might evolve into the actual process of mahamudra meditation, I find it helpful to consider the metaphor of a rock pool at the seashore. If I look into a rock pool my first experience is that I see the colourful things that are there, the seaweed, the fish, the creatures in the pool. They are the objects of my attention and I see them but do not become specifically aware of the water itself. In mahamudra, we may begin with an awareness of what is arising within our experience, feelings, sensations, thoughts, sounds and so on as I described in the Chapter 6. This capacity to witness the arising and passing of these experiences is important to stabilise awareness. Gradually, awareness settles without becoming drawn into the objects arising and then we begin to open and become more spacious. We need to give ourselves time to stabilise this experience so that we are not too distracted by thoughts and for our awareness to become more relaxed and open. The 'mantra' I find myself repeatedly saying when guiding this process is to 'let the body relax into a sense of ground and awareness to gradually open'.

When we have steadied this quality of awareness we can begin to make a subtle shift. Coming back to the metaphor of the rock-pool, what we begin to do is shift our attention to be aware of the spacious nature of the water itself. We need to open our attention to rest in the natural space of awareness itself. We are shifting the entire orientation of awareness from one that is observing what is arising, to the space within which phenomena arise. We might describe this subtle shift of attention in a number of ways; we open to, rest back into, lean back into or drop into the spacious nature of awareness itself (Appendix 7). Once resting in that space of awareness, feelings, sensations, thoughts and images will arise, but they pass through like 'clouds passing through the sky'. We remain aware of the sky. We open to the clarity of non-dual awareness which has always been present yet obscured by our ordinary 'hallucinating dualistic mind' as Lama Yeshe would call it.

As our experience deepens we begin to recognise a further subtlety in our understanding of the nature of mind which I have already alluded to. The unfolding flow of present spacious awareness may at first have a subtle sense of witness that 'observes' this process. A subjective sense that subtly witnesses the spacious nature of awareness as it continually unfolds. At a certain point this subjective sense of witness gradually fades and we are left with a direct experience of non-duality. In this experience there is neither awareness nor subjective witness. We open our awareness to a spacious quality that is beyond our notions of mind or subjective awareness.

To make this shift of awareness requires a capacity to let go and drop our normal, albeit subtle, holding to the sense of 'me'. Recognising the emptiness of self helps in this process but at some point, the subtle instinctual holding onto or contraction around 'me' needs to relax and let go. It is at this point, however, we may discover we are not so able to actually relax, let go and open because something blocks us. Psychologically what we are beginning to encounter is an aspect of what is sometimes called early or primary patterning that shapes the way in which we contract around a sense of self. As our sense of self forms in early months of life, it is affected by how safely held we feel. This is our experience of holding by our mother or primary care giver. When this is unsatisfactory we need to find a way to hold ourselves. This causes a contraction that will hold on to a sense of self because it is not safe to let go open and just be. This can remain present in us on a cellular level despite great amounts of meditation. Coming to this final frontier of letting go is therefore a necessary and valuable point. Here we finally begin to touch into the most subtle levels of holding onto our sense of self. We are confronted with the need to let go and open to the space of non-duality, like a drop of water dissolving into the ocean.

The process of mahamudra in relation to tantric practice helps us to encounter this threshold time and again as we dissolve our sense of self into emptiness, non-duality. As Lama Yeshe put it, "If you can touch your fundamental pure nature…. (then)… the usual self-pitying wrong conception - I am hopeless; I am impure; I am bad; I cannot do anything; I cannot help myself, dissolves."[17] Gradually we begin to loosen this self-contraction and can then rest more and more deeply in our innate empty nature, the ground of being, like dissolving into the ocean.

When we begin to meditate in this way it can facilitate a change in our tantric practice. Tantra is a practice that involves many visualisations which could be understood as arising within the space of non-dual awareness. There are also many occasions within the process of practice when visualisations naturally lead us to the experience of non-duality. Two particular examples of this are at times of 'dissolution' during the process of self-generation, something I will explain later in Chapter 13, or immediately following the recitation of mantras. If we are able to sit with a settled mind at these times we can go deeply into those experiences rather than restlessly move through them and stay caught in our conceptual mind. When we can rest in clear spacious awareness and emptiness, the space of non-duality, then it will always be experienced as the underlying ground of practice or more appropriately the space within which the deity emerges. The forms and appearances of tantric visualisations are like the clouds that emerge in the sky, the clarity of the sky is always there in the background. It is like the musical composer who is aware of the silence within the music or the creation of the visual artist that is aware of the space within form. When we understand this and can rest in the natural clarity of awareness, then we see that the process of deity practice is a display of radiance that manifests within it.

As we increasingly have a capacity to rest in the natural clarity, spaciousness and brightness of awareness itself, then we have a basis for tantric practice that will bring freshness to our experience. It will mean that visualisation and mantra practices enhance this experience, as I will describe in Chapter 12, because we can return to it time and time again as the space within the form. When teaching this approach in the US at Vajrapani Institute, it was interesting to hear the response of some of those who attended. Because they were not used to a style of practice that opened up so much space to rest in clear awareness, at first it was unfamiliar and uncomfortable. They were used to moving on to the next thing to do in the process of recitation. They were restless and the mind would not easily settle. Gradually, however, over a series of retreats the response changed. They began to describe how spacious they felt within practice and how much it was allowing a real settling into meditation.

When we enter the practice of tantra it is extremely important that we begin by learning to meditate in the quiet spacious clarity of awareness. It helps to have a conceptual understanding of emptiness as well but this does not mean we are necessarily able to meditate. From my own experience and from the experience of many I have taught, the practice of mahamudra is a valuable starting point. I am often surprised when I meet people who have been practicing tantra for many years and have complicated sadhana practices to perform and yet have never been taught how to meditate in the clarity of awareness within their practice. When I speak with them it becomes apparent that they often find great difficulty going beyond the conceptual mind. I am then not surprised when they say they are not fully getting a taste of the practice. When we cannot settle more deeply with the effect of deity practice, visualisation and mantra recitation then we do not *feel* the 'juice' that is potentially there. Our mind and its energy does not become pervaded by the power of the practice and we do not digest and assimilate its effect. It is not surprising then, after a period of time, we begin to lose heart and inspiration. In our daily life it requires great faith to keep going, but faith alone is not enough. We may recite endless texts describing visualisations of deities, but if our mind cannot become soaked in the felt-sense of practice. there may be little transformation and it can become just mechanical. First, therefore, we must learn to rest in the natural clarity of awareness itself.

When Lama Yeshe was alive and teaching aspects of deity practice he would often describe a visualisation process and say, "Then just let go into the space of non-duality". He was continually reminding us to touch into this ground of awareness and drop below the conceptual mind. I have always found his example an inspiration when introducing others to deity practice. He enabled a quality of space within the form of practice through his emphasis on mahamudra.

A greater emphasis on a basic capacity for mahamudra meditation and not just conceptual reflection is an important ground for tantric practice. Early in my practice I was not alone in having a tendency to be in the head and disconnected from my body. If we are like this then we can spend a considerable amount of time just doing our mediation practice in our heads. This experience is countered by coming back into the body and grounding in basic present awareness. In this respect mahamudra is something we can do at the beginning of the path if we are guided skilfully into it. It is also something we do in the middle of our tantric practice and it comes to its deepest fruition in the completion process. To begin with it is important to return to an awareness of body sensation and feeling. This awakens our relationship to the underlying energetic vitality that is so important in tantra. This then leads to a natural opening into the clarity and spaciousness of awareness and the nature of mind itself within mahamudra practice. All these stages are an important ground for deity practice and without them we may wonder, some years down the road, why our meditation is not as effective as it could potentially be.

9

A Psychological Process

I HAVE BEEN LEADING meditation retreats now for more than 30 years. In that time, I have also worked as a psychotherapist. Living between these two worlds has gradually brought me to see what our Western psychological knowledge can offer to our experience of Buddhist practice and tantric practice in particular. As my understanding has grown I have begun to see some of the most important ingredients in how we hold our psychological relationship to meditation and tantric practice. As I have said previously, the process of tantric practice is intended to bring to the surface aspects of our unconscious life that need to be awakened, transformed and integrated. If we practice skilfully, in an embodied way, whether we like it or not, this is what will begin to happen. What has been held or buried in the unconscious and the body begins to emerge and what is in the shadow begins to manifest. Inevitably this is seldom comfortable because what often awakens is not wonderful, blissful realisations, but rather the contents of our shadow, our emotional wounds and sometimes buried trauma. From my own path of practice, particularly in retreat, I found that whereas I was hoping for special realisations described in the teachings, instead I went through all kinds of painful emotional processes. As these were drawn out from the depths of my unconscious, they gradually began to be released, digested and healed.

I do not wish to imply in this that only what is uncomfortable will come to the surface. Within the unconscious there will also be blissful, joyful and insightful experiences that begin to awaken. Many of these emerge as we go through a psychological process that can begin in an uncomfortable way but release wonderful feelings as some kind of resolution takes place.

As I have worked with others it is very clear that a similar process goes on for most of us. The questions that arise will then be, how prepared are we to see this as the actual process of the practice? Are we ready to face these aspects of ourselves and begin to work with them with kindness and compassion? Do we understand what are the most useful and skilful ways to be with what arises to enable healing to take place?

As I have expressed in *The Wisdom of Imperfection*, while we receive guidance on the various aspects of practice as a *path* that unfolds, there is seldom an explanation of the underlying psychological *process* as we might experience it subjectively. It is very clear to me that knowledge of the dharma doesn't necessarily mean we are able to be with our psychological process in a skilful and transformative way. It is all too familiar within our Buddhist world to have some reticence or even fear of emotional process. We can often see it as something that needs to be contained, overcome, even avoided or transcended. If we grow up in a family or cultural context that does not sit comfortably with our emotional life then we will inevitably bring this attitude into our Buddhist practice. The danger with this view is that it will create conditions that are not naturally conducive to transformation. Even those that lead meditation retreats may unwittingly create an atmosphere that doesn't really welcome emotional process. We need to remember that the purpose of tantra in particular is to transform every aspect of our nature, not to reject it as unacceptable and not to put a veneer of supposed spiritual experiences over deeply buried emotional wounds.

When Lama Yeshe was alive I recall going to see him before I went into a three-month Vajrasattva retreat. He gave me one piece of advice that was so simple it was very easy to overlook and yet was perhaps the most profound thing he could have said. He said, "Whatever comes up just let go". It took me many years to really understand the significance of that comment and even today it is perhaps the most profound teaching I ever received. It has huge implications if we truly feel the subtlety of what he was advising. In some respects, this has been a central principle to my own practice and how I have subsequently led meditation retreats. Because of this I wish to describe what are perhaps the most important things to hold in mind when we practise tantra for the sake of our psychological healing.

When we practise tantra we place ourselves into a container or alchemical vessel that has certain ingredients. Retreat especially is an alchemical process that takes us through various stages. At first, we begin to adjust to the containment of retreat. As we settle into practice we begin to see or feel what we are bringing into that retreat space. For example, I often find myself struggling with a residual stress, tiredness and toxicity in my body that becomes apparent when I begin to meditate. As we go more deeply into the retreat space, the cooking process begins. As this 'heats up', things come to the surface that are aspects of our inner life often held in the body. This is natural and to be expected. We can even say that this is what is supposed to happen as whatever is to be transformed starts to be activated. This process can be uncomfortable and even disturbing. We are beginning to experience things arising, some of which perhaps we would rather not be see. Strong feelings may come, some of which may feel hard to be with, others may be blissful and even overwhelming. These will often bring with them mental activity that can be particularly disturbing if we are trying to meditate and want things to be quiet and still. Instead our inner life is becoming busy and out of control.

This cooking process can be especially intense during retreat, it may even cause us to want to get out of the vessel and run away. We may feel difficult emotions and wonder, "What am I doing here?" When I am leading a retreat, it is at this point that I will often need to remind people to stay with the process and trust that all is unfolding as it needs. It is part of the process. If we can allow this to pass through, some kind of resolution can begin, enabling our inner energetic reality to start to change. We begin to feel a sense of the transformation. In the context of retreat, I have seen this process happen often, whether it is over a month a week or just a weekend.

To enable the process of transformation in practice, whether in our day to day life or within retreat, there are some significant things to be aware of. Firstly, to heed Lama Yeshe's advice to *just let go*. What this means is not simple. We need to adopt an inner relationship to what arises within that does not judge or try to get rid of it. It is an attitude that is accepting and compassionate. It is also one that does not contract around what arises in a way that fixes and makes it into something that becomes too solid, too frozen or too formed. This can apply equally to our positive experiences as well as the painful ones. If we are fearful of our emotional process then we will tend to react to it and contract, suppress or dissociate from it. We can distract ourselves with stories and mental wandering. None of this helps the process of what is unfolding to follow its natural course of awakening, healing or transformation.

As I said at the beginning of this book, one of the central prerequisites for the practice of tantra is an understanding of emptiness. This means that we stop solidifying and freezing our experiences into something that becomes stuck. We often habitually want to control and contract around what arises within to feel safe or to feel we can cope with it. This may have been the most healthy way we could deal with painful experiences in our life, but ultimately it does not transform it. Transformation happens when we allow its emptiness to be. This means letting what is arising have the space to go where it needs to go. When we become more comfortable with this process we begin to feel the natural fluidity of everything that is arising and passing within our body and mind. We naturally start to feel its empty, transitory, fluid nature. We are after all continually changing moment to moment, and tantra works because it is a way of responding to that changing, transitory, empty nature.

Within our meditation, therefore, we need to be truly present with what is arising as a result of our practice. We need to hold an attitude that allows whatever is there without judgement or fear that it should not be there, and without contracting and grasping at it. It is a natural part of a process unfolding. We need to have the courage and openness to let what we feel arise in its rawness and allow its underlying energy the space to move through us. Transformation can then happen.

In my own retreats I saw this especially in relation to times when something very painful had emerged. I have also experienced it in relationship to times when pleasant and inspirational feelings arose. I remember vividly an occasion when as I began to work through a painful process that was deeply connected to my sense of identity. As this moved through I began to feel an incredible sense of elation. My tendency to contract around this elation took me off into all kinds of fantasy and excitement. My energy became more and more excited and I could barely contain it. Eventually I slept that night, but when I awoke I had dropped into a very depressed place. My energy had collapsed. To me this was a painful example of where I had not heeded the advice of "whatever comes up let go".

As someone holding the space of retreat for others this feels such an important thing to do. If I am afraid to allow emotion to arise because I feel it is not acceptable in some way then I block the process for those I am supporting. I need to hold a free and secure space that allows people to go through whatever they need to go through. If I can make this safe with a sense of love and compassion then those who are there can begin to relax and open. As they do so, they can allow their emotional life to be as it is and give it space to arise and transform.

If we consider that at the heart of Buddhist understanding is the notion that suffering arises through reaction and grasping, that is to say we contract and block a natural process. When we let go and open, this allows the fluid nature of our inner reality to move through us and heal. If we can maintain this way of being then our tantric practice will bring great healing potential liberating us from suffering. It is important to remember in this process that our intellectual conceptual mind is often an obstacle to the transformation that is possible. If we continually analyse and think about our emotional process, even our dharma knowledge can just create more attempts to make things different from how they are. It perpetuates a dualistic attitude that says this feeling is ok this feeling is not.

What I am describing here is a way of practice that goes beyond that judging duality and allows whatever arises to be as it is. When we totally open to its nature and let go, it is free to become liberated and healed. It moves through us and is transformed in its empty fluid nature.

10

The Deity as a Window

I HAVE DESCRIBED two aspects of meditation that are important to cultivate so that deity practice has a fertile ground in which to grow. The first is a capacity for a deeper awareness of the movement of feeling and its underlying energy within the physical body. The second is the ability to increasingly rest in the nature of clear spacious awareness, the nature of mind. These are two dimensions of the same process in meditation. Once this is established, when we then turn our attention to deity practice it will be much more effective. Perhaps we need to return to the question: what is the purpose of a deity?

I recall many years ago in Bodhgaya, India, hearing H.H.Dalai Lama respond to a question from a group of Westerners. Someone asked, what is the point of visualizing a deity? His answer was interesting and, I am sure, was particularly in response to this group which contained many people from the Theravada tradition. He said that when our mind is aware of the relative appearances of our reality, it is not able to be aware of emptiness. Then when our mind is aware of emptiness in meditation it is not able to cognize relative appearances. When we visualize ourselves as a deity, however, we are able to be aware of the form of the deity and emptiness at the same time. The mind can hold or cognize these paradoxical natures simultaneously; emptiness and appearance. One way that we can understand the significance of this is to recognise that a deity inhabits a realm that is metaphorically on the threshold between two dimensions of reality. Sitting on this threshold it acts as a kind of portal or gateway to another view of reality.

In the Tibetan tradition it is common to speak of two levels of truth: the level of relative appearances or relative truth, and ultimate truth, the true nature of those appearances. Relative truth relates to the world of forms and appearances, ultimate truth is the dimension of no-form, of emptiness and non-duality. In Buddhism these are not separate realities, they are two dimensions of the same experience, the union of appearance and emptiness. Our difficulty from a Buddhist point of view is that we are not usually able to cognize these two at the same time. This is because to gain the subtle realization of the empty nature of appearances requires considerable exploration and meditation. Our mind's disposition to see appearances as solid, enduring, truly-existent phenomenon is very strong and habitual, despite their true nature being empty of self-existence. To truly see that appearances are simply the moment to moment play of emptiness can be a difficult thing and take many years of meditation.

From a tantric perspective the ultimate nature of reality is known as dharmakaya. This is the ground of our reality. It is the natural, empty, spacious, clear-light nature of mind, from which all appearances manifest as the play of emptiness. Metaphorically, we can say that there is a threshold between these relative and ultimate dimensions of reality. This threshold is the paradoxical place of both form and emptiness simultaneously, inseparably, within a space of non-dual awareness. It is upon this threshold that appearances come into being from moment to moment, as the expression or play of clear awareness and emptiness. This threshold, therefore, is not an inert liminal space, it is a dynamic space that has tremendous creative energy or vitality. This vitality in the tantric tradition is associated with the *lung* or energy-wind as described in Chapter 6. This is the life vitality that moves through us and the world in every moment of its manifestation, as appearances emerge within the sphere of dharmakaya. In its pure aspect this energy is known as sambhogakaya, the dimension of energetic vitality that pervades our existence. One expression of this energy is understood to be the five elements or five lights of earth, water, fire, air and space, from which all appearances are created. We may be largely unconscious of the presence of this energy but if we begin to attune ourselves to it we will recognise its nature. It flows through our body and the environment and is expressed through the elements and runs beneath our emotional life.

It is upon this paradoxical dynamic threshold of form and emptiness that the deities of tantra abide. They are a direct expression of the creative vitality of sambhogakaya. When we tune into their energetic presence we begin to open to that quality and can feel it in our body and mind. The deity, whose form is the play of light energy within the sphere of emptiness, enables us to hold an awareness of these two levels of truth together.

It is unfortunate that most of us don't readily experience or recognise the innate empty ground of reality; the radiant clarity of dharmakaya. We may have glimpses, but it is largely obscured by our ordinary mind's pre-occupation with habitual, dualistic, conceptual confusion. Dharmakaya becomes an unconscious ground of being, and our lack of relationship to it means we are effectively shut off from the very essence of our true nature. Many of us have a deep yearning to return to that relationship because we know it is there in potential. This is often part of our sense of spiritual calling. But to restore the relationship it is helpful to have some kind of bridge or gateway into that reality. Then we can begin to open to its presence. In the tantric tradition this is the role of the deity, which sits on the threshold between our ordinary reality of appearances and the ultimate nature of dharmakaya. When we meditate with the presence of a deity we can begin to access what is beyond its light energy appearance. It then becomes a gateway or window into the ultimate nature of reality that is ordinarily inaccessible to us.

One way we may understand this is through the metaphor of a stained-glass window. Many times, I have stood in a church or cathedral and gazed up at the beauty of stained-glass mandala images or images of the saints. I find it fascinating that when I look, the image may at first be relatively dull and two dimensional until the sun shines through. Suddenly I find myself bathed in sunlight and the image comes alive. The colours become radiant. If I consider where that radiance comes from, however, it is the sun on the other side of the window. It is through this intermediary of the window that I connect to this source of light. In the same way, a deity is a window through which we can come to recognise our innate wisdom nature beyond form, our experience of clear-light dharmakaya. The deity is alive and vibrant with light and radiance because the clear-light nature of pure radiant awareness shines through. A deity gives us the potential to open to this nature in our being and receive its blessing and inspiration. It is the subtle form through which we can connect directly to the source.

When we visualise a deity, it is as though we are looking into that window beyond which is the vast sphere of clarity and emptiness. If we can open to this awareness we will begin to awaken that wisdom in our nature and receive the blessing that comes through. In this way we make a connection to what we might call *Source*. When in the process of practice, we transform into the deity, it is as though we actually sit upon that same threshold. Then we open to the creative nature of form and emptiness as it is expressed through the deity, bringing this into our experience from moment to moment. Effectively, we become a vehicle or channel for that quality to come through us. We become the window.

What the window metaphor tells us, is that the deity's form is the relative appearance. It's true nature is the union of dharmakaya and sambhogakaya that shines through. In this sense it is a vehicle for something and not exactly the thing itself. It is the finger pointing at the moon.

Since a deity is the gateway through which the emptiness of dharmakaya and energy of sambhogakaya 'communicates' to us, it becomes very powerful. That power is an expression of the dynamic vitality that is present on the threshold between form and emptiness. It is also imbued with the blessing of the Buddhas who have awakened fully, and the meditators who have given such care and devotion to its practice.   When I began to paint tangkhas (Tibetan icons) while I was in India I realised that the precision and consistency of the images I was painting had a purpose. This was to provide a focus within meditation that could enable a consistent alignment with the quality we wished to awaken. As an archetypal expression of our innate buddha-nature each deity brings with it a profound sense of meaning through the qualities that are exemplified in the symbolism of the form. For example, Chenrezig is an expression of compassion, Manjushri of wisdom and Vajrapani of power. They are imbued with what Jung called numinosity, a sense of awe and fascination. Here it is important to remember that a deity is not merely an image of buddha-nature, it is a direct emanation of it.

As I will describe more fully later, a deity is also a manifestation of what we might call the inner guru, and when we open to this we receive 'blessing' and inspiration. This blessing means that our mind becomes inspired and energised, enabling us to deepen our experience of qualities we need in our journey. It will help us cultivate the qualities of the deity such as wisdom, compassion, strength and so on. Ultimately this relationship will open us to our innate clear-light nature of blissful wisdom and will imbue all that we are and what we do with that quality. When we connect to this source, we become a vehicle for its manifestation in the world, through our physical embodiment.

11

Initiation

FOR US TO ENTER into the practice of tantra it is necessary to receive some kind of initiation or empowerment. Traditionally this process follows a number of possible forms which may be relatively brief or alternatively extremely complex. The simplest is known as a *lung* or oral transmission of a mantra or text associated with a specific deity. The second is known as a *jenang* or permission to practice. A third is known as a *wang* or empowerment, which may be relatively simple but with some practices is very complex and carried out over several days. While it is usually considered that we can only practise a particular deity once we have received one of these ways of entry it is worth considering what is at the heart of initiation.

The reason we need initiation is partly self-explanatory. Initiation is the first or initial spark that gives rise to the beginning of something new. It is like the moment of conception or the moment of ignition of a flame. It could be seen as the initial germination of a seed that begins the process of emergence of a new plant. Initiation begins to awaken and germinate an aspect of our nature already present within us, but in what might be seen as a dormant state.

A deity therefore is potentially present as a latent seed within our innate nature. Each of us has buddha-nature or a natural buddha potential. A deity is an expression of this buddha potential that, once awakened, can act as a catalyst for transformation. For this to come to life it needs some means of waking it up through a process of initiation. Once the flame is ignited it is then for us to gradually allow the fire to grow.

If we consider these metaphors we can see that the moment of initial awakening can happen in a formal setting transmitted by someone who has already awoken that experience. It could, however, be ignited spontaneously by other means. This may, for example, be through a dream or some form of vision, which is certainly how most of the tantric deity lineages began. There was a time in India when several of a group of highly evolved meditators known as the 84 mahasiddhas experienced specific visions of deities such as Vajrayogini, Chakrasamvara and Hevajra. There have also been more recent meditators in Tibet who received visions of tantric deities and as a consequence have begun new lineages of deity practices. The deity Chittamani Tara is one such example.

Following their initial vision, these yogis were able to practise and introduce others to their experience through the process of initiation and empowerment. The lineage of transmission of these experiences has then been maintained over time, and it is this continuity (Tibetan: *gyu*)[18] that we are able to tap into when we also receive empowerment. Here the terms initiation and empowerment have significantly different implications. Empowerment implies that a transmission of the potency of a deity experienced by the lama is passed on to the disciple. The disciple responds to this by deepening its experience through practice.

When we receive an initiation or empowerment something extraordinary can happen. The energetic field created in this process by the initiating lama can open us to an experience of the deity that affects us deeply. What the process of initiation does is to open the window I have spoken of in the previous chapter. The feeling of inspiration and awe we may then feel in the presence of the deity can be very powerful. Lama Yeshe used to say that we can experience significant realisation at the time of initiation if we are well prepared and open to receive the experience. He said this is why it is often helpful to repeat that process with a particular deity several times through our life. He felt it will deepen each time, bringing an increasing intimacy with the deity.

Initiation or empowerment is taken very seriously within the Tibetan world and various protocols have been established in the different traditions as to how it is to be followed. These protocols create a formal structure and system around the transmission of tantric practices that protects and maintains the authenticity of the tradition. They are also to ensure that the recipient of the initiation maintains their relationship to the deity in a clear and consistent way. Part of this is expressed when taking certain vows, such as the bodhisattva and tantric vows, which can often be required before receiving empowerments.

Over the years I have seen that difficulties can arise when we embark upon the process of receiving empowerments, particularly in relation to higher tantra (Skt: *maha anutara yoga tantra*). I experienced some of these myself in my early years as a Tibetan Buddhist and think it may be useful to name them. There is often a feeling that an initiation is a rare and important event that should not be missed. This can lead to a subtle pressure to take something that we may or may not be prepared for. It is easy for many of us to naively receive empowerments and not actually know what we are doing. What especially concerns me is that often only cursory guidance is given beforehand as to the complexity of what is being entered into. As a consequence, we may have little understanding of what is going on during an empowerment, in part because much of it is in Tibetan. Often only relatively brief descriptions of complicated processes are explained. Having translated one of these long initiation texts while in India, I became very aware of how much I was missing during empowerments. I have often heard people new to this experience describe how it was powerful and inspiring, but they still did not know what was happening. Even so, they have technically 'received' an empowerment and therefore have to fulfil the requirements the lama gives in terms of commitment.

Unfortunately, there can then be a danger of these commitments becoming somewhat onerous when applied too tightly or rigidly. Increasingly, in the West, Tibetan teachers understand that we are not able to follow quite the same strictness of protocols as there were in Tibet. Part of this is in relation to the nature of the commitments that are asked of those who receive initiations.

Once we receive an initiation and the seed has been germinated, the commitment given is intended to sustain a relationship to that deity so that our experience gradually grows. This is called the *samaya* that we take at the time of initiation and implies both a bond with the deity but also with the lama that gave the transmission. How we fulfil or maintain that *samaya* can happen in a number of different ways. The most common way is that we are expected to perform specific practices, rituals, prayers or mantras associated with the deity. This will mean that practitioners will often gradually accumulate a series of prayers and practices they are expected to do as a daily routine. This may be a very inspiring and fulfilling process but there can also be the danger of becoming overwhelmed by the amount of practices that need to be done. Speaking with friends and peers, they have said that so much time is taken fulfilling these commitments, they feel they do not give enough time for actual meditation practice. This can be a huge problem if we have found ourselves with many commitments to different deity practices accumulated over the years.

I was recently reading an article in which several lamas, including both the late Gelek Rinpoche and Zazep Rinpoche, felt that in the west there is a great danger of us taking too many empowerments that we may not then practise in any depth. They could see that it is not the number of practices we have that is important, but the depth into which we go with any one practice. This problem becomes especially acute when we are expected to fulfil commitments to many deities that require the recitation of sadhanas. This can be very time consuming and easily become dry and mechanical.

The way in which tantric initiations are given means that we commit to a relationship with a deity that remains through our life. Trying to integrate deity practice into a Western lifestyle and especially, as I have experienced myself, into lay family life can be quite a challenge. Many or most Western practitioners are lay and have relatively conventional working lives which can often make it difficult to create space to practise. At its most detrimental I have known people suffer a huge sense of guilt and anxiety because they are not fulfilling something they have been told to do. If we come to the point of realising we are involved in something we simply cannot fulfil it can bring great inner conflict. To hear the Tibetans speak so readily of the downfalls of breaking commitments and the kind of suffering we will encounter, can also be very disturbing. This is especially problematic for new practitioners who take higher tantra empowerments and lack an understanding of what they have committed to in terms of the complexity of practice. This is rather like signing a contract first and then being allowed to read what we have signed for afterwards.

There are I think a number of solutions to most of the difficulties I have described above. One is to prepare the ground well before embarking on this journey and hopefully what I am writing in this book will also contribute to that. Learning some of the meditations I have introduced earlier can help and also getting to know what tantric practice is about. It is helpful to persistently ask questions of those who have some experience of initiations, to make sure we are clear about what we are getting involved in. When we fail to do this, we may regret it later down the line. Another solution is to be careful about the number of initiations we receive and not to rush in just because a high lama arrives giving a special empowerment.

Some Tibetan teachers are more hard-line about commitments than others, and as new practitioners we can be especially vulnerable to the line they take, often because of a lack of experience. Fortunately, there are lamas who hold a somewhat more compassionate and less rigid view. H.H.Dalai Lama is one such teacher. When a friend found she simply could not relate to or do a particular higher tantra practice she had received some years earlier his advice was very sensitive. He told her to respectfully take the text of the practice, wrap it in cloth and place it on a shelf with the wish or prayer that at some time she may be able to practise it.

When I heard this something in me relaxed. I felt that we are so fortunate to have someone with such a gentle touch in how we as Westerners should approach this path. This is not to say that we should not take the practice of tantra seriously and do so with the genuine desire to do the best we can. What felt so powerful about the Dalai Lama's response was that he is giving the message that we should not turn these guidelines for practice into a rigid dogma based on fear. When we do this, it has a very detrimental effect on our relationship to our own spiritual life and also to this extraordinary tradition. As I recall hearing a Tibetan doctor once saying, it can become a kind of spiritual sickness.

Having received an initiation, the familiar requirement, as I have said, is to perform certain recitation practices to uphold our commitment. These may be brief such as a mantra which we may find relatively manageable in our daily life. The danger when commitments become more involved, is that it can become a mechanical recitation of prayers, while half asleep or at great speed, just to get them done. Unfortunately, I have in the past found myself in this position. If we find ourselves doing this it is worth considering a deeper relationship to the practice. If we go beneath this superficial level and find what is actually at the heart of our commitment, it is the inner relationship of devotion and the profound honouring of the sacred nature of what we have received. This is partly conveyed by the term often used to describe a special relationship to a particular deity. It is called our *yidam*, literally our 'heart-bound' deity. A deity is intimately connected to our heart as a relationship to our innate nature. When we receive an initiation, we are opening ourselves to something in our nature that has profound implications and which is in essence the source of all the deities, not just one. If we have a taste of this significance and let ourselves be touched by the process then the true commitment is to that quality awakening in our nature. If we lose sight of this, or in some way do not believe in or trust in this aspect of our nature, then we are truly losing our samaya. I am reminded of the true meaning of the word sin in Christianity, which is a sense of losing sight of or turning away from God. We could see something very similar in the notion of commitment in the tantric tradition.

Once we receive an initiation and the seed of an experience begins to grow, to turn away from it or lose relationship to it is very unfortunate. There can be a deep and painful dislocation from the heart of our spiritual life. I have seen this happen with a couple of friends, owing to a rift or break in relationship to a lama that was at one time important. It left them feeling lost and painfully out of relationship to their practice, but perhaps more seriously out of relationship to their spiritual core. Because the deity practices that become 'heart-bound' have such a depth of meaning as well as connection to the lama who gave us the transmission, any break in that relationship will be very painful. It is for this reason that we should be extremely careful from whom we take initiation, but also be diligent in how we protect that inner relationship. It is perhaps important to also consider how many initiations we choose to take, when we may only be able to practise a few in any depth.

The recitation of prayers when heartfelt, helps us fulfil the maintenance of our relationship to the deity and through that to our true nature. If this becomes just a mechanical recitation we can lose the heart connection. If, on the other hand, we try always to hold in our heart the precious gift of our innate buddha-nature and the awakening of the deity as the essence of our spiritual life, then I feel we hold our samaya. Ultimately it is our relationship to the essential nature of our clear-light mind of non-duality that is the true samaya. As Tilopa expresses in the *Song of Mahamudra* also known as *Ganges Mahamudra*:

He who keeps the Tantric precepts yet discriminates betrays the spirit of samaya.
Cease all activity, abandon all desire,
Let thoughts rise and fall as they will, like ocean waves.
He who never harms the non-abiding,
Nor the principle of non-distinction upholds the Tantric precepts.

What this verse points to is a very subtle understanding that there is the relative samaya conveyed in the form of the recitation of texts, precepts for practice and the pitfalls of not upholding them. There is also a deeper recognition that if we open to the innate non-dual nature of our reality, we see these are just superficial forms. The true samaya is to our innate clear-light nature.

What this verse points to is the understanding that there is the relative samaya conveyed in the form of the recitation of texts, but also the ultimate samaya. He is suggesting that our relative samaya can be broken by a discriminating mind that becomes caught up in dualistic thinking.

12

The Sadhana

DEITY PRACTICE IS CENTRAL to tantra and over the centuries many meditators have attained profound insights and experiences through this path. As I have said earlier, in India after the time of the Buddha, there were a number of yogis known today as the 84 Mahasiddhas, that dedicated their lives to tantric practice. Many of them were the originators of specific deity lineages, initiating a transmission of experience that has been unbroken for hundreds of years since the time of the Buddha.

The historical movement of tantra, from India, often through Nepal and into Tibet, is interesting in that it helps us to be aware that these practices have evolved and changed. With tantric deity practice there is a living lineage that continues to this day. What now comes to the West is a form of practice, while originating in India, has over the centuries been shaped and elaborated by the Tibetans. They have created the form of practice we encounter today, with richly detailed descriptions of visualisations, prayers and rituals known as a *sadhana* or 'method of accomplishment'. They have also written many extensive commentaries on these practices. This process has led to a rich and colourful way of practice that is inseparably interwoven with Tibetan culture. H.H.Dalai Lama on one occasion said, however, that this was not exactly how tantric practice would have been carried out hundreds of years ago in India. Their practice, he suggested, would have been primarily visualisations, not the recitation of extensive complex texts. These texts and commentaries emerged later as the practices became developed and systematised, by the Tibetans in the context of monasteries. Today we can see that the transmission of tantra to Japan, Nepal and China created very different forms. What most of us experience as the form of tantra as it comes to the West is, however, primarily coloured by the Tibetan culture.

Once we have received some form of introduction or initiation to a deity we are able to embark upon the practice of a sadhana. A sadhana is the description of an unfolding visualisation process that enables us to gradually bring a deity to life within our psyche. Over the years there have been certain gifted lamas in Tibet who delighted in the poetic composition of these sadhanas, many of which have become the primary texts upon which practices are based. These texts can be full of lengthy liturgy of prayers, offerings and detailed descriptions of visualisations, that may take several hours to perform as a recitation. In the context of Tibetan monasteries, one can see the value of this, with large groups of monks spending many hours chanting these texts together. They needed a form that contained the essential ingredients for the cultivation or generation of the relationship to the deity, and because they were chanting these practices together they became rich in devotional liturgy.

As I began to embark upon my own practice of tantra some forty years ago, at first I found this richness and complexity of the tantric sadhana very inspiring, but also somewhat overwhelming. It was in the early days of these practices becoming accessible to Westerners. Sadhanas were usually chanted in Tibetan transposed into phonetics, with a relatively crude translation either alongside or beneath the phonetics. It rapidly became clear to me that I was trying to do a combination of things that were actually very difficult to bring together. As I did not understand Tibetan well, to get the meaning of what we were chanting I would try to read the English at the same time. I was then attempting to visualise what we were chanting. On top of this I was hoping to meditate. It was clear to me that the chanting had an effect on my mind, but I did not feel that it readily enabled me to meditate as I would have liked, and much of the detail of the practices was lost.

In time these practices have been translated more skilfully into English. This makes it possible to read a sadhana in English, certainly for our own personal practice, even if this is not so easy within groups. In group settings sadhanas often continue to be chanted in Tibetan, although relatively recently some Western practitioners have tried, with varying degrees of success, to transpose English translations into some kind of chantable form.

While these traditional sadhanas are quite extraordinary and often contain extensive detailed visualisations, there is a question of how manageable they are for Westerners and Western mind. Having spent many years engaged in my own practice and a lot of time in retreat following a relatively traditional approach, I began to find the complexity problematic. It also became apparent that when it comes to meditation, the elaborate sadhana is not so helpful. Initially I found that the best way to transform my sadhana practice into something that was more meditative was to memorise the text. This often meant memorising very long texts that would normally take at least an hour and half to do. Having done so, however, it did enable me to have a deeper meditative relationship to practice. What still remained problematic was shifting from my conceptual mind to a deeper felt quality of experience. At a certain point I began to feel full to bursting with all the forms and busyness of the way I was practising. I could feel something inside me becoming desperate for space, for quiet and stillness. I began to seriously consider that I needed to drop my practice and do something radically different.

What I began to see was that for meditation purposes the continual recitation of a detailed sadhana was becoming problematic. I needed do something very differently but it was not clear at first what that needed to be. I felt that I was not really deepening into a felt experience of practice, nor was my mind really learning to settle particularly well. When I was in retreat, my retreat mentor Gen Jampa Wangdu related something very interesting from his own experience. He said that meditators will begin with the more detailed long sadhanas, then gradually move to the shorter abbreviated form and then eventually go to an extremely brief form that had almost no words. This meant that the long sadhana had the purpose of filling in the detailed information about practice and what was being visualised, but the brief forms were for actual meditation.

He described how the sadhana in its simplest form then became just a series of visualisations triggered by sanskrit syllables, something which accords with what the H.H.Dalai Lama had said regarding the early meditators in India.

The Purpose of a Sadhana

There is a principle at the heart of sadhana practice that is not always clear when we are doing long and complex forms. The sadhana is a development of visualisations that take our mind though a particular evolution. It is intended to guide the mind along a pathway that leads to a qualitative felt shift in our inner reality. It is a transformational pathway. As such, the purpose is to set up what might be seen as a new habit or pattern in the mind that becomes increasingly instinctual. Like learning to drive a car, at some point we just do it naturally, we don't have to think. Similarly, through a constant repetition of a sadhana we set up a kind of groove into which our mind settles and follows naturally. Once this is established in our awareness as a natural stream of movement, then we are able to relax much more deeply into the process and drop beneath the conceptual detail. The words become secondary to the actual unfolding process of visualisation. The sadhana gradually becomes a natural pathway for transformation because of its repeated activation.

For a sadhana to become a pathway for our mind I feel it is important that gradually we have the evolution of a practice memorised. This has a number of advantages. Perhaps the most important is that we do not have to refer to a text and in doing so come out of the depth of our meditation. A more practical reason did make good sense for me, however, when I was in India. I had a friend who was a monk and over many years had accumulated a lot of practices he was committed to perform each day. To do this he had a considerable number of sadhana texts, some long and others brief. One day he arrived from Delhi very distraught having taken the overnight train. On the train he had had his luggage stolen and the thing that distressed him most was that all of his practices were in his luggage. For him this was a complete disaster because he had only a few of them memorised. Now he was seriously afraid he was going to break so many of his commitments with dire consequences.

It was this experience that made me decide that from that point I would memorise all my practices in a form that was practical to meditate upon without the use of texts.

Over the past 30 years or more of leading meditation retreats with Westerners it is clear to me that many of us have difficulties with the traditional detailed style of sadhana practice. Many people I have taught in retreat find they can be too intense and a great strain on their mind, sometimes causing a tension that is not helpful. Perhaps the Tibetans have the capacity for this kind of practice in a way that we do not, and certainly chanting sadhanas together in the monastery must have its own effect that is very powerful. For meditation purposes, however, our mind is less used to this kind of concentrated conceptual practice and needs something more spacious and less complex. There is also a danger that if someone has little feeling for the deity in the sadhana then it is very difficult to make a connection. Sadhana recitation then becomes just mechanical.

This led me to conclude that it is necessary to find a way into this kind of practice that is more conducive to our Western mind so as to actually *feel* the process of transformation. In my own retreats I increasingly found simplifying the essentials of the sadhana, as Gen Jampha Wangdu had suggested, was helpful. When I have found myself in the position of guiding others with these practices, this issue has become even more critical. It is in answer to this dilemma that I found myself continually referring to the way in which Lama Yeshe taught. Fortunately, in the years before his death he seemed to understand this problem and consistently suggested that it was more important for us to get a 'taste of the practice', as he would put it. This meant going below the intellectual conceptual mind and actually getting a feel of the deity. His view was that if we are to meditate more deeply on the practices then working with either brief sadhanas or key segments of the sadhana would be more useful. He wanted us to actually meditate upon the practice rather than just do recitation.

He once said: "I also think that it is not necessary to read all the words of a sadhana if you perform the meditations. If you remember the process from beginning to end and have a complete mental picture of all the meditations, you do not need to recite the words. Once you have performed the meditations, what is there left to do? Words can definitely be an obstacle."[19]

The structure of the Sadhana

Figure 4

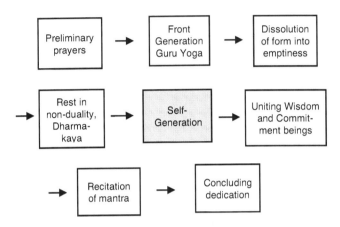

When teaching, Lama Yeshe took an important step, which consisted of two things. Firstly, when he was teaching deity practices such as Vajra Yogini and Manjushri, he would simplify some of the liturgy to abbreviate the lengthy verses of praise and requests for blessing and so forth in the longer sadhanas. Secondly, he would often break sadhanas into smaller sections so that we could actually meditate upon them to get more of an experience. He would say, "Today I want you to take this bit of the sadhana and really go into it in meditation to get a feel of it". This felt very significant.

In my own practice I began to see that for the sadhana to become a more meditative experience it was helpful to get to the essence of the practice. To make this possible we need to understand the key elements that make up the 'bone structure' of a sadhana around which elaborate liturgy has been written. While in India I spent a long time translating the sadhanas of one particular higher tantra practice into English. In this process, it was fascinating to see the way in which these sadhanas are structured and how they consistently follow a formula, as I have shown in Figure 4. Here we can see how *self-generation*, where we become the deity, is central to most complete sadhanas. There is a process that leads up to this and one that subsequently follows on from it. In the preceding process, the deity is visualised in front, often as a practice of *guru yoga*, which I will explain later. There then follows what is called a dissolution into emptiness before arising as the deity. Many simple sadhanas only have a *front generation* practice which can have elaborate prayers and offerings. Following the self-generation there can be various visualisations that lead eventually to the recitation of the deity's mantra followed by some form of concluding process of prayers and dedication.

Once I understood this formula, it was then more obvious what Lama Yeshe was doing when he split these practices into sections or stripped away the complexity of liturgy to reveal the essential form. It is now very clear to me, having taught some of these practices to people in the context of retreat, that a less complicated, more spacious and contemplative approach has been of greatest benefit. This spaciousness gets lost when too much complexity and excessive liturgy is included. The question is, can we hold to the very essence of a practice and bring that into our experience?

Integrating Mahamudra and Deity Practice

To answer this question, I would like to describe a way of entering into a sadhana practice that is different to the conventional approach. As I have already expressed, if we begin the process of deity visualisation from a state of awareness primarily bound within our ordinary conceptual mind, then our meditation will not readily go into great depth. This may mean that if we do the sadhana in what seems to be the familiar way, reciting or chanting a text with very little settling, then it would look a little like the upper line (Conceptual mind) in Figure 5. We can see from this that we are not settling either into the body or the more subtle nature of mind. The result is we continually stimulate conceptual thinking and allow little opportunity to slow the process down and to drop deeper.

As Lama Yeshe would often emphasise, if we slow the process down and open up the space for settling, as in the second line (Body awareness), then we have more likelihood of feeling the effect of practice, particularly within the energy-body. If we can settle into quiet present awareness within the field of sensation and feeling in the body, before we introduce deity practice, then a change begins.

By practicing a sadhana that has less words, it is possible to open up spaces where we again return to the experience of present awareness as a way of deepening the felt experience. We can then more easily digest or integrate what is happening. This process is conveyed in the

Figure 5

3 Levels of Practice

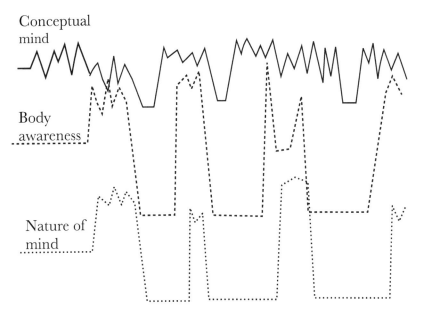

Conceptual mind

Body awareness

Nature of mind

second line (Body awareness) of Figure 5. Here we are doing less conceptual recitation and instead dipping into direct felt experience whenever possible. The spaces where we drop below the conceptual into the felt process can be opened out and lengthened to suit our own personal intention. In my own practice this is where I began to bring a sense of space back into my mind that had become lost by the intensity of conceptual recitation. My meditation became alive again once I could let my mind relax and drop into the felt sense.

For those who have never meditated in this way before, the experience of a slower more spacious sadhana practice can at first feel challenging. Many of my students who have previously been used to reading or reciting a sadhana have said that the capacity to rest and quieten, dropping below conceptual mind, was unfamiliar. It revealed their inner restlessness. It is for this reason it is helpful to begin with the basic meditations of quiet awareness in body feeling and sensation to gain the capacity to stop, settle and rest. As I said in Chapter 6 this is the practice that actually enables us to directly digest and feel the effect of our practice as we go along.

As we become more comfortable with practicing in this way we can potentially go deeper, drawing on the practice of mahamudra. It is for this reason I have emphasised in Chapter 8 how helpful it is to have first cultivated some capacity to rest in the nature of spacious awareness itself before taking this next step. To go deeper we bring to the beginning of the sadhana the experience that comes from mahamudra, meditating on the nature of clear spacious awareness. This is conveyed in the third line (Nature of mind) of Figure 5. Once we are able to settle in the mind's innate clarity of spacious awareness we begin to introduce the presence of the deity. To do this, again, we do not want to 'rise up' too much into the conceptual mind. With experience, however, it is possible to begin to introduce the deity into the space of awareness in the way a cloud may emerge in the blue sky, its nature is not other than the sky.

When I introduce this in guided meditation I find it helpful to change the language I use to describe what is happening. When I use the phrase "visualise in the space before you" I have found many people try to see something with their eyes. Many struggle with not feeling they are getting it right because they can't visualise well. On the other hand if I say, "within the space of awareness there arises", it conveys a very different sense. We are allowing the deity to emerge within the nature of awareness itself as a radiant movement of the energy of the mind. It is not other than the mind and its energy, radiance and clarity appearing within the medium of the mind. There is also less emphasis on having a clear image and more on the felt presence of the deity. To do this we can use a minimum of concepts and have the desired effect. If it is helpful to use a few concepts to evoke the image of the deity they need not disturb the experience of meditation like the metaphor of the fish swimming through water, it does not disturb the water.

To follow a sadhana practice in this way requires a number of things. First, we need to have a clear knowledge of its evolution so that we know the unfolding process of practice. This is often where we start with a more conceptual experience and then begin to drop the concepts once we know what is happening and what the deity, etc, looks like. We then begin to strip away the complexity of words and move through the visualisations in a more fluid, less conceptual way. We also need to slow down and stay with the felt experience of what is happening. In retreats I lead, I prefer to initially guide people through a sadhana practice as a meditation process that does not require that they read any text. This enables a much deeper relationship to practice and the deity as a felt experience, something reading a text often hinders. Once they are familiar with this in a sadhana they may then take this experience and gradually memorise it. They can then use it in their own practice referring to a text or audio recording only when needed.

We therefore need to change the emphasis of practice away from its form and more to its flow and the space that opens up within that. To do this we may need to let go of the idea of counting lots of mantras and to have either decided to do so at some other time or to have already done it previously. Personally, I was greatly relieved when I had done my 'counting retreats' because I felt I could really start to meditate. The purpose of the counting retreat is to activate the vibration of the deity within our nervous system through the quality of the mantra. This can be extremely powerful but perhaps there needs to be a kind of 'health warning'. If we do a counting retreat in an intense, often excessively driven and busy way, I feel it's value is extremely debatable. These retreats are sometimes called 'close placement retreats' but I am not always sure how 'close' they really bring us to the deity if our mind is tight and full of chatter as we try to recite mantras as fast as we can.

We could say that in essence the intention of deity practice is to begin to liberate and transform the energy contained in the body and awaken our awareness to particular qualities. To do this we need to settle increasingly deeply into the body and the spacious nature of awareness. Lama Yeshe would repeatedly describe points in a sadhana where he would say, "Just let go into the space of non-duality." When we give ourselves the space to do this we can experience the potential for transformation that is there. If we don't we may find our practice loses its 'juice' and becomes dry and mechanical.

I have been describing a way of practice that can be experienced on three different levels beginning with a conceptual process then settling more into the body and finally resting within the nature of awareness. This may give the impression that these are three distinct and separate approaches, in practice, however, this is not necessarily the case. With experience we may find that within the process of one meditation we can move through all these levels. In retreats where I introduce a sadhana as a guided visualisation, people move out of the ordinary conceptual mind and settle into the body at the beginning of the meditation. This leads to an increasingly subtle relationship to the felt effect of practice within the energy-body, which in turn leads to a more natural opening into the space of awareness. We could perhaps say that this is the purpose of a sadhana, to gradually lead us to more subtle states of embodied energy awareness.

When we allow more space within sadhana practice we return again and again to the felt sense of the process of transformation. As our practice becomes pervaded by spacious awareness we can increasingly see the deity's nature as a radiant yet empty reflection of the mind, emerging and dissolving within the medium of awareness.

Entering into the process of sadhana practice is something that needs guidance. This is why the relationship to a teacher who has experience of the practice is important in the tantric tradition. There may be teachers with intellectual knowledge but this is not enough, particularly with regard to this Eastern tradition meeting Western mind with its particular needs and tendencies. I feel this is still very much a learning process. Something that has helped me in this, is asking a question that I never felt was asked in the traditional context. When I have guided students through certain visualisations in a retreat setting, I will often ask: "How was that for you?" Their response to this can be very helpful. It gives me the opportunity to explore what touches them more deeply and what doesn't. It also gives me the opportunity to discover individual differences in how practices can be integrated. That makes it possible to make practice more 'person-centred', something I will explain in more detail later. It also gives people the chance to talk about the difficulties they might have and know this is a natural part of the process. Sharing their experience gives others new insights into how they can practise so that they learn from each other. I think the result has been incredibly productive and has really helped me to teach. I feel I am learning all the time how these practices affect us and can be integrated more skilfully. What becomes very gratifying is when I hear people who have practised in this way for a while, say to me, "This really works".

The points I have been making about the sadhana suggest that there are two important ways in which it is practiced, which need very different forms. One is in a group setting where the richness of liturgy may be entirely appropriate for the recitation or chanting of deity practices. The other is in the context of retreat or private meditation practice when we are trying to go into a deeper meditative process. In this situation a more brief essence of a sadhana is helpful especially for Western mind.

13

Front Generation

IF ONE STRIPS AWAY some of the complexity of many sadhanas, at their heart are two primary processes. One is the invocation of a visualised deity in the space in front of the meditator, or *front-generation*, often associated with a practice known as *Guru Yoga* which I will discuss later. The second is *self-generation,* where we actually transform into the deity. These two processes are the core of the practice and all the prayers and offerings are then added around them, often as a devotional embellishment.

Front-generation is where we begin to cultivate a relationship to our innate buddha-nature through the visualisation of a deity in the space before us. There is an obvious duality in this because we are creating an apparent separation. To consider Jung's view however, we are inviting a manifestation of the Self in front and recognising our ego's relative position in relationship to it. To clarify this, I think it is helpful to return to Jung's understanding. In *The Psychology of Buddhist Tantra* I describe a map of the psyche that sees the ego as a subordinate aspect of our nature in relation to the Self (see Figure 6).

Through our life our relationship to the Self as our innate centre of wholeness, goes through different phases. Earlier in life the ego

Figure 6

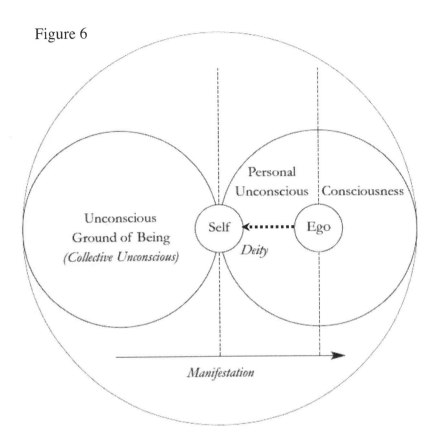

needs to become established as the stable centre of our ordinary identity in the world. From a psychotherapeutic perspective, a necessary aspect of this process is that the ego emerges from a ground of being in which it is immersed. We could see this as immersion in the mother-ground, where mother embodies an all-embracing environment. In Buddhism this ground of being is our innate dharmakaya which, interestingly, is also known as mother clear-light. According to the psychologist Michael Washburn this emergence of the ego from what he calls the 'dynamic ground' requires that we partially or completely close down our relationship to it.[20] As we do, a threshold between ordinary day to day consciousness and the unconscious gradually begins to form. Effectively we can say that the ground of being, that mother-ground, or mother clear-light, has become submerged in the unconscious and is veiled from consciousness. Once the ego is established as the centre of conscious life, however, one of the downsides of this development is that it has become separated from the core of our nature. Jung called this core the Self, our centre of wholeness. From a Buddhist perspective we could call this our buddha-nature. This separation means that the ego considers that it is the centre of its world, when in actuality it is not.

From Jung's viewpoint, at certain times in our life in the process of individuation, the Self begins to assert its presence, giving the ego the suspicion that perhaps it is not the centre. This may be expressed in a deep yearning for spiritual awakening and for the sense of meaning it can bring. It is as though we know there is something 'other' in our deeper nature and we embark upon a journey to discover it.

If our ego identity is strongly established as a controlling centre of our life, the return of the Self is less comfortable as we discover that there may be other forces at work that are more potent and not in our control. This kind of experience can happen at any time, but is especially felt in mid-life or in times of what might be called spiritual crisis. Whenever it happens it will often be disturbing and unsettling as our ego loses a sense of control and centrality. Whether the re-emergence of the Self is disturbing or a welcome discovery, we open to an awareness that there is a deeper centre of spiritual being that is actually unfolding our life. We could say that the Self has always been there in the background, while the ego lived with the illusion of its primacy.

The relationship between the ego and the Self is crucial, as shown by the arrow in Figure 6. How this is expressed in our life may vary, but it will always carry with it some sense of deepening respect for and surrender to the presence of the sacred nature of the Self. According to Jung the Self is the carrier of the images of the divine as they are projected into our spiritual life. These have manifested in all spiritual traditions and in Buddhism and tantra in particular they are present in the aspect of the deities we practice.

In the tantric tradition, the relationship between the ego and Self is expressed in the practice of front-generation where it becomes increasingly alive and inspirational. If we translate this into Buddhist language we can see that the relationship between the ego and our buddha-nature has a similar dynamic. We can also begin to understand the importance of what we call 'taking refuge' as an inner re-alignment with our core nature, our buddha potential.

This relationship begins as we invite the presence of the deity into the space before us. To appreciate the efficacy of this visualisation I want to return to something I said in an earlier chapter. We could see the deity as being like a stained-glass window. As such, it is an opening to another depth of awareness that is not always accessible to us. Just as it is the sun-light radiating through the glass of the window that generates its radiant colours, so too it is the nature of what is 'behind' the deity that gives it its potency. The deity is the window to the experience of the innate ground of being, of dharmakaya. When we make this connection, we can open to receive the blessing that comes through like the light through the stained-glass window. It is important to understand that the deity is not an image or representation of Buddha-nature, it is a direct emanation of it. In the process of front-generation we are recognising that our own innate buddha-nature is intimately and inseparably connected to that same nature of all the Buddhas.

Once we have developed this front-generation visualisation, we can begin to cultivate a relationship that awakens a more devotional space. This is deepened through particular practices that are a reflection of the importance of the deity in our life. These take the form of prayers, making offerings and prostrations. Traditional prayers can be lengthy and elaborate and may be very beautiful, often falling into three different aspects. One will be an expression of what is sometimes called 'praise for the deity', which usually involves homage and veneration towards the qualities of the deity and how significant or important the relationship is to us. A second aspect of prayer often takes the form of requests for blessing and guidance, or that we may receive realisations or qualities valued on our spiritual path. The third form of prayer can often be an expression of gratitude and appreciation for the presence of the deity in our life as our guide and protector. Traditionally these prayers have frequently been composed by lamas who are venerated for their poetic capacity. They may be very elaborate and devotional in one respect, but in another are not particularly personal. However, it is the personal link that may be equally if not more important if we are to get a feel of the relationship to the deity. From my own experience I often felt that making this more personal, without the complexity of liturgy became more effective. I would sometimes make some of the formal prayers and then explore my own prayers and open my heart to the deity in relationship to what felt most pertinent to my own life and spiritual process.

In a sadhana front-generation, prayers are usually followed by a system of offerings. These are made as a part of the expression of gratitude and devotion towards the deity, as well as to request blessings. This could be seen as a kind of etiquette, that if we are going to request to receive certain things from a deity then we should also offer something as part of that exchange. A deity doesn't need anything from us, but this is important in terms of our own inner attitude. Traditional offerings often follow a formula that includes certain hand mudras and specific chanted verses of offering. These offerings follow a form that has been passed down since the days when these practices were performed in India. They represent the same offerings that would be made to honour the arrival of a visiting dignitary such as the local raja or king. In relationship to a deity they could be seen as an expression of gratitude. In a traditional sense they are a way of generating what is called merit, an accumulation of positive karma that will support and ripen our practice. From a more contemporary sense this process of offering enriches and enlivens our vitality and the potential to experience the benefits of practice. The offerings and prayers we make are an expression of relationship and are there to awaken a sense of intimacy and connection with the deity.

When we begin the process of front-generation the visualisation may at first feel relatively separate from ourselves. In my own practice, because it was oriented towards the recitation or reading of a sadhana, this sense of separation could feel difficult. This became especially noticeable if I was working with a Tibetan text and then attempting to read the English and visualise. What began to bring greater closeness, was when I memorised the visualisation process so that I no longer needed to read a text. To repeat something that Lama Yeshe emphasised, once we know the sadhana and the visualisations, we can begin to drop some of the words and simplify certain details. Once I had done this I was able to invite the deity into the space of awareness within my meditation in a very different way. The important ingredient that began to grow in this relationship was a greater felt sense of connection or intimacy with the deity's presence. When I was able to meditate more within the felt experience of the body and open to the space of awareness my practice radically changed.

In Chapter 11 I was describing different depths of meditation we can experience before we invite the deity. If we are able to settle deeply in the spacious nature of awareness before we begin deity practice then we can invoke the deity from a different place. Rather than just imagining the deity arising in the space in front of us, we can feel the presence of the deity within the space of awareness. Then we are not separate from the deity, instead we are seeing it as an emergent quality of our own spacious awareness. This subtle distinction may sound insignificant but in practice it makes a profound difference. In our meditation we need to open and let the presence of the deity touch us. We learn to receive the deity as an emanation of the Buddhas, and to some extent this is facilitated by the way we visualise this connection. Often this is done by imagining light emanating from the deity towards us in a similar way to the light radiating through a window. It is our openness to begin to receive this connection that nourishes us like receiving the light from the sun that warms us. As we let this presence touch us, the separation diminishes and the feeling that we are of one nature begins to grow.

There are two further practices that are often included within the context of front-generation. One is the practice of prostrations, the other is a practice called the mandala offering. What these two share in common is a way in which we surrender ourselves to the deity. This is particularly relevant within the practice of guru yoga as I am going to describe in the next chapter, where the deity becomes our guru-deity or Yidam, our heart bound deity.

Prostrations may be seen as a practice we do as a simple gesture of homage, expressed with the hands held with palms together at the heart, or they may be much more active. Here we can also enter into a practice I have described at some length in *Preparing for Tantra*. We begin to make physical prostrations that reflect an inner disposition to surrender our ordinary ego's sense of centrality in our life to the centrality of the deity. It is the gesture that affirms that, although we may believe we are the authors of our spiritual journey, in fact it is the deity as an expression of buddha-nature that is truly the source. Jung spoke of the ego's experience of becoming relative and secondary to the Self at the heart of our life's individuation process. In the experience of making prostrations to the deity we are carrying out a ritual expression of this 'relativisation', as he called it. This process further supports the devotion and intimacy we begin to share in our relationship to the deity. Prostrations are a significant practice as a means of purification as well as the accumulation of merit on the tantric path. They are seen as one of the main 'preliminary practices'.

The mandala offering, I have also described at length in *Preparing for Tantra* so I do not intend to go into great detail here. What is important in this practice, is the quality of surrender it generates. This is achieved by a visualisation of the whole of our sense of totality in life, that is to say all that we are - with our qualities and difficulties, all that we have achieved, all of our material life, as well as those things we aspire to - we totally offer to the guru-deity. It is the gesture that says, 'I place myself in your hands', and we make that same shift of surrender as with prostrations.

All of these practices gradually deepen and open our connection to our innate nature inseparable from the Buddhas, manifesting in the form of the deity. As we open, we receive more inspiration and vitality to go forward on our path. We also increasingly clear the obstacles that can be in our way. This sense of inspiration and connection is further enhanced by the last aspect of front-generation practice, where we begin to recite the deity's mantra.

This is often seen as one of the key aspects of our relationship to a deity within a sadhana. It is this practice of mantra recitation that has sometimes meant that tantra is given the name *mantrayana* or the 'path of secret mantra'. It is important to remember that a mantra is intended to attune our energy to the quality or vibration of the deity. This can be especially valuable if we are someone who does not visualise easily or who takes time to open up to the felt connection. Coming back to Lama Yeshe's wish that we gain a taste of the deity, it is often through the mantra that I have found this happens. Even when my visualisation capacity is poor, the quality of the mantra opens up the presence of the deity as a felt sense. This does mean that, rather than the mantra being a small or rapidly performed part of the sadhana, it needs to be given enough time. One of my frustrations with the lengthy recitation of sadhanas in Tibetan was that often in a group we would chant a text for three quarters of an hour and then, when my concentration was ebbing and my knees becoming uncomfortable, we would get to the mantra. This would be recited for a few minutes and then we would quickly finish the sadhana and that would be the end. Alternatively, in retreat I could become so caught up in rapidly counting mantras, that I did not give time and space to the experience the mantra generated.

The recitation of mantra is a prime example of where we can readily make the transition from conceptual mind to a more subtle quality of awareness if we allow it time. When we recite or chant a mantra it helps to temporarily clear the conceptual mind. Although the mantra is a significant part of practice, what can be even more important is the kind of experience we get when the mantra stops. It is here that we need to 'just let go' and open to the space of non-dual awareness and experience the nature of mind. This is a practice sometimes known as *samadhi* beyond or after sound.

In the practice of the sadhana there are two significant experiences of the deity that are not always explicit. One is the nature of the deity as a visualised form, the other is the felt taste of the deity as a quality of presence without form. The deity, as I have said earlier, is a gateway or window to a certain experience of the innate nature of mind, to dharmakaya. When the mantra stops, at this point we can open that gateway and experience even for a short moment our innate nature, flavoured by the quality of the deity and the vibration of the mantra. It is a time of complete union of our mind and the deity as a quality of presence beyond form. As our mind opens to its natural clarity, this will be a quality of awareness, but significantly, it is also a *felt* experience. Furthermore, each deity and mantra practice will bring a subtly different felt flavour and this is what we are wishing to 'taste'.

We could say the point of deity practice is to develop the capacity to visualise clearly. From this different point of view, however, the true nature of the deity beyond form, is the intimate inseparability of a felt quality with the nature of our own mind. Lama Yeshe, in *Becoming the Compassion Buddha*, repeatedly emphasises the meditation on what he calls the mahamudra deity[21] at the end of mantra recitation, as resting in the nature of mind. From a mahamudra point of view this is one of the ways in which the nature of mind is revealed to us. It is also how we come to deeply feel the transformational nature of the deity as it affects our energy-body. We recognise this transformation, healing and purification of the energy-body particularly because of how it *feels*. In this respect it is the felt-sense within the body that tells us so much about our practice and its effect.

When we get the balance right between the form of a sadhana and the opening of space within it, we will experience the effect of practice in deeper and deeper ways. I have tried to show an example of this in Appendix 8. Leading many retreats over the past 30 years it has become increasingly clear to see what actually touches people's experience and what does not. Much of this has grown from the feedback that comes from those who attend and find certain approaches really work and others do not.

When we meditate with a sense of ground within the body or within the nature of clear awareness, we will increasingly bring the quality of the deity into our experience. We will become one with the deity and its nature. If we do not have this ground to begin with then our deity practices can be just in our heads. They become a mental phenomenon that does not actually connect to the very essence of what is being transformed, namely, the energy-body or our emotional body. This is extremely important when we consider the second approach to the sadhana, which is the practice of self-generation.

14

Guru Yoga

IT IS OFTEN SAID in the Tibetan tradition that the heart of the path and the source of all realisations is the guru. In traditional teachings, from the beginning there is an emphasis on devotion to the guru as the root of the path. It is then said that to receive his, or occasionally her, blessings it is important that we should see the guru as the Buddha. The idea behind this comes in part from the view that the Buddha is still present for us manifesting in the aspect of the guru. It is also believed that if we see the guru as Buddha we will receive the blessings accordingly.

Traditionally there has been much emphasis on the outer guru because this has been very important in the hierarchy of the Tibetan tradition. The physical person has been the primary object carrying the notion of the guru, but this is a relatively superficial way of seeing things. It is helpful to understand that within tantra, the guru is considered on three levels: outer, inner and secret. The outer guru is the physical presence of a teacher, the inner guru is the growing relationship to our own inner wisdom often seen within the tantric tradition in the aspect of a deity. The secret guru is the essential nature of the mind or our innate dharmakaya.

The terms lama and guru are not direct equivalents although this is often the way it is conveyed in the West. Tibetan lamas are often part of a lineage of power, authority, status and wealth that carries huge importance in Tibetan culture. The emphasis that has grown historically on the reincarnation or *tulku* of a lama is an aspect of this power structure that can have many political implications within the institution of Tibetan Buddhism. Finding a lama's re-incarnation to continue this lineage then becomes of major importance. Many of the Tibetan tulkus around today are genuinely realised beings and of great significance as carriers of the lineages, but the system itself has many pitfalls and is far from meritocratic. The term tulku in Tibetan is the translation of the Sanskrit word nirmankaya, or emanation body, which implies that someone is a fully awakened Buddha. The way this word is being used for the re-incarnation of a lama can be somewhat misleading, because not all tulkus are fully realized beings and many demonstrate very human flaws.

The emphasis on deference and surrender to the authority of the outer guru has been central to the way in which the Tibetan tradition has evolved and been preserved. This has its own rationale that is supported throughout the Tibetan teachings. Great significance can be placed upon the disciple's surrender to the guru as a necessary step within the path and this is usually expressed as surrender to the outer guru. As Buddhism comes to the West it enters a culture that has few examples of this kind of relationship and it is important that we look more deeply at its psychological nature and its appropriateness for Western mind in this time. If we become involved in a guru/disciple relationship and can genuinely trust the integrity, authenticity and psychological health of the lama then this can be a very valuable experience. Difficulties arise, however, when a lama in whom we place our trust, perhaps with the view that this person is a Buddha, turns out to have problems, or to not be trustworthy.

While many of us naturally seek out a relationship to a teacher because we feel we need guidance, the question is whether this traditional emphasis upon the guru is something that is always appropriate for Westerners. Here it is perhaps important to distinguish between teacher and guru, where a guru carries much more of an ideal of perfection. The nature of the guru/disciple relationship is easily misunderstood and can lead to a great amount of confusion. Even H.H. Dalai Lama has recently said that from his point of view the teachings on the guru as perfect should not be emphasised for Western practitioners[22], and certainly, until we understand its implications more deeply, there needs to be considerable caution. He has been particularly concerned about the view that holds the physical outer guru to be a perfect Buddha only to then discover that he or she may be behaving in ways that are not perfect. This can lead to considerable confusion when we are told that a teacher's mistakes are actually 'showing the aspect' of negative behaviour as though it is therefore acceptable. Equally, we may be told that wrong behaviour is just our projection and allow things to go on that are not beneficial.

The relationship between gurus and disciples can have complications, many of which I have explored in *The Wisdom of Imperfection*. For what I wish to explore here it is important to say that, for the purpose of tantric practice, an outer teacher is very necessary. Otherwise there is no way to be guided into its depth and intricacy. This relationship, however, should be held carefully so as not to become too caught in idealised projections that fail to see their human nature. A relationship to a teacher can carry a powerful emotional charge: it can also hold all manner of parental projections causing us to become quite childlike. When we see these tendencies, we should be extremely cautious so as not to become caught in a blindness that does not see the underlying psychological complications that are present in the relationship.

I feel it is also important to consider that many Westerners do not have what might be described as a physical guru. Many people find they meet Tibetan teachers but do not feel drawn to relate to them in such a specific way. Those who have Western teachers may also not be so comfortable with the 'guru' label or indeed the guru projection. The question this may bring up is whether we are then unable to practise tantra and whether there will be some kind of limitation in the path. Personally, I do not think we should see the absence of a physical guru as a limitation. To follow the practice of tantra most certainly requires guidance from a teacher with experience. To have an actual physical *guru*, however, may be unnecessary if we understand the nature of the guru more deeply. As I said at the beginning of this chapter, within the tantric path the guru is understood on three levels, namely outer inner and secret.

The outer guru is human even though he or she may have extraordinary qualities. What is interesting psychologically in our need for a guru is that our psyche projects an inner ideal of wholeness and enlightened wisdom onto the outer person. In doing so, we effectively turn teachers into gurus. This process is largely unconscious and happens when we least expect it. Because of this we have little control over how we then respond. Before we know where we are we will find ourselves with starry eyes praising the wonders of the guru. If we are doing this we are almost certainly caught in the beguiling nature of the guru projection in the same way we may find ourselves falling in love.

To make a gradual shift from an emphasis on the outer guru and our idealised projection to the inner guru is not always a comfortable journey. It can involve or be initiated by some element of disillusionment, which may be completely natural. A deeper understanding of the guru as an inner aspect of our nature comes as we begin to take back our projections. It may also be that we begin to take more account of our own inner wisdom and personal responsibility for our life rather than leaning so much on the outer person. As this process happens, we are in a sense beginning to grow up and as Jung would call it, individuate.

Any teacher that is skilful, will wish to enable his or her students to begin to grow up and find their own inner wisdom. This requires of the teacher a genuine capacity to empower disciples. If empowerment still means that we are dependent totally on the outer person as our ultimate resource then there is no actual empowerment taking place. The shift from outer projection to inner guru supported by the outer person is a very important step in which we begin to "trust in our inner knowledge wisdom", as Lama Yeshe put it.

The shift from outer to inner is facilitated by our relationship to the deity. As this happens we need to understand that the innate pure nature of the teacher's mind and the pure nature of our own mind are unified in the aspect of the deity. We have placed this innate nature into the hands of the outer guru to hold for us until such time as we can own it for ourselves. When we understand this, we can begin to re-own this inner quality, helped by seeing that the deity is a reflection of our own true nature as inner guru. The essence of *Guru Yoga* is to recognise that the outer guru's inner nature and the nature of our own mind are unified in the deity. This is considered a very significant aspect of the tantric path as it begins to generate a clear relationship to the guru as our own innate nature.

In the West as we come to terms with all the psychological complexities of relationships to outer gurus, we can see that one of the most important changes can be the shift to place greater emphasis on the inner guru. When we make this change it can begin to solve some of the complications that manifest with our confused and immature relationship to gurus generally. If we understand how to practice guru yoga skilfully then we need not get caught up in the terrible trap of feeling that our teachers are supposed to be perfect and yet are not always getting it right for us. Essentially, they have the same innate pristine nature that we have, present within a fallible human form. Recognising the deity within the teacher and within ourselves as the same nature means we can hold a sense of openness and respect without the idealised illusion of the teacher as perfect.

The shift from outer guru to inner is facilitated by the deity in tantra and the practice of guru yoga. What this implies is that any of the front-generation deity practices can be a practice of guru yoga. What makes front-generation into guru yoga is the particular way of understanding the deity to be our own innate buddha-nature, inseparable from our teacher's true nature and that of all the Buddhas. When we link these three things together we tap into a powerful resource that is less dependent upon the outer guru and his or her idiosyncrasies and shortcomings. This enables us to maintain respect for our outer teachers, even when they show their human side, without losing the depth of our connection to the essence of what the inner guru brings. Furthermore, if we do not actually have what we might see as an outer guru, and this is not uncommon in the West, we are still able to hold the presence of the deity as our inner guru, inseparable from all the Buddhas. This can bring a depth of experience that is, I feel, just as profound. It is unfortunate that sometimes we are given the impression that we ought to have an outer guru to practise and that we may then go on a kind of hunt for the guru. If we have this deeper understanding we can see that this is not so crucial. As I have said earlier, it is true that we cannot practice tantra without guides and teachers, but the guru can be on a different level altogether.

The guru-deity becomes an important presence and resource in our practice. It is interesting to consider that there have been some prominent historical figures that seemed to emphasise the guru-deity relationship. Tsong Khapa the founder of the Gelugpa tradition was dedicated to Manjushri as his guru, an the Indian master Asanga was devoted to Maitreya as his guru-deity.

With guru yoga we could say that we reclaim our inner guru rather than projecting it outside onto a person. This does not mean that the outer relationship does not continue to have value and significance. It does mean, however, that in the process of individuation we begin to have an empowering sense of our own resourcefulness and inner wisdom. Our journey can be guided by an inner alignment to our true nature and not so dependent upon an outer person. When we seek an answer to some question of our life journey we will have a greater inner resourcefulness to listen to the answer from within, "trusting our inner knowledge wisdom".

There is also a point in this journey where we need to recognise something I have heard Lama Zopa Rinpoche say many times: "The true meaning of the guru is the innate dharmakaya nature of the mind." Again, it is interesting that we may hear this statement many times and yet still be somewhat fixed on the outer guru when we hear the word guru. To go deeper we need to recognise that the intrinsic primordial nature of our own mind and the outer guru's mind are also of one taste. Essentially the outer guru's true nature of mind is dharmakaya, and this is inseparable from our own innate dharmakaya nature. Our teachers may have varying degrees of realisation of this nature but it is nevertheless inseparable from our own intrinsic nature. This then is the secret guru described from one perspective as the unified nature of bliss and emptiness and, from another, as the nature of non-duality. This is the true or ultimate meaning of guru where the others are the relative meaning.

For some the relationship to the secret guru can feel very natural and does not require the facilitation of the inner guru-deity. If we do not so easily access this deep sense of the secret guru in our being, then the deity acts as a kind of intermediary. It is then in the practice of front-generation guru yoga that we find this facilitated. As we understand and experience these distinctions more deeply it gradually takes away the emphasis on the outer guru as someone who needs to be perfect and instead re-orientates us towards a more symbolic yet very powerful recognition that the guru is the deity and is our own true nature. As this happens it need not damage the relationship to outer teachers, in fact it may actually serve to make it more authentic since it is based less on our needs, expectations and fantasies.

The understanding of these different levels of the guru is expressed in the practice of guru yoga and is considered a significant aspect of practice for the traditional accumulation of merit. Perhaps we could translate the term merit into something that is more immediate by seeing it as the cultivation of inspiration and energy to practice. Guru yoga is a way of opening to the guru-deity with devotion, dedication and a sense of surrender so that we gradually become a vehicle for its inspiration and vitality to manifest in the world through our life. As we open to the deity we open to our innate nature, gradually receiving its presence as a source of health and vitality.

As this experience deepens it becomes a valuable resource when we need guidance or support. I became very aware of this when Lama Yeshe died in 1984. At first, I was dismayed at the terrible loss of someone who had given me so much and who seemed to be so attuned to my practice and who I was. I really felt that Lama Yeshe 'saw me' as no-one else had ever done. Following his death, I feared that my connection would somehow diminish and fade but, to the contrary, something else seemed to happen. My practice of guru yoga became such a natural internal opening to a deeper nature of the guru on a level that has remained a source of insight and inspiration. Guru yoga is a gateway to opening to our own innate clear nature; the danger is when we become caught on the outer projection as the primary feature in this, we are unable to go deeper and discover our own reality, our own inner truth.

In actual guru yoga meditation, as I have said, the front-generation of a deity is often the main way of practice. In some sadhanas this can be extremely elaborate and complicated with extensive prayers, praises and offerings. These may suit many people and within a group process can be very inspiring. In terms of our personal private practice we can consider a more meditative approach. Once again it is extremely beneficial to spend time settling as deeply as one can into meditation within the awareness of the felt sense in the body, quieting the mind to be present and spacious. It is within this space of awareness that we bring the presence of the deity as the guru. When we invite the deity into the space we are effectively opening to the presence of the ultimate guru, dharmakaya manifesting as the guru deity. This is an important moment and needs to be given time to rest into with awareness. There is then a potential intimacy as we open our heart mind to the inner and then secret guru.

15

Self-Generation

THERE IS A POINT in the practice of many sadhanas when we
make a shift from visualising the deity in front, to actually becoming
the deity. If I return to the way Jung described the relationship
between the ego and Self (Figure 6), what we could say is that we are
beginning to shift the centre of our awareness from ego to Self. In
this sense we are moving from a relatively limited small sense of
ourselves to the very centre of our totality. Jung would not have
considered this to be possible because he would see it as a serious
inflation. However, in Buddhist practice this becomes possible
because we go through a process where the ego is dissolved into
emptiness.

In Buddhist understanding we shift our awareness to identify with
our buddha-nature, or perhaps we could say our divine nature rather
than our ordinary nature. I recall Lama Yeshe once saying that when
we do this we change the way we emanate our reality from our
ordinary ego identity to our innate clear nature in the aspect of a
deity. He said that if we are identified with a low-quality sense of self,
that is what we will emanate. If we identify with our innate wisdom
nature then that is what we will emanate.

In the practice of self-generation, we bring into the present an immediate relationship to our innate buddha potential in the aspect of the deity. We often think of the Buddhist path as an evolution towards a state of awakening that unfolds over time, and yet within the tantric tradition the paradox is that we can identify with our innate buddha potential right now. For this reason, tantra is sometimes said to bring the result, Buddhahood, into the present. When we shift our awareness to being a deity, we bring into our reality qualities that are latent within and expressed archetypally in the form of the deity. Our ordinary form and identity then become a vehicle or vessel for these qualities to manifest in our life through whatever we do.

While the front-generation practice brings a more intimate relationship and opens up a dialogue with this aspect of our nature, self-generation immerses us directly in its quality. We begin to embody or inhabit the deity. To make this shift, however, we must first dissolve our identification with our ordinary ego identity. If we do not do this we will end up with an ego that thinks or imagines it is divine. This state of inflation is not beneficial.

To make the transformation that occurs with self-generation, we go through a process that gradually dissolves our ordinary sense of self and ordinary appearance into emptiness. This is done very skilfully within the sadhana, in that we bring the mind into an awareness of emptiness or non-duality from which the new identity as the deity then re-emerges. I began to describe this in Chapter 11, but here I wish to go deeper. If we consider Figure 7, what we are doing is making a transition where we shift awareness from the realm of the ego across into the left-hand circle representing non-dual awareness or dharmakaya. From that place we then re-emerge as the deity having dissolved identification with the ego.

At the root of this process is the knowledge that from a tantric point of view all relative appearances are in actuality emanations or projections of our mind. We could see this on two levels. Most of us recognise, especially when we are emotionally agitated, that states of mind, create our experience of reality as we project our inner psychological disturbance onto the world around us. Our values, beliefs and emotional states all colour our reality through projection. But projection is more subtle than that. From a tantric point of view our entire reality of ordinary appearances is a projection or creation of our primordial clear-light mind, sometimes called causal mind.

When we recognise that all appearances lack any substantial inherent nature, we see the illusion in which we are bound. Lama Yeshe used to call it our 'hallucination reality'. In the process of dissolution, we acknowledge this empty nature and begin to draw back the projection. This is not a kind of withdrawal in the sense of avoiding reality like a snail that draws in its horns when it touches something uncomfortable. We dissolve the projection because we see

Figure 7

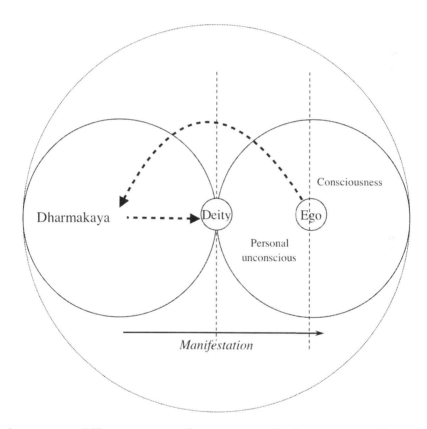

the empty and illusory nature of appearances. In the process of this practice these appearances are gathered back into the source - causal mind. In this visualisation we dissolve our mind's entanglement in the reality of our ordinary daily life. Our engagement with this world of dualistic appearances has been temporarily released. This can feel like a relief from the chaos and confusion that arises from our ordinary identity and its connection with the world of appearances. For a while we rest in the state of non-dual awareness and relax.

This meditation reminds us that the source of our world of relative appearances is our primordial clear-light mind or causal mind. While we are ignorant of this fact we hold the appearances that we see as solid real and 'out there'. Once we recognise that this reality is not other than a manifestation of clear-light mind, we see through the illusion of a solid creation and recognise its empty nature. It is sometimes said that so long as we fail to see this truth, appearances are the basis of samsara; once we recognise they are the product of causal mind, appearances are the basis of nirvana. These two are the same reality of appearance but seen through completely opposite states of mind. This is the difference between *rigpa*, in Tibetan, meaning seeing and *marigpa*, not seeing or ignorance. Thus, when the mind settles in the clear spacious awareness that remains following the process of dissolution we know this as the underlying ground of our reality, dharmakaya.

In many sadhanas the way the dissolution process begins is with prayers to a deity visualised in front as a typical 'front-generation' practice described earlier. This deity is then brought to the crown of the head and descends into the heart chakra, blessing the heart-mind. This is then followed by the process of dissolution. In my earlier years when I participated in sadhana recitations in groups, this was often done relatively quickly making the experience brief and not particularly deep. I always felt frustrated by this, and in my own practice wanted to approach it in a different way and give time to slow the whole process down.

When leading this practice in retreats I spend time returning to an awareness of the body and its felt sense before starting any dissolution visualisation. Resting quietly in this way for some minutes prepares the mind for the process that follows. It is worth giving this time. Within that more settled subtle awareness and presence in the body, we then visualise a form in the heart which begins the dissolution process. This form is most often a *seed syllable* such as a Hung, Hrih or Tam depending upon the deity. A seed syllable is a Sanskrit letter that symbolises the source, our innate causal nature of extremely subtle clear-light mind. It could be seen as a combination of light and sound that is the seed from which the deity grows or emerges. This quality is present in the heart chakra and is recognised as the source of all appearances projected into our reality. If a Sanskrit syllable such as the *Hung* shown is difficult to imagine then a small sphere or drop of light will work as well.

Allowing time to settle our awareness into the experience of this syllable in our meditation helps what follows. Light emanates from this syllable or drop, expands and gradually fills the body pervading every cell. It then radiates out through the skin into the environment around. This is not our ordinary sense of light that is obstructed by solid appearances, it is a light  that passes through matter and expands out into the vastness of space. Without becoming drawn into conceptual mind, if at all possible, we imagine that all appearances lacking any inherent substantiality, being by nature empty, then begin to dissolve into light. That light is then gradually drawn back as the world and the environment and so forth dissolve eventually into the body. At this point it is helpful to again consider that our entanglement with the aspects of our life have temporarily dissolved.

The next step relates to the ways in which we tend to hold to a solid sense of our identity and all the beliefs and ideas we have about ourselves. This can also relate to the view we have of our body. The body, our ordinary appearance and identity then also melt into light and dissolve into the seed syllable in the heart. For example, the syllable Hung as shown. This has the effect of dissolving the solidity with which we contract around often negative self-images or self-beliefs. We are left with just the seed syllable resting within the space of awareness. The seed syllable itself then gradually dissolves upwards until all relative appearances have dissolved into emptiness, non-duality like a clear sky. We consider that they have dissolved into dharmakaya as the source. I have given an example of this way of practice in Appendix 9.

Once appearances disappear into the space of empty clear awareness then we can simply let go into the non-dual nature of awareness. At this point Lama Yeshe stressed that we are more likely to gain a taste of dharmakaya, the ground of being, if we can drop all the concepts and descriptions and simply meditate. This experience may not be for long at first, but as we relax and deepen, this spacious quality of awareness opens up and becomes more stable.

In the commentaries on higher tantra it is explained that this visualisation is also intended to replicate a process that happens at the time of death when our relationship to the world of appearances also dissolves. The activity of the five elements in our body that activate our world of appearances, gradually dissolve back into the heart from where they came and no longer function. At the point of death, we experience what is known as the clear-light of death. This extremely subtle state of mind is present just before our consciousness leaves this body at the time of death. In meditation we do not die, but this visualisation is a valuable preparation for this journey when the time of death actually comes.

I have always found this dissolution meditation to be one of the most extraordinary aspects of the tantric path. In many ways it is the heart of the sadhana and as such is a very significant aspect of meditation. As someone that has always valued the depth of meditation possible within the practice of mahamudra, this is a very useful way of entering into the space of clear non-dual awareness. In my own retreats and daily practice, when possible, I try to sit in this space for up to half an hour before moving on to the actual emergence of the deity. What this does is to really immerse my mind in the state of non-duality as deeply as possible, letting go of the subtle identity of an I. This softening of the contracted sense of self can then carry over into daily life and bring an extraordinary taste of the clear nature of mind free of the proliferation of relative confusion and appearances.

As I have suggested earlier this restful awareness in the state of non-duality leads to a release of the entanglement we have with the relative world we normally inhabit. If this entanglement is particularly disturbing or challenging it is possible to let go of some of the habitual reactivity that occurs. This habitual process is 'wired' into our nervous system and will not release unless we can relax into the spacious nature of awareness the dissolution process facilitates. I have felt as though the locked-in structure of my reactivity softens and is able to let go. Relaxing into the space of clear awareness, as I have said in Chapter 8, is the practice that goes to the heart of our normal contracted mind that holds onto and blocks the natural fluidity of reality unfolding. Letting go into this place is a profound liberation of all of this subtle habitual reaction.

There is also another level I find this meditation subtly affects in relation to the body. Having dissolved our identification with the body and our self-image, the way in which our mind holds and identifies with a sense of our form has been temporarily loosened. This has a significant effect on the energy within the body and the way in which we solidify, even subtly, our physical body's form. Although we have dissolved the appearance of the form of our body, our body is of course still present. It is not the object of our awareness because we are resting within a space of emptiness or non-duality. The effect of this upon the energy-body and our physical body is nevertheless happening as we gradually relax more deeply. My own sense of this is that there is a softening and loosening of the contraction in the energy-body which enables the energy to move and find its own natural flow. It is like water finding its natural flow. When I 'return' from this kind of meditation, if I have given time to the process and relaxed deeply into the space of non-duality, emptiness, then I will feel an enhanced quality of ease and bliss within the energy in the body.

If we adopt a more meditative approach to the practice of sadhana then this experience is very significant. The deeper we go the more the sense of transformation can then take place as we emerge as the deity. Here it is also important that we do not suddenly return to the conceptual mind in a way that pulls us out of that space of awareness. When I lead meditation retreats, something I try to do at this point is to guide people out of that experience with as few words as possible so that they can meditate rather than think. The emergence of the deity then becomes much more deeply felt within the energy-body.

Figure 8

The self-generation process in its simple form often begins with a lotus, moon and seed syllable arising of within the space of dharmakaya (Figure 8). This syllable represents the re-emergence of our own consciousness. The syllable then radiates light out in all directions inviting the blessings of all the Buddhas, which returns in the form of light. Finally, the syllable transforms and we arise as the deity. We then hold a subtle identification as the deity with all of its attributes, sometimes also within the context of a mandala. If we do this on our own and are not reciting a sadhana in a group, it is extremely helpful to do so without reading texts or without too many words. The description of the process is useful at first to remind us of the visualisation, so that we get the details right. After a while they can be a hindrance to the actual process of meditation. It is helpful then to have memorised the process with fewer words. If we can do this we can re-emerge as the deity without shifting away from the deeper space of meditation awareness which is really the aim of the practice.

If you are familiar with detailed recitation of sadhanas, it would be worth exploring the process in the way I have described. If you have the sadhana memorised this may help, but essentially begin to let go of the text. Let the emergence of the syllables and symbols leading to the eventual arising as the deity be done as a visualisation. Don't be too disturbed by not always getting every detail right, the important experience is to feel the quality of the transformation and let it become something that you can meditate deeply within. Forget the conceptual process and immerse your awareness in the presence of the deity as a felt experience intimately connected to the energy in the body. In effect, we are trying to slow the process down and meditate as deeply as possible in the space of awareness in the aspect of the radiant form of the deity. The phrase that is often used at this point is to hold 'divine pride' or confidence as the deity. This means a very subtle level of feeling 'I am the deity', but without the ordinary ego identification because we have dissolved this away. By remaining in a less conceptual awareness, we can unify the feeling aspect of the energy-body with the deity. They become pervasive of each other and inseparable.

The process of dissolving appearances into spacious non-duality and then re-emerging as the deity becomes a very different experience when we have the capacity to meditate more deeply in the empty nature of mind. It is for this reason I have emphasised, in Chapter 7, that before embarking upon this kind of tantric approach we first develop a capacity to rest in the clarity of awareness with some degree of settling, some degree of tranquil abiding. This unfortunately is often not emphasised in the urgency of counting mantras and the strict adherence to the complexity of the traditional way of practice. In my experience it is this shift in emphasis, that can be of great benefit to us as Westerners. It brings a deeper relationship to the essence of the practice, gaining what Lama Yeshe called, a 'taste of the chocolate'.

Once we arise as the deity, there are various things one can do, which in higher tantra practices, are often quite elaborate. This may involve making offerings and prayers. It can also involve a process known as 'merging wisdom and samaya beings'. What this means is that we invite the wisdom nature of all the Buddhas in the aspect of the deity to merge with our own experience of self as deity. This is to remind us that our deity nature is one with that same nature of all the Buddhas. It gives a sense of empowerment and inspiration so that we receive the blessings of the Buddhas.

All of these rituals can enrich and augment our practice in a very beneficial way but can also be abbreviated when necessary to make our meditation less cluttered with activity. There is always a danger, at the points of deep meditation, that when many elaborate things are added, they begin to detract from the depth of the practice. There may be times when we can enjoy doing these things because they bring inspiration, or we may choose to abbreviate and stay with the deeper meditation. Personally, I have often found I wanted to stay with the depth of meditation that has been generated rather than go back into too much conceptual liturgy.

Mantra Recitation

One of the most beneficial aspects of the self-generation practice is the recitation of mantra. Again, this can be brief or it can be extensive. One of the traditional ways in which mantra recitation is taught is to go through a process of counting large numbers in order to activate its quality in our nervous system. I have spoken of this at some length in *Preparing for Tantra* when referring to the preliminary practices or *gnon-dro*, where it is often required that we count hundreds of thousands of recitations.[23] From my own experience, I have no doubt as to the benefit of this process, but we can easily make this the goal rather than the experience that can come with mantra in a different way.

We could say that there are several orientations to the process of mantra recitation within self-generation practice. One is where we fulfil some aspect of our bodhicitta commitment to serve the welfare of others. This is achieved by visualising that we are sending out light from the heart as an expression of love and compassion to heal and bless others. We can visualise this light-energy goes out to those we are close to who may need support in some way, or more generally to all those we live and work amongst. We could also radiate light to go out and heal the planet. The second orientation is directed more towards the effect on our own inner experience in meditation.

The beauty of mantra recitation is that it begins to attune our energetic nervous system to the vibration of the deity. We can do this for some time and begin to feel its effect. Unfortunately, it is also easy for our mind to become distracted and wander even during the recitation of mantra. This is especially problematic if we are reciting vast numbers at great intensity with the aim of counting. If a mantra has a particular chant then it will often enable us to avoid the wandering mind. It also has a significant effect on the breath. Chanting a mantra can put us into a trance-like space that will have a very important effect when the chant stops. Here we can rest with a quiet mind in the space of awareness that follows. This will have a felt quality that pervades our energy-body. Sometimes our breath will become very subtle following a chant and almost feel for a short while as though it has stopped. The point of this experience is to really let go and rest in that quiet mind. As I have said earlier, it is one way in which we can be directly introduced to the nature of pure clear awareness.

With mantra recitation it can be extremely beneficial to move to a quieter inward listening to the sound of the mantra. This is something that we can only begin to do as our mind is more deeply settled. In his book *Becoming the Compassion Buddha*, Lama Yeshe describes some of the mantra practices that are found principally within *kriya tantra*, where mental recitation is commonly used. When we move the focus of our attention into meditating on the inner quality of sound then we can touch into subtle states that will begin to have the effect of bringing the energy into the central channel primarily through the heart chakra. [24] One such meditation is connected to a visualisation of a flame in the heart. We then listen to the sound of the mantra emanating from the flame. Concentrating upon the flame and sound of the mantra the mind and its energy-winds begin to gather towards the heart chakra. With practice this leads to the energy gradually entering into the central channel, giving rise to a blissful clarity and stillness that is empty in nature. This in time awakens the experience of our clear-light mind. In another practice, following this meditation upon fire and sound, we visualise the deity melting into light and absorbing into the flame which also dissolves into the sound of the mantra. This sound then also gradually dissolves into a spacious awareness of emptiness and bliss.

The beauty of mantra recitation is not just the recitation itself but the period immediately following, when the mantra stops. This is the 'samadhi at the end of sound' I have described in a previous chapter. In the clear spacious and often blissful awareness that arises as the sound ceases we can really *feel* the quality that the mantra leaves. When we do this, we will begin to gain a taste of the quality of the deity as a felt sense that pervades the spaciousness of awareness. What we will notice is that each deity has a subtly different feeling flavour. If we practice a deity such as Tara then there will be a particular 'taste' following the mantra. If it is Chenrezig it will be different again. These differences are very subtle and will only really be felt if we slow the process down and sit deeply in the effect of the mantra. It is then that we could say we open to the true nature of the deity as a felt quality in the spacious nature of awareness itself.

Within the practice of self-generation, we come to embody the quality of the deity within our nervous system. Our energy-body begins to resonate with the vibrant quality of the archetypal nature of the deity. Traditionally there has often been an emphasis on the visualised form or appearance of the deity but we should not overlook the way in which we will *feel* the deity as it begins to wake up within. Gradually this becomes something we can feel through our day as a subtle quality that informs how we are.

Self-generation is a profound practice when we begin to meditate deeply within the experience. When we do not slow down and drop below our conceptual mind to rest in the quality of felt experience we can miss the potential that is there. If we get out of the mental process into a more embodied heartfelt experience, we can begin to feel the transformation the deity brings within our energy-body. What I have described in Figure 5 in Chapter 11 is extremely important here. If we can begin our practice with an awareness of the body and mahamudra, our experience of deity meditation can touch us deeply as this aspect of our nature wakes up. This is not so dependent upon having to have clear detailed visualisations, it is more the real felt experience in the body and therefore within the energy-body. It is often said that in the generation-stage we imagine the deity, but in the completion-stage, the energy-body becomes the deity. While this may be true, we could also see that if we can meditate upon the deity in the way I have suggested above then even within the generation-stage there will be a deep felt-sense of the presence of the deity in our energy-body. The energy of the deity is alive and awake within us and coming through us in every aspect of our life.

16

Embodiment

HAVING BEGUN THIS EXPLORATION of the practice of tantra by emphasising the significance of the body, I wish to return to that same theme within the three kayas. We have addressed the experience of dharmakaya, as we come into relationship with the empty, non-dual nature of mind. When we consider the deity and its energetic nature we are entering a relationship to sambhogakaya. What then is the basis of our relationship to nirmanakaya, which is normally considered to be the emanation body of a Buddha? We can think of this as just an attribute of a Buddha, as the *fruit* of the path, but we can also see the significance of nirmanakaya as it is reflected in our capacity to embody and therefore manifest our buddha-nature in the world right now. In one respect one could say that these three kayas are already perfected right now. They are primordially pure but this is obscured by the defilements of our dualistic mind and ignorance. We could see this as the nature of the *ground* that needs to be transformed. What we recognise, however, is that on the *path* of transformation, we are in the process of refining and awakening our relationship to these three in our being. We may then talk about the cultivation of the nature of mind and our energy-body with relative ease. What does this mean in terms of cultivating our nirmanakaya?

Our physical body is always present within the context of our practice when we are sitting. It is often the part of us that almost gets in the way because the knees hurt and we are restless, our back hurts, then we may need a pee. Often, we want to get to the point where our body behaves itself and sits still and 'shuts up'. Indeed, it is true that the more comfortable and relaxed our body becomes the more readily we can sit. In the yoga traditions the physical process of yoga is considered a preparation for the raja or king yoga which is sitting. We may consider that the kind of physical processes we engage in are secondary to the real business, which is meditation and cultivating a dharmakaya/sambhogakaya experience. But this is far from the truth.

The rituals associated with tantra are often described in relation to samadhi (mind), mantra (speech/energy) and mudra (body movement). An example of this is when offerings are said to be blessed by samadhi, mantra and mudra. Here we see the relationship between the three kayas expressed through the process of practice. The samadhi element of this blessing is in the mind, where we visualise the creation of the offerings emerging out of emptiness. This visualisation is accompanied by the recitation of mantras to bless the offerings. For example, the sanskrit mantra OM ARGHAM AH HUNG is chanted, blessing the offering of water for drinking. Here the mantra, although an aspect of speech, is an expression of the energy body. In this way it is used to create an energetic environment that blesses the offering. During this ritual process, the third element is the use of mudras, or gestures with the hands, which are physical expressions that empower the energetic blessing.

How we move is intimately associated with our energetic expression as well as having an influence upon our environment. We do not always recognise the significance of this, but it is well understood within the practice of tantra. Mudra is the body's language of expression and the many different mudras practised within tantric rituals have a profound symbolic significance. In most sadhana practices there are places where particular movements, usually of the hands and arms, are performed as part of the practice. There are also practices that are more like dances, where the participant brings an expression of the entire body into play. Lama dancing is such an example where the meditator is embodying a deity and then moving in particular ways. So too are the beautiful deity dances practised by the Newaries of Nepal.

What is of particular importance is the link between how we move and the energetic dynamic that is present as we do so. We could say that the body provides a vessel through which the two processes of mind and energy are able to be embodied. Perhaps we could go further and say that as dharmakaya begins to manifests through the energetic nature of sambhogakaya it needs to come to ground and expression in nirmanakaya. It is interesting to consider that if our energy is not expressed through the body as nirmanakaya then something is incomplete. It would be like a lightening conductor that is not connected to earth. We can see this reflected in the way many of us have a very ungrounded, disembodied relationship to our 'spirituality'. Either we are very heady so that our energy becomes upward moving and disconnected from the ground. Or alternatively our energy may feel sluggish and blocked resulting in exhaustion. One way we can recognise this is when our emotions become stuck, then the flow of our energy becomes held in the body and cannot move through to a complete resolution. This resolution can begin as we come closer to a more embodied way of being. The shift towards a more embodied way of living is usually a gradual one that requires a readiness to engage with the emotional experiences that may have caused disembodiment in the beginning.

This gradual shift towards embodiment is facilitated through the movement work that Anna brings into the context of the tantric retreats we teach together. Our emotional life, as described in an earlier chapter, is a direct reflection of our energy-body, our sambhogakaya nature and, in part, is the material that we work with in the process of our tantric practice. In Anna's words:

"As our meditation practice becomes a more embodied process, feelings and emotions inevitably arise. The containment and safety of being on retreat both holds but also intensifies this, the movement aspect, therefore, is included as an invitation to explore and transform what arises. As an underlying principle I encourage participants to bring the qualities of compassion and equanimity to support their process, alongside movement exercises that bring awareness to the body as a resource. I find movement to be a flexible and open medium through which it is possible to facilitate more congruency between mind, emotions and body.

The body could be seen as the place where we cannot hide. Our posture, our way of moving and our speech, all reflect who we are and who we have become in response and in relation to what we have experienced and met in our lives. My observation is that the more we build awareness of what is healthy and nourishing in relation to our body, the more the stuck aspects, emotionally and physically begin to loosen their hold. With this in mind, on retreat, initially we focus on building resources through awareness of what supports us. By beginning to allow the body to 'speak' though movement, we can drop deeper and it becomes more possible for the energy held in these stuck places to be expressed or released. This can result, ultimately, in a quieter and stiller meditation practice.

It would be easy to assume that our 'history' and where we have contracted around our emotions is a problem to be solved. If we look at this from a holistic point of view, however, we can see that the opposite is the case and that it is often though our suffering that we develop our individual gifts and potential for expression. There is much wisdom to be gained though the experience of being with our own difficulties and often an increasing compassion towards others in their suffering.

By opening to the body, in as much capacity as can be tolerated, it is possible to gradually liberate the energy that is held and through this our latent embodiment naturally unfolds. A key aspect of our increasing embodiment is learning to attune to the underlying rhythms of the body, beneath our reactive, patterned behaviour. As we learn to listen more deeply, we become increasingly able to contact these rhythms and respond to how the body is guiding us to move or be. This builds our relationship to and trust in the essential health of our evolving process, which can be extremely helpful and supportive. A compassionate and safe space enables an openness to this natural relationship to the body, where we honour our need to move, or be still. It also encourages a greater acceptance of our emotional reality as we align more completely to ourselves and the energy within our body and being.

In our Western world it might seem radical for us to allow what feels nourishing or satisfying as we are so relentlessly programmed to take control of our body, rather than listen to its needs. But as the Buddha said, 'when hungry, eat, when tired sleep'. As we connect to the natural rhythm of the body, we discover that it has its own 'inner 'breath', which, in its own time brings body and emotions back into balance. We will see that it is through pushing or holding back our energy that we have become out of touch with this inner rhythm. As we restore this relationship we will find it also has a profound effect on how we align with the rhythms of nature, so that we are more attuned, both internally and in relation to who and what is around us."

(Anna Murray Preece : 28.10.18)

We are all out of relationship to our body to some degree and we could say that the process of our tantric practice is the gradual deepening of our capacity to embody our true nature. As this process unfolds it inevitably brings to light the aspects of our emotional life which make that embodiment a challenge. But to repeat what Anna said above, it is not helpful to see what arises in the process of practice as a problem to be overcome. It is this emotional process that needs to gradually be worked through, so that our experience of disembodiment can begin to heal. It helps to see this as a natural expression of our practice not as a sign of an obstacle.

While embodiment can be important for the transformation of our emotional energy into a healthy expression, it is also important in our relationship to the deity within the tantric path. For our experience of the deity to become alive in our life it must also be something that we begin to embody. In effect it needs to be brought through into nirmanakaya. When it is not embodied it is as though the electrical circuit is not complete and the energetic charge that is present in opening to the deity is not being grounded to earth. In my own journey one of the most obvious expressions of my lack of embodiment was in my *puer aeturnus* tendency, as I have described at some length in *The Wisdom of Imperfection*[25]. My relationship to my deity practice, rather than supporting my embodiment, encouraged my tendency to go into 'spiritual flight'. I did not wish to be sullied by earthly relationships and saw my path as the gradual separation from the 'worldly life' of work, relationships and the body. When, however, I became aware of the level of disembodiment it promoted, I needed to look at its underlying causes - my fears and anxieties - and begin to work with these. Through this I was slowly able to bring my practice to an increasingly embodied place, radically changing how I related to my spiritual path, my emotional life and my tantric practice in particular.

This process made me realise that it is for each of us to look at the underlying roots of our disembodiment and begin to work with them. This may not be a comfortable process for some of us because we are returning to some of the emotional experiences that caused us to be disembodied in the first place. For our tantric practice to grow and deepen, however, this is a path worth following.

Embodiment of the deity is a profound opening to the deity's presence to come through. In terms of our usual understanding of tantric practice, it could be seen as the process that happens when we are in a deep relationship to the deity, whether this is within front-generation or self-generation practice. Many years ago, I was staying in Bodhgaya in India and was doing my prostration *ngondro* in front of the Mahabhodi stupa. While there I met a lama called Adze Tulku, who was a lay lama living with his Nepali wife and working at Magada University. I had asked him to help me translate the verses of the Heruka *tsog*, a ritual offering practice. One day I asked him how he experienced the deity (Heruka) in his daily life. He replied, that as he walked around he had the sense of Heruka's blue light energy body passing through his physical body. When he looked at his hands he felt the blue energy in his hands. I found this description fascinating because he was not saying he visualised himself as the deity with all the implements and attributes, rather that he felt the blue light energy within his body. This reminded me of something Lama Yeshe had said when he was teaching Vajrayogini at Tushita retreat centre in Dharamsala. He advised us between sessions to just imagine Vajrayogini's red energy in our body.

Traditionally we are taught to visualise ourselves as a deity in our daily life, however, if we can begin to be aware of its felt-sense then our experience will become more embodied. To feel the energetic nature of the deity within our body feels more grounded than imagining I am a deity with twelve arms and bone ornaments trying to cook dinner or do the washing up.

In my own practice, when I come out of meditation naturally my awareness returns to my ordinary body. If during the meditation I generated as a deity, my body is the vessel in which the process of transformation happened. As a result, within my physical body I can also be aware of the felt-sense of the energy-body of the deity. One inhabits the other and I begin to feel my body to be a vehicle or channel through which the deity is moving. If I can retain this felt connection, rather than a visualisation, then that feeling can be present in my body through my day. Whatever I am doing can become pervaded by a sense of the deity's energetic presence.

This is where our body becomes the nirmakaya expression of the deity embodied in our life. I am reminded of Lama Yeshe's comment, that if we are identified with a low-quality sense of ourselves then that is what we emanate, if we identify with the deity then that is what we emanate.

A point can be reached in our practice where we recognize that the three kayas are simultaneously arising and present in each moment. In dzog chen, it is sometimes said, dharmakaya is the natural, empty, spacious nature of rigpa, sambkogakaya is its radiance and nirmakaya its spontaneous compassionate expression. It takes time and practice to awaken to that reality, but we all have the potential to do so. It may be veiled by our obscurations of body, speech and mind but the essential ingredients are there within us. As we begin to clear the veils of obscuration we see that all appearances are the 'play' of dharmakaya. We also see that the relationship between emptiness and form has a dynamic vitality that pervades our experience in each instant. We are by nature a continually changing, living, creative expression of the three kayas. Unfortunately, our suffering arises from our failure to recognize this reality.

Embodiment is like completing an electrical circuit. It is the fulfilment of the process of our life where what begins on a subtle level as dharmakaya moves through the dynamic energy of sambhogakaya and then comes into manifestation through embodiment in nirmanakaya (Figure 9). This movement is happening all the time, in every instant and not just within our own continuum but in the world around. We can see that the whole of reality is an expression of this same process, moving from the subtle formless nature of dharmakaya through the vitality or creative energy of sambhogakaya into the forms and appearances of nirmanakya. In our tantric practice, as we arise as the deity, we step into alignment with this creative expression and can become the vehicle for its manifestation in the world in all that we do. If we wish to live our lives in the service of others this is perhaps the most profound way that we can live. We open ourselves to the source of vitality in our nature that will come through us as an emanation of our buddha-nature and be of great benefit to others. This is our embodiment of bodhichitta.

Figure 9

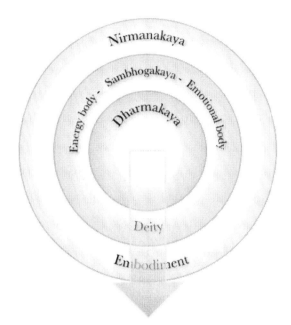

Manifestation

(This diagram is adapted from the MA. Dissertation of Anna Murray Preece. 2017)

Part Two

A Journey of Depth

I SOMETIMES HEAR the question asked whether spirituality and psychotherapeutic work should be brought together. Are they compatible? It is as though there is a belief that spirituality is somehow separate or different from psychological process. This may in part stem from a notion in the West, particularly from Christianity, that the 'spiritual path' is associated with a journey of ascension and transcendence. This is often seen as a movement towards the rarefied heights of purity, goodness, clarity, light, love, ecstasy and altered states of awareness. In my early years as a Buddhist practitioner, when I began to train as a psychotherapist, I would often receive from my peers a view that we did not need to do psychotherapeutic work, the dharma was enough.

Personally, I have always felt uncomfortable with this view of spiritual elevation, because while, on the one hand, it may be inspiring and uplifting, on the other, it can overlook the darker, more painful side of our reality. I have never been happy splitting the elevated brightness and purity of what is deemed 'spiritual' from the suffering and struggle of our human fallibility. I have sometimes felt spiritual idealism, purity, piety and correctness leave me deeper and deeper in the dark, feeling impure and far from holy. I think this is in part why I was moved to write *The Wisdom of Imperfection* as a kind of antidote to spiritual ideals of purity and perfection. In that book I make the observation that while in the Buddhist tradition there is a clearly defined path to attain realisations, there is seldom an explanation of the psychological journey that will go on within or beneath it. For me this psychological process has seldom been as straightforward as the path might suggest, nor has it ever been so filled with inspiring realisations. Rather it has often been a painful process of working with inner struggles, emotional wounds and painful self-beliefs as I gradually grow and transform. I am not sure that the Buddha was intending a path towards holiness but rather towards awareness, authentic being and liberation.

It is interesting that C.G. Jung, the archetypal psychologist James Hillman and others have wanted to emphasise an entirely different journey that could be seen as a polarity to the spiritual path. They often called this the journey of the soul or of soul creation[26]. This was the downward, deepening path into the dark unknown corners and crevices of our psychological nature, where mysteries lie that also need to be awoken. They saw this as a feeling journey that would be shaping and colouring the experience of our human nature as a source of authentic being. They also saw this taking us deeper into the body and what is held there within the unconscious. Of course, in Buddhism we do not consider the existence of a soul as some kind of inherent nature, but this is not how Jung and Hillman meant soul either. Equally, one could say that in Buddhism there does not appear to be an equivalent word to 'spiritual' and yet we liberally use it. Jung considered the spiritual path to be one that emphasised a masculine upward movement towards consciousness and light. He considered the path of soul to be more associated with the feminine as a journey of descent into the unconscious and the depth of our being. This is not the journey up the mountain but rather into the deep, moist caves and shady, mossy grottos in the valley. It is not a journey into the upper world but rather into the underworld, into the dark. It is not a journey of illumination and ecstatic visions, but of stripping away and revealing our raw, sometimes painful, inner depths as a route towards wisdom and compassion.

When I was first involved in the Tibetan tradition, I was seeking a path strongly influenced by an ideal that spirituality would free me from my emotional pain and lead me to some kind of transcendent state beyond worldly struggles. I believed that through Buddhist practice I would gain liberation, and all kinds of realisations, even enlightenment, although I was not always clear what that might mean. I had a very idealised spiritual side of my nature that was seeking liberation through what I might now call spiritual flight.

While I was in India in retreat, however, I found that it was far from being a path that took me into ecstatic heights of transcendent joy and bliss. For a considerable amount of my time I was doing the opposite. During certain periods of my retreats I found myself going into painfully depressed states. I felt as though I was being gradually taken to pieces and my inner life torn out of me like organs being ripped from my body. There was a sense that whatever I held onto in myself was being stripped away. My ego's world was being dismantled and dissolved into emptiness.

It is sometimes said that for a tantric practice to be most effective it needs to bring the process of death and rebirth into the path. One way this can be seen is within meditation practices that follow the evolution of the death process itself. In a different sense, however, at the heart of tantric practice is the recognition that our journey is one of psychological death and transformation or death and re-emergence. When we look more deeply into this experience we see that it can be a necessary and valuable aspect of our journey. This will not be an easy path. It is often painful and yet is both profound and transformational. Many of us go through this process but do not always have the support or guidance to know how to be with the experience. Instead we may think something is wrong and that this should not be happening. With the right guidance, support and understanding, however, we can discover that this is a completely natural aspect of the journey and that we need to 'trust in the process'.

One way that we might understand this is as a 'journey of depth', where we go more deeply into our nature and begin to transform. As this happens it is seldom a path of glowing realisations that flow from our practice, at least that has never been my experience. It is a journey of both uncomfortable as well as extraordinary discoveries as we go deeper and deeper into ourselves. The understanding of this psychological process in tantric practice is not always obvious and can also be disturbing if and when it happens. It is not usually an aspect of the teachings we receive and those who are intellectual scholars alone may be unable to guide us. This is not a journey of the mind and the intellect it is rather one of a depth of feeling and relationship to the body and emotion as we unravel our psychological life. This can be rich and beautiful as well as painful and challenging and from my own experience I would not wish to avoid it.

This is a journey that brings us into an intimate relationship with our raw, authentic, fallible human nature. When we touch this, if we can learn to hold it with kindness and compassion it can deeply affect how we relate to others. We will see others with compassion and care because we recognise that same depth and pain that needs to heal. It is my own experience of this process that is partly what motivated me to become a psychotherapist.

We may seek a path that takes us to heights of transcendent realisations, but if we do not at some point journey into the depth of our being, we will not heal and transform much of our emotional and psychological wounding. It will remain there beneath the veneer of our supposed spiritual realisations. It was Jung who once said that we do not become enlightened by imagining ourselves as beings of light, but rather through transforming the shadow.

In Part Two therefore, I wish to look at this journey of depth as it can be experienced through tantric practice. When we understand the journey into our psychological nature, we will see how important it is for us in the West. This could be understood as the psychological meaning of what is known in the tantric tradition as the path of 'mother tantra'. We discover that within tantra there is a path that takes us into the depth of the unconscious through a process of psychological descent.

What naturally follows is a further journey that leads us back into the world again through a process of re-emergence and manifestation. How we return to the experience of form and embodiment is expressed in what we creatively manifest in our life. This is reflected in what could be described as the psychological meaning of the path of 'father tantra'.

To begin with, however, I think it can be helpful to explore the notion of what in the West we call the unconscious and how it is relevant to our understanding of tantra, even though there is no such term in the East. It is our relationship to the unconscious that much of the tantric process touches and awakens. Here we begin to understand the idea of depth and descent as we go beneath our ordinary conscious mind into the dark unknown unconscious regions of the body and mind to transform and awaken.

17

Levels of Consciousness

W HEN I BECAME INVOLVED in both the worlds of Tibetan
Buddhism and C.G.Jung in my early twenties, I was struck by the
resonances between them. I began to see, however, that these
traditions approached the nature of the mind or consciousness in
very different ways. Before I begin to explore 'the journey of depth'
I feel it would be helpful to clarify two differing views of
consciousness, one that derives from the tantric tradition and the
other from Jung. When we understand their difference, we can also
begin to see how these views offer significant insights into how we
experience tantric practice as a psychological process. I have tried to
convey these two in Figure 10 and I think it is important to not try
and make a direct equation from one view to the other as though
they completely correspond. Creating this map, however, helps to
show how, if we use a different language, it brings about a very
different relationship to our mind.

   Jung's view was born out of a time when the notion of the
unconscious began to enter psychological language, originating with
Freud. It became extremely valuable in conveying how aspects of our
inner life are not accessible to us because they are beyond or beneath

Figure 10

Jung's View	Tantric View
Consciousness	Gross Consciousness

- -

Personal Unconscious (Emotional Patterns. Shadow)	Subtle Consciousness

- -

Collective Unconscious (Transpersonal Ground)	Extremely Subtle Consciousness

- -

Pleroma (The unmanifest wisdom of God – Sophia)	Clear Light Dharmakaya 'Source'

conscious reach and therefore 'unconscious'. This does not mean they do not affect consciousness but they do so from within the unconscious. This means that the unconscious is effectively a *location* that contains certain aspects of our nature. Jung's map of consciousness is a structural map, where there is a threshold between consciousness and the unconscious. Consciousness cannot, by definition, cross that threshold, we can only bring what is in the unconscious gradually into consciousness. This view explains why Jung did not consider meditation a particularly useful thing for Western mind, because we would, he thought, go unconscious.

Jung's notion of the shadow is consistent with his map of the unconscious. The shadow relates to aspects of our nature that, having been repressed, 'dwell' in the unconscious and have a life there in the dark. These repressed aspects our nature can, when they are triggered, emerge into consciousness and strongly effect our emotional life.

In Buddhism it is less easy to assert that something abides in the mind either on a conscious or unconscious level. Experiences in the mind arise as interdependent transitory phenomena that do not endure through time. The nearest equivalent to the idea of shadow in Buddhism will be the presence of what are called *samskaras*. These might be described as karmic emotional patterns. They are propensities or tendencies that when triggered manifest in a constellation of feelings, perceptions, and habitual reactions. They do not specifically constitute a level of shadow because they are not held in the unconscious through a process of repression. They are, however, present yet dormant on a level that remains unconscious until they are activated. They then come into the foreground of awareness shaping and colouring our experience. In this sense they could be said to 'dwell' in the unconscious.

The tantric view does not create a structure of the mind. It is more a reflection of a process of awareness unfolding moment to moment. Rather than there being a threshold to the unconscious as a location, it recognises that our gross ordinary mind is not able to see what is unfolding on a deeper, more subtle level and is therefore unconscious. If we are able to quieten the busy-ness of our ordinary mind, we will gradually become aware of a more subtle process going on. This is experienced as the movement of our inner feeling, emotional life and habitual patterns of thinking and reacting. In meditation, rather than 'going unconscious', as Jung saw it, we are able to enter into an increasingly subtle awareness of inner processes.

Where these two views share a common ground is that both recognise that much of what is below the threshold of consciousness is buried or held in the body. This means that as we descend beneath gross consciousness we are opening to an increasingly subtle level of felt-sense of the processes within the body. In the therapeutic world today, it is recognised that the body is where we discover and re-awaken trauma within the unconscious. It is also understood that we can gradually become aware of more subtle levels of body process as we explore the healing of trauma. Effectively the therapeutic world begins to shift from the map that emphasises the unconscious to one which relates more to a subtle process of awareness.

If we follow this map downwards, Jung recognised through his work with patients that there was another far deeper level of the unconscious that influences our conscious life. This he saw in the manifestation of what he recognised as universal archetypes, or primordial psychological patterns; aspects of our unconscious life contained within what he named the *collective unconscious*. He saw these archetypes as roots of meaning and ordering templates that influence and shape conscious life from deep within the unconscious. They manifest in our dreams and are expressed in our creative life in symbols and images. It is this domain of the collective unconscious that underlies the mythical reality that lives through us and shapes our psychological life in subtle yet very powerful ways. This notion of an archetypal domain of the collective unconscious has a significant parallel in the 'extremely subtle consciousness', the source of the tantric deity. We see the tantric deity as a latent potential of the most subtle level of consciousness awakened through initiation and then cultivated through meditation practice. They are also archetypal in that they personify universal forces within the deepest level of our nature.

The primary difference between these two views is that Jung's collective unconscious is what he called the 'dark background' of our conscious reality, whereas in the tantric view this dimension of our mind is awake, bright and clear. It is not unconscious, rather it is our ordinary gross mind that is asleep or perhaps we could say unconscious. Effectively the maps are opposites. This means that the journey we are on from the Jungian view takes us into the unconscious darkness to illuminate what is living there by bringing it into consciousness. From a tantric point of view, it is a journey that gradually reveals the natural wisdom and radiance of our innate nature through meditation. Having said this, we can see that, even within the tantric view, owing to the dominance of gross consciousness, we are not readily able to access these more subtle levels of consciousness. They are said to be obscured by ordinary consciousness which means that they are effectively unconscious. While Jung's map is a description of the structure of the psyche the unconscious is, as I have suggested before, a kind of location. The tantric map is more a description of the process of the mind's capacity for levels of consciousness or levels of awareness, as an active moment to moment experience. Hence, Jung speaks of the contents of the unconscious whereas in the tantric map we are speaking of increasingly subtle processes of awareness. By definition, for Jung one cannot experience the unconscious, one can only gradually make what 'dwells' there more conscious. In tantra, what meditation does is enable a deepening into more and more subtle levels of consciousness, eventually reaching clear-light mind.

Jung's collective unconscious and the tantric extremely subtle clear-light consciousness cannot be seen as direct equivalents even though it is in this domain that we see the emergence of the archetypal forms of deities. Although it is not well known, Jung also saw a deeper level of the unconscious which he called the 'Pleroma', described as the unmanifest wisdom of God, or Sophia, and saw it as a void or nothingness beyond time and duality[27]. In many ways this can also be seen as an echo of the tantric dharmakaya, the wisdom ground of being from which all appearances emerge.

I have introduced these maps of the mind or consciousness because it feels important to give some clarification before I go into the notion of descent in more depth. We can then see this process from both a tantric and Jungian point of view where the comparisons give some interesting understanding. When I teach I am aware that in my use of language, I often shift from one map to the other relatively easily. I am also aware that in the psychotherapeutic setting sometimes it is very helpful to come from Jung's map and at other times from the tantric map. The two convey helpful ways of approaching a similar experience and bringing to light different reflections on its nature.

18

Meeting the Unconscious

IN THE PREVIOUS CHAPTER I began to describe two maps of
the psyche that are very different and yet have some interesting
overlaps. We saw how Jung's structural view leads us to recognise
levels of the unconscious that 'contain' aspects of our psychological
life. This is in contrast to the tantric map that sees degrees of subtlety
of awareness as a moment to moment process. There is a further
significant difference between these two views in how we approach
what dwells within the deeper levels of our consciousness. To explain
this, I want to make a distinction between the process of *visualisation*
used in tantric practice and what Jung described as *active imagination*.

Jung's relationship to the unconscious was very different to what
we see within the tantric tradition. His orientation was to allow the
unconscious its natural creative expression, to reveal its wisdom and
insights through the power of symbolic image and metaphor. The
tantric tradition has, by contrast, created an incredibly rich system
out of the symbolic life of the psyche and turned it into a formal
spiritual practice. Jung suggested that in the East they do not
consider creative imagination useful because they have turned
imaginal reality into a spiritual path. In the West we have a

somewhat ambiguous relationship to it. We value the imagination as an expression of individuality, it is the source of so much creative innovation in all areas of life, but we also exploit it relentlessly.

It is interesting to consider that even though there is a powerful relationship to the symbolic world in tantra, imagination as a creative expression is not really valued. Instead the important process is passing on the lineage of symbolic forms in as exact a way a possible so as to preserve the lineage of a tradition. As a tangkha painter (Tibetan icons) I became very aware of how tight the creative process had to be. There is very little room for personal expression except in the surrounding landscapes and how the actual painting process itself could be done. In Tibetan art and crafts generally, the emphasis is on precisely reproducing particular symbolic forms whether it is in the temples, ritual furniture and implements or the painting of icons. By contrast, in the West we are very concerned with originality and free individual expression of creative imagination.

When we begin to approach the tradition of tantra, symbolic life is given far greater importance than we tend to consider in the West. We do not hold it to be very real and tend to consider that images and visions may have meaning, but still have little more reality than just imagination. But imaginal reality has power. The deities visualised in tantra are 'real' in the sense that they are an expression of our energetic reality, our psychic reality. They carry a power that has an effect and is not just imagination. In *Kindly Bent to Ease Us*, Herbert Gunter makes the point that a deity doesn't just symbolise our Buddha nature, it is a direct emanation of it.[28]

Through the work of Jung and other archetypal psychologists and in the tantric and shamanic traditions we learn that our inner world of the imagination has great potency, it has energy and has an effect. In tantra if I imagine a deity to be present its energetic power becomes present. Our imagination brings a reality into being that in Jung's terms draws on the innate potency of the archetypal domain of the unconscious. In tantra this is the domain of the energetic vitality of sambhogakaya, where the deity is not merely symbolic, it has a living reality. The deity is experienced as a direct manifestation of the energetic undercurrent of our reality and will be felt as such. It will bring with it archetypal qualities that have particular potency to affect us. We cannot then separate the imaginal from an energetic experience, they are reflections of the same phenomenon. Jung recognised this in what he called *numinosity* where images that emerge from the unconscious bring with them a certain potency or charge and a fascination.

For many people the practice of tantra will naturally begin to awaken this numinosity and inspiration. This is facilitated through the process of practice that continues from the time of initiation. For those who already have a very active relationship to the archetypal symbolic world, tantric practice may feel very natural. In my own experience I found myself living between two worlds. I have always had a very lively and active inner life of creative imagination expressed in my art and interest in myths and fairy tales. Jung's work always fascinated me. At the same time, I was powerfully drawn to the tantric tradition and its deities. Something seemed to resonate within me around these forms and images. In many ways I think I was looking for a more formed system, to give greater clarity and cohesion to my symbolic life. It was, as Jung suggested, as though the Tibetans were practising what I could only imagine.

Increasingly, however, I meet people who are drawn to this tradition and yet struggle to gain a real alive connection to the qualities of a deity through visualisation. This can easily reflect Jung's view that the visualisation of an Eastern deity was imposing an image upon the psyche that may not touch us deeply. Receiving an initiation may inspire this connection, but this may not always last when we begin to practice a traditional sadhana. If this is so we may need to wake up a relationship to the symbolic world of the unconscious as a bridge to tantric practice. When the process of formal deity visualisation does not bring a sense of connection, I have begun to see that it can be helpful to activate or re-awaken our imaginal reality in another way. Jung's approach to the activation of the unconscious was not through direct visualisation but through what he called *active imagination*. I have found that what this approach can potentially do is bring our own inner life more into relationship to the forms of the tantric tradition. This in itself can help to bridge worlds both in terms of archetypal meaning as well as a felt connection.

Visualisation and Active Imagination

The dilemma I am describing, as to whether a deity touches us, is partly connected to the difference between *visualisation* and *active imagination*. In tantra we are constantly using what we usually describe as visualisation, while in Jungian work we use what is more likely to be called active imagination. These two are very different in nature and yet they both utilise the mind's capacity to create vision and image. From both a tantric and Jungian perspective this is possible because the mind's energetic vitality and luminosity is such that it generates inner vision that can take the form of images and fantasies. We see the power of these images because as they arise they will bring with them a kind of charge that is often felt very strongly. Fantasy for example, is often highly charged and that charge has a kind of motivating force that is often hard to resist. Jung sometimes described the energetic quality of an archetypal image as its 'archetypal intent'.

In his alchemical studies Jung described this as the power of *spirit*. According to many medieval alchemists, spirit was an immaterial 'substance' that inspired and illuminated our psyche, giving rise to inner vision and creative imagination[29]. In tantra this capacity is an expression of *lung* or energy-wind which is refined and cultivated in the process of deity visualisation. Some people are extremely adept at the process of visualisation, others seem to find this process extremely difficult no matter how much they may try. Unfortunately, because the process of visualisation is so important in tantric practice, it can be very hard for those that find this difficult.

Active imagination is an altogether different story. The way this is often used is in the creation of what might be called imaginal journeys or guided imagery. Having spent many years creating and guiding this kind of journey in the process of psychotherapy workshops, it is interesting how much this helps to awaken our natural imaginal capacity. Even those who hitherto felt they had no ability for this kind of thing often surprise themselves. This may not automatically make us great deity visualisers, but it does enhance the sense of their reality.

With active imagination, what we are doing is allowing the mind to begin to enter a magical reality of imagination. This brings our awareness into a more subtle state that begins to touch into the unconscious, allowing it to 'communicate' through symbols and metaphors. Active imagination requires much less control than the process of visualisation and is often something that, with the right conditions, people can do even if they are not very good at visualisation.

To create a less controlled state of mind to allow imagination to unfold it is often helpful to lie down and deeply relax. As the mind quietens and deepens towards a more dreamlike space it is allowed to spontaneously give rise to images or an imaginal process that can be partly guided by conscious awareness. We are on the threshold between consciousness and the unconscious. Working with exercises in active imagination I will usually create the rudiments of a story line that begins to initiate the imaginal process. This creates an environment within which images begin to unfold in response. In this way there is a level of interaction with the unfolding of images, a subtle dialogue.

When we consider these two orientations: visualisation and active imagination, we can see how the first could be seen as the imposition of an image on the psyche and the second as the free expression of the psyche. A visualised deity image is, of course, not *just* an imposition upon the psyche and can resonate deeply if we have awakened the connection. It is clear that many Western practitioners do not always find this visualisation process to be easy. In this case, exploring some form of active imagination can help.

Perhaps some examples of this will make the connection clearer. During a retreat Anna and I led in the UK one year, I wanted to explore our relationship to the five elements: earth, water, fire, air and space. These are personified in the tantric tradition as five dakinis, or five female deities. I decided to bring together some of my background of transpersonal psychology, working with active imagination, into the tantric process.

I began by guiding a simple visualisation, imagining that we are standing within a walled enclosure or garden with four exits. Each of these exits would be a doorway out into the elements. We spent a while becoming familiar with the garden, how it appeared, its condition and so on. I then guided those participating to go to each of the exits in turn where a dakini of each element would come to meet them and guide them through the element. During their own imaginal journey, they would explore their relationship to each element as well as a feeling for the quality of that dakini. After a period of perhaps seven or eight minutes, I brought them back into the walled garden leaving the elemental dakini outside. After a short while they then went to the next exit to meet and explore the next element, guided by that elemental dakini. We proceeded through the elements giving time with each to discover how they experienced that element. At the end of this journey I suggested people made simple drawings and notes of their experience.

Following this meditation, I asked people to begin to describe what they had experienced, which was a combination of two things in particular. First, they said they had a much clearer sense of why the elements are symbolised in the aspect of dakinis. This in turn brought to life a closer feeling of the presence of the four dakinis when visualised in the heart, within the conventional Vajrayogini sadhana.

Perhaps more importantly, however, was the way this exploration opened up their own relationship to the way the energy of the elements affected their life emotionally or psychologically. It gave an opportunity to see how the elements live through their experience and how they may be uncomfortable with some elements while others were very familiar. This in turn enabled a greater sense of their potential strengths and weaknesses and what needed to develop.

When I reflect upon the months I spent in retreat engaged in practices that incorporate the dakinis of the elements, I never felt I made that kind of relationship. It was not until many years later doing this sort of exercise that they truly came alive for me.

More recently I wanted to explore another meditation using simple active imagination to help people begin to make a connection to a particular deity. The deity, Vajrapani (Figure 11), embodies an aspect of our innate power and effectiveness to engage with our life. Some of those on the retreat had difficulty relating to Vajrapani because they struggled with their own relationship to power. I therefore wanted to introduce a way to explore their experience of how power might be more healthily brought into their life.

After settling in meditation in the usual way I then asked them to imagine that they were walking through a familiar landscape. This gradually led them to a wilder forested landscape and a path that led to a sacred place deep in a forest. Entering this sacred space, they sat and waited for the deity to come to meet them. I suggested he would come to them in a form they would be able to relate to personally.

Once the figure arrived I asked them to have a dialogue to explore what would help them to have a beneficial relationship to their own power. There were other aspects to the meeting that included being given an object that related to how they could be more effective in their life. After this meeting I guided people back to the meditation space.

I introduced this guided imagery journey to begin to stimulate an imaginal process that was an expression of their own inner reality, rather than simply imposing a deity upon it. Afterwards many people said that it enabled a connection to come alive in a much more personal way. They felt they could enter into a more magical reality, rather than just visualising the deity. Some expressed how it brought to awareness where their relationship to power had been detrimentally affected, particularly in relation to father authority in early life.

Over the years I have explored this active imagination approach in relation to other deities such as Manjushri and Tara. This process will, of course, never substitute for the nature of the sadhana as a more formal practice. It may, however, go some way to creating a bridge that deepens or enables a more personal experience. Those I have guided in this way have expressed how it has enabled a more alive relationship to the deity, rather than the somewhat static experience of visualisation. The purpose of bringing the imagination alive in this way, is to enhance our relationship to a practice that may not automatically connect to our Western experience. It is understood within the tantric path that the deities we practise are present in the depth of our psyche, they need to be awoken so that we can feel a genuine personal connection. With the process of active imagination, there is the potential to discover this more personal relationship, helping to bring alive a deeper connection to what is already in our nature.

Figure 11, Vajrapani

19

The Gods in our Diseases

THERE IS A MEMORABLE EXPRESSION that comes from Jung: 'there are gods in our diseases' or that 'the gods have become our diseases'. It was James Hillman who later spoke about our inner daemons that could either be a resource and guiding presence in our life or they would become potentially demonic.[30] What both Jung and Hillman were saying is that while we are unaware of the archetypal forces within us, they can unconsciously influence or dominate our lives. They can then become part of our inner dis-ease. When the forces they embody are not given credence in our life and honoured for the powers that they are, they can become destructive. The energy they contain can become unhealthy and manifest in damaging ways for us both individually and collectively. Jung would often cite the god Wotan, which he believed was an underlying influence in the German psyche during the Second World War. It became a monstrous collective force whose archetypal intent was bent on power, domination and cruelty. Wotan symbolises the authoritarian patriarch that seeks power at the expense of love and that when thwarted will destroy what obstructs, even his own children. Unrecognised and unchecked this force he felt possessed the collective psyche of the Nazi regime.

In British culture when the gods, so to speak, of ecstasy and spiritual intoxication have no natural outlet in a healthy way they become a basis for addiction and drunkenness. When the erotic aspect of our nature does not have a healthy channel, its repression can easily manifest in addiction to pornography and sexually abusive behaviour.

There are archetypal forces in our psyche that will live though us and dominate our lives without our knowing, if we are blind to their presence. They become our psychological disorders and will remain so until they are recognised and begin to be consciously integrated. For Jung, this is in part the task of the process of analysis. Once the archetypes begin to be consciously brought into our lives they can become more humanised and healthy. As they become integrated they can then recede into a less dominant place in our psyche. Their energy naturally becomes part of who we are in a healthy way. If we do not embark on this process of integration, these archetypal aspects of our psyche become hidden within our shadow.

It is our lack of relationship to the powerful world of the archetypes in the West that is a cause for concern. This is significant when we consider the idea of an Eastern spiritual tradition and Western psyche. It is not easy for us in the West to have a healthy and appropriate relationship to the gods or daemons in our psyche. It is possible through the insights of Jung to begin to acknowledge their presence, but this psychological knowledge can still lack something if there is no method or ritual of transformation. Jung saw this method is largely missing in Western culture.

I am reminded of something Robert Johnson said in *The Psychology of Romantic Love*. He considered that in the East the images of our inner archetypal life are placed in the temple not projected into our relationships. Johnson was particularly referring to the images of the masculine and feminine or *anima* and *animus*. This could equally apply to what Jung saw as the archetypal shadow. This becomes very clear to me when I reflect on an experience I had many years ago while I was in India.

In early 1981, I had the good fortune to stay for about a month in a small monastery associated with the dharma protector Mahakala, to carry out a fire ritual retreat. This monastery was on the side of a small range of mountains close to Bodhgaya, where the Buddha attained enlightenment. While I was there I would often go into the small temple at around 3.00 the morning when the abbot was performing his prayers to Mahakala. Standing at least six feet tall in the centre of the temple was a magnificent statue of Mahakala, his wrathful black face staring down. The only lighting in the temple were small butter lamps and its walls and ceiling were painted black making it a dark and mysterious cave-like place. To add to this atmosphere, all along the walls where painted images of offerings formed out of pieces of the body placed in skull cups.

What was extraordinary about this Mahakala temple is that, from one perspective, it is a temple to the shadow in all its power and darkness. In this way we see how the Tibetan tradition place into the temple what we in the West cast into the shadow as demonic and evil. They see its sacred nature and do not split between light and dark, good and evil in the same way we do in the West. When Younghusband, a British explorer, went to Tibet in the early 1900's he must have seen similar temples which, convinced that the Tibetans were demon worshipers, led him unsuccessfully to try and convert them to Christianity.

It is this split in our psyche that leads us to bury the powerful and darker aspects of our archetypal life in the unconscious. While we remain out of relationship to the presence of those archetypal patterns they will, nevertheless, continue to have an influence over our life but often in ways that are unhealthy. One could say that the psyche, our psychological totality, is always attempting to wake us up to its presence. The problems we encounter psychologically are the symptoms that manifest through that process. We can also see that the film industry makes good use of this enshadowed side of our nature in its superhero and horror movies. We seem to be endlessly stimulated by these powerful images. Within our deeper nature lie archetypal forces that are seeking an outlet, rather than being blocked and distorted. These are the gods in our diseases. In the practice of tantra we are brought back into relationship with this archetypal world in a way that potentially connects us directly to their source. They are returned to the temple. The deities that are a manifestation of these powerful forces can provide a natural vehicle for their awakening.

Jung believed that the archetypes within the collective unconscious brought with them a powerful intentionality, he called 'archetypal intent'. This is a deep often irresistible undercurrent or force that will affect our behaviour for good or ill. This undercurrent can be like an unconscious compulsion that drives us to behave in ways that are sometimes very disturbed. He recognised that for these archetypal forces to be healthily awoken in our psyche, rather than remaining unhealthy and potentially demonic, they need a channel for transformation. He also considered that for an archetype to 'speak' to us and become more consciously meaningful, awake and integrated it helps to have a connection to an image within our conscious world. In this way our symbolic imagination becomes a reflection of our unconscious world. This can bring what may have become demonic into our awareness, with the potential for transformation and integration.

In tantric practice we discover a means of working with this unconscious archetypal energy. The wrathful deities of higher tantra in particular provide a very natural expression for these forces in our unconscious. In *Symbols of Transformation*, Jung speaks about the way in which the energy of instinctual passions such as aggression, anger, sexual desire and so on need a channel of a similar nature to what is to be transformed.[31] With anger for example we find this in the deities Vajrapani or Yamantaka, who are able to magnetise and hold that energy. Vajrapani (Figure 11) has a roaring, snarling, ferocious form like a powerful warrior or wrestler. He is muscular and potent and in one description I recall him being described as having a hairy body. In one period of Indian art at a time when the Greeks were in parts of India, Vajrapani was sculptured in the style of Hercules. Here we have a symbolic channel for the powerful, potentially violent, aggressive energy that can lie deep within us and yet is often not expressed healthily. While it is not given a channel to transform it will manifest in uncontrolled anger and violence. Behind this is the god in our disturbed energy, which in tantra is the deity of power, strength, effectiveness and confidence, symbolised by Vajrapani. Once this energy is given a clear means of expression it can be harnessed and brought into more conscious integration. I know from my own experience that often behind my expression of anger and frustration is almost always a blocked or distorted sense of my power. When I feel disempowered or unable to assert some sense of my 'truth' then it can come out as anger. If I can open to the root of that anger and contact the underlying force within it then I recognise my power and my potential to assert my truth. This is the meaning of Vajrapani.

Another example arose when discussing this process with a group of women during a retreat. They wondered whether there was any natural means of transforming the wild passionate aspect of feminine energy within Christian culture. Rather than having a channel of awakening and transforming this energy, they felt it tended either to be submerged into the shadow as unacceptable, or to come out as part of a culture that would perhaps drink excessive quantities of alcohol and want to party wildly. Neither of these options they felt gives a healthy means of awakening and transformation. Recognising this lack of a natural means of liberation and transformation, many of these women said they found ways of working with that energy through a relationship to nature, through movement and dance. It is within the practice of higher tantra and the deities connected to the dakini practices such as Vajra Yogini, that we find a very significant means of transformation. Vajra Yogini is a deity that harnesses the wild, fiery, passionate and erotic side of the feminine. She enables us to awaken this energy in our nervous system, giving it a means to liberate and become a basis for profound wisdom.

It is important that we understand that Buddhist deities are archetypal so long as we do not fall into the disposition that they are *merely* archetypal images and therefore not 'real'. This takes away their sacred significance, their magic and their power. The deity is a manifestation of buddha-nature that has an archetypal quality reflected in its appearance as an image. The deity has power, it has its own reality that needs to be valued and understood as a force in our life that we must begin to relate to. When we do, it brings the capacity to awaken energies within ourselves giving a means to transform and liberate them in a healthy way. As they are woken up, however, they need to be held in a safe container, or channelled skilfully, so that they can be embodied and integrated. Then they become part of our human reality rather than being demons that dominate us.

The Alchemical Vessel

Jung considered that to bring these deep forces back into awareness was like the re-awakening of the dark gods. He said that when the dark god arises from the depth of the psyche it needs a strong vessel to be able to hold or contain the energy that emerges. He was speaking of the alchemical vessel within which these forces can awaken and be contained, so that they become consciously integrated. When we engage in tantric practice therefore, we need to consider that the vessel or container that holds our practice is very important. This is something the tantric tradition takes very seriously and we define the alchemical vessel that holds the process of awakening in a number of different ways. I have referred to this in some detail in *The Psychology of Buddhist Tantra*[32]. It is defined partly in terms of the ethical or moral boundary that we place around our practice. In higher tantra these boundaries are the tantric vows taken during the initiation process. In the lower tantras at the very least one is expected to hold the Bodhisattva vow or vows, as a moral container. This is in part to ensure that our quality of intention for practice is to awaken for the welfare of others, not just because we have some desire for powers. The vows are defined in this way so that as these powerful aspects of our inner nature are activated, there is an ethical framework in which they are held. In this way others are protected from any harm this activation may potentially cause.

The vessel in tantra is further defined by the boundaries of retreat, within which we may do this kind of practice. The term for retreat in Tibetan *sam la do* means to 'sit within boundaries'. This boundary holds the energy of practice in a container that enables it to awaken and transform. It is what Dora Kalff, the Jungian sand-play therapist called a 'free and secure space'[33].

An aspect of this secure space is the presence of someone, a guide or mentor, who can act as a holder of the vessel. During my retreats in India it was re-assuring to know that one of my teachers, Gen Jampa Wangdu, was keeping an eye on how I was, even though he was some distance away. I always knew that if I was struggling with what my meditation practice was bringing up, I could walk down the mountain and see him. When leading group retreats I also see the importance of holding the vessel skilfully, with compassion and psychological understanding. This allows people to go through whatever process is necessary and trust in the safety of the container. When we are able to create the right conditions for practice the effect is profound.

Finally, and possibly the most crucial way of understanding the vessel of transformation returns us to the recognition that the body is the primary vessel within which the transformational process is taking place. As I emphasised in Chapter 16 there is a natural process in the relationship between the three kayas. Our energy moves from the subtle level of dharmakaya through the expression of sambhogakaya into the embodied sense of nirmanakaya. If we do not in some way complete this process then we will be left with a lot of energy awakened in our system but with no means to embody and ground it. This is one of the dangers of tantric practice when it is only performed as a mental process. This is also important because the physical body is the container within which all the embedded trauma, or emotional wounding within our nervous system lives. From a tantric point of view this is the stuff of transformation and we need to give the energy that is woken up a means to be digested through the body. Because of this, once again I want to emphasise the importance of ways of working with the body through meditation, but also through movement and exercise so that grounding and embodiment takes place. Without this we will never experience the full benefit of healing and transformation.

As we relate to the deities of tantra they can evoke aspects of our nature that may be painful, frightening and uncomfortable to face in ourselves. We should not assume that when we practice even a peaceful deity like Chenrezig, the Buddha of compassion, that all is going to be blissful and easy. When Anna and I have led retreats on this practice it has often been surprising how much rage or pain can emerge in people's experience as a result of practice. We may be surprised, but if we understand how the psyche needs to open, so that what is in the unconscious can be allowed to flow through, then this is quite natural. Indeed, we could almost consider that if it is not happening then there may be something not right. It is for this reason that I am sometimes suspicious when I hear people say they have had such a wonderful retreat. In my own experiences of retreat, they were seldom entirely blissful and most often quite challenging, as shadowy aspects of my unconscious came to the surface.

What becomes problematic is when we do wrathful tantric practices without working through the body and its energetic nature. Intensive visualisations and mantra recitation practices that stimulate our energy, need to be grounded. If this doesn't happen, rather than being a healing process, it can potentially perpetuate psychological problems that remain unresolved where the energy becomes 'backed up' in the body. When I was in long retreat I found the need to work with physical energy practices such as yoga was crucial if my energy was not to become stuck. These deities evoke powerful forces from the unconscious that can be transformed into what might be called wisdom energy. But as these are indeed 'dark gods being awoken' from the unconscious and we need to take care in how we practice them. What I want to stress here is the need to come back to the principle I have spoken of in Chapters 6, 7, and 8. To really transform, digest and integrate what arises we need to be practicing in an embodied way.

The gods in our diseases are forces that can be awoken within our energy-body and transformed given the right conditions and channels. It is regrettable that in the West these channels are not always easy to find, especially within the context of our spiritual life. Christian society has a history of splitting us from our shadowy side, repressing as evil and demonic these aspects of our psyche. So long as that is how we relate to them, they have no other direction to go. They become dark and powerful, living in our sicknesses psychologically, physically and collectively. Given the appropriate context, however, there is a natural potential for transformation. Tantric practice places these 'gods' back into the temple where they can be honoured as qualities to be awakened.

20

The Journey of Descent

I WAS ONCE VISITED by a client who described her experience of an awful phase in her life where she suffered a terrible sequence of bereavements. Over a period of a few years she lost her beloved son and then her partner of many years. These deaths were a devastating blow and she was in a state of grief and despair that felt interminable. Her relationship to her Buddhist practice became very tenuous at this time as she struggled to find a way to be with the continual emotional turmoil that would at times overwhelm her. Her formal deity practice, she said, became little more than a mechanical ritual that meant very little and did not really touch her or give any solace. Regretfully, some of her Buddhist peers were encouraging her to use a thinking process to bring herself out of the pain so that she could move on. Something that clearly hadn't helped.

From my perspective I felt that it was important she gave what was emerging emotionally the space to move through with open present awareness. I suggested she began to ground herself more in her body and to see the emotional distress she experienced as a natural flow of grief that would gradually free itself if allowed to be as it was without judgement. As she explored this she said she felt as though her normal sense of self was gradually dissolving into a pool of tears. As she cried she began to open and in this opening she started to feel layers of pain and grief mixed with a deep sense of love. The image that repeatedly came to her as she stayed with her feelings, was of an ocean of sadness that was in part her own but also something vast and collective that she was opening to and descending towards.

It was not easy for her to trust that if she began to let go of her ego's need to contract and control, she would settle into something that was deeper and more holding. 'Trusting in the process' was hard for her at first. As she began to let go she contacted fears and anxieties that were part of her early childhood and her mother's inability to be a safe presence. She had great courage, however, and was willing to stay with that process. I began to see that my client was, through the experience of her grief and pain, being opened to something that was very profound.

As we explored this experience the image that came to my mind time and again was of a drop of water dissolving into the ocean. I am aware that this metaphor is often used in the tantric tradition. It signifies the way in which our ordinary individual sense of consciousness gradually dissolves into the deeper ground of our being, our clear light nature or dharmakaya. It is significant that two of the primary metaphors for dharmakaya are the ocean and the great mother.

It was some years earlier when in the middle of my psychotherapeutic training I read a book called *The Descent to the Goddess*, by Silvia Brinton Perera[34]. In this book she describes the mythical journey of the Sumerian moon goddess Innana descending into the underworld and explains the psychological significance of the process of descent. As Innana descends through the various levels that lead to the underworld she is gradually 'taken to pieces' and dismembered. Reaching her final destination in the depths, she is found at the feet of her sister Eriskegal, the dark goddess of the underworld. Eriskegal is in the pain of labour when Innana arrives. At a crucial moment when Eriskegal's pain is unbearable, the upper world god Enki sends some small creatures into the underworld. They have only one task to perform which is to honour her pain, reflecting with compassion "Woe to your pain". As soon as they express this, the situation begins to change. Innana passes through a process of death transformation and is then once again reborn into life in the upper world. Brinton Perera makes the observation that these small creatures created from dirt beneath Enki's fingernails are like the therapist whose humble role is merely to be present with compassion.

This myth is often seen as an example of the journey of what is considered the sinister, left-handed, descending path. It is associated with the feminine and the journey of descent into the dark and the unconscious, in contrast to the upward moving path into the light and brightness of consciousness and the intellect. In the Western mysteries this is often feared by the masculine principle that holds to light and the experience of spiritual ascent and purity rather than this descent into the dark unknown.

This is, however, a route along which many of us are taken in our 'spiritual' journey and it is seldom a comfortable one. I experienced this process at a certain point while I was in long retreat. I had descended into a very painful phase of practice that was accompanied by great anxiety and depression. I felt as though my sense of identity, my sense of self, was being gradually taken to pieces and stripped away. I often found myself tearful and wanting to scream out in despair. I used to go to a large rock close to my retreat hut and lie down, wanting to let go and 'die'. There I opened to the pain and totally let go into it. The grief and tears flowed through me and the pain began to soften and dissolve. As I allowed this I felt as though I died into a state of spacious openness. Gradually the pain faded and I experienced a deep sense of spaciousness pervaded by a feeling of peace.

When I reflect upon this psychological journey it is interesting to see that within the practice of tantra, there is a path which echoes much of what I am describing. The path of 'mother tantra' is traditionally described as the gradual clearing of the obscurations that prevent us from opening to our innate clear-light nature, the primordial ground of our being, our natural dharmakaya. This journey is also described as the left-handed path of descent into what we might describe in psychological language as the unconscious. Of course, there is not a concept of the unconscious within the Buddhist tradition but this term can usefully apply. As we descend our sense of self is gradually dismantled and we soften the contraction around the grasping at *me*. As we open, our experience of spaciousness and non-duality increases. Eventually awareness dissolves like a drop of water into the ocean of clear-light, dharmakaya.

When I studied this aspect of practice in traditional teachings I am aware, in retrospect, that there was no psychological description of the kind of internal emotional process that might accompany such a journey. There is no discussion or exploration of how the processes we go through in practice might feel on the inside. How painful or disturbing it might be to descend and be gradually 'taken to pieces'. In my own experience this sometimes led me to consider that I was doing something wrong. I was not gaining glowing blissful insights and awakening, I was experiencing the sense of being broken down and dismembered. For this reason, I have felt it necessary to bring this kind of psychological understanding into the context of Tibetan practice. It is the only way I can make sense of the internal process I and many others I speak with go through in some form or other.

In this descending journey that eventually returns us to the ground of our being, we may meet many levels of unconscious resistance. We can encounter the primary patterns that have evolved as a means of finding safety and ground in relationship to our early experience of mothering. We will meet the patterning that causes us to hold on, to contract, to control and not let go. We may fear letting go because we do not trust that if we do so we will find a safe sense of ground. This, for many of us, echoes a lack of safe holding in early infancy.

We may experience this as a painful re-awakening of emotions that have been buried in our nervous system from very early in our life. We can pass through layers of emotional experience as we touch into our early wounding, which may be held in the body and energy-body. For many of us this can be a disturbing and even overwhelming experience and is a time when it can be helpful to seek support of someone we trust who can hold us with compassion. This may be a therapist or mentor who is familiar with the psychological process we are going through.

It has become clear to me that if we are to follow this journey of descent that these patterns in our psychological makeup are part of the process. They are the aspects in us that have to be gradually released and passed through, so that we may finally begin to rest in the open ground of our being. At first, we may not trust that it is safe to open and let go. In time this becomes more natural and we begin to realise that there is actually nothing to trust and nothing to rest in. We open to the space of dharmakaya the great ocean, the great mother. We let go into what is sometimes called the 'groundless ground'.

The gradual re-awakening of deeply buried aspects of our nature is concomitant with the awakening or return to our experience of the body. If we have lived a disembodied or dissociated life, where the body is lost in the background of our experience then this will bring it once again to the foreground. In my own journey of descent, the painful emotional process I went through brought me into stark relationship with the feeling life in my body. I had no choice but to fully feel what was going on.

As my experience of my body began to re-awaken I felt as though what was locked away and frozen began to melt. This returned me to a direct experience of the moment to moment fluid nature of my physical being. There was also an existential element in this journey. I felt I had lost the solid ground of my familiar world which put me into relationship with the uncertainty of my existence and the fragile, fluid nature of my physicality. This time of liminality, where my sense of form and reality were unsure, insubstantial and impermanent, was full of anxiety. I was faced with the truth of my emptiness, my lack of substantial and enduring nature. This experience brought to the surface all the anxiety I had suffered through most of my early life was. I felt a terrible sense of groundlessness, like an abyss I would fall into and be annihilated. As I stayed with this process, I found myself increasingly preparing for what I feared or knew was going to happen. At some point this reached a natural peak, and all I could do was break open and let go. This letting go was a release of the contraction I had experienced in my being as I tried to hold onto my sense of self. Suddenly my anxiety was gone. It was as though I had fallen through space and to my amazement, landed softly in a place of peace.

This descending path can take us deeply into our inner life and into the body. Having gone through this in my own journey and worked with the process with clients, I can see that we may embark on this path several times in our life, going gradually deeper. Many of us go through periods of descent during which we discover and digest aspects of our nature before returning to the surface. My experience is that this is often at times of crisis and may be accompanied by some level of depression. Jung saw depression as a time when our natural life vitality was held within the unconscious and therefore unavailable to us in our conscious life. Within the unconscious there is, however, still a process of digestion going on. As we go deeper our tendency to hold onto a sense of self can increasingly soften and dissolve. This does not happen all at once and sometimes the journey is slow and gradual, at others it is steep and rapid. There can be a way in which this process becomes almost familiar as through our life we descend and return, to heal and restore.

With more experience of meditation, we develop resources that make the process far more 'manageable'. We can learn to let go. To be with the emotional processes in a way that does not hold on but allows them to move through. It is as though we are learning to let go and slide into the water rather than fight against it. Ultimately, we are discovering how to surrender our solidified sense of self and like a drop of water, dissolve into the ocean. The more we are able to let go, the less painful this will be.

This dissolution of our substantial sense of self as we descend is particularly associated with mother tantra. It is seen as the esoteric path, the left-handed female path and is associated with the dakinis who are often considered to be guides on this journey. They are the messenger dakinis, female practitioners who are profoundly experienced in this path of awakening. This path is very natural to the female psyche, however, men who have been through this process can also be very adept at guiding others. I feel it is important to recognise that is not a path we can study intellectually, it is a path of direct felt experience.

In the West, as I have said earlier, there is also this left-handed path, the 'sinister' path, a path of descent that spirals counter-clockwise into the depth of our being. In Western mysteries this is the opening to the great mother who is both the dark abyss, but also the blissful presence of love and wisdom. She can become the dark abysmal mother when our ego suffers the existential fear that cannot let go of a sense of self. The ego fears its ultimate demise, seeing the spaciousness of the ground of our being as a dreadful abyss into which we will fall and be devoured. When the ego releases its hold, it is a descent that can begin to free us from pain and anxiety, as we open to be held by the great mother.

In both the East and West therefore, this path is known. In the West it has been both feared and misunderstood by the masculine principle that wants to hold a sense of form and control, or that wants to ascend into light and purity. Feared because it is associated with the mysteries of the feminine and the natural wisdom of women. This led to the endless persecution of witches in the middle ages as the church patriarchy attempted to assert its authority. Psychologically, however, the masculine habit of control and rational thinking cannot hold at bay the pull of this path of descent once it begins to draw us. In our culture there is great emphasis on being happy and competent, where depression or break-down is often frowned on. But as I found myself, depression is sometimes part of this journey where our energy, our joy and lightness have indeed gone underground.

If we can understand the significance of this journey it will have profound implications for any of us that go through some kind of 'dark night' descent. While in tantric teachings the path of mother tantra is often described as the path towards our clear-light nature, 'mother clear-light', what may be less obvious is how that may be experienced psychologically. The journey becomes less painful as we increasingly discover how to open and let go. This is a natural process of healing many of us will go through.

As a psychotherapist I have seen this journey in the therapy and mentoring context on many occasions and experienced it myself. If we can see the journey of descent as something that is natural and necessary and trust in its process then there is much to be learned as we re-emerge at the other end. And we do re-emerge, or perhaps it is more appropriate to say there is a re-emergence. Who we are and how our relative self re-emerges is not always clear. How we then re-engage with the world is something that takes time and care. It is as though our form returns and we become a person once again, renewed and different. No-one is the same when they return from the experience of descent into mother ground, but that is the beauty of the journey.

Figure 12
The Journey of Descent and Re-emergence

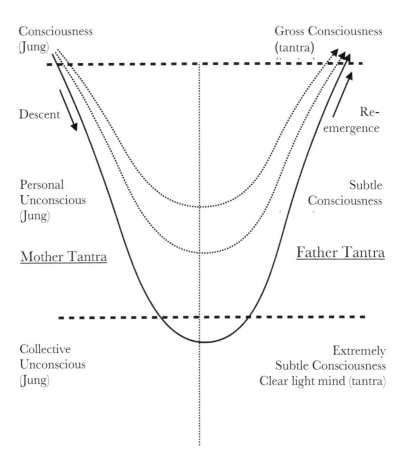

In this diagram I am plotting levels of descent and re-emergence in the context of the two parallel perspectives of consciousness I have explored in Chapter 17 and Figure 10. This is to show that we could understand the nature of that process from either perspective.

21

Death and Transformation

WHEN WE LOOK at many of the deities of higher tantra, the repeated use of skulls in their symbolism becomes very noticeable. In their simple meaning, these skulls symbolise death and transformation. On a more subtle level they symbolise the clear-light nature of mind that arises at the time of death, just before our stream of consciousness leaves the body to move into the intermediate stage. This is the 'clear-light of death', experienced when the energy-winds absorb into the heart chakra at the time of death and the extremely subtle state of clear- light mind arises.

While there is in the tantric tradition a profound understanding of the actual process of death, there are different levels in which we may experience this journey of transformation. When I referred, at the end of Chapter 17, to the comment Lama Yeshe made that 'something has to die', he was not referring to my actual death. He was responding to a very important aspect of my journey in relation to my ordinary identity and sense of self, that needed to die.

In the process of tantric practice, at the heart of the sadhana is a repeated experience of dying. On one level this is the process I have described in previous chapters, of a gradual dissolving of our relative identity and relationship to form and appearance prior to self-generation. On another level it is a simulated preparation for death itself. It is sometimes said that for a tantric practice to fulfil the requirements of true transformation, it needs to bring the process of death, bardo and rebirth into the path. Within the traditional teachings, what this means is that death is transformed into the path to experience dharmakaya; the intermediate or bardo state is transformed into the experience of sambhogakaya; rebirth into the experience of nirmankaya.

If we look at this in terms of our inner process, we are going through a gradual dissolution of our experience of relative appearances and identification with our form, into the clear-light nature of mind. This clear-light mind is sometimes described as 'causal mind'. This refers to the fact that from a tantric perspective all the appearances of our world are seen as an emanation or projection of our subtle mind. We are therefore, in effect, turning off the projector, withdrawing the projection. In meditation, we then rest in a state of awareness that is free of projected dualistic reality. We may remain in this meditation for long periods and allow the sense of freedom from entanglement in the relative environment to deeply sink in. Eventually from this state of non-dual clear awareness, the vibration of relative appearances starts to move. Our energetic nature begins to awaken an intention to manifest, which then re-emerges into form.

In this process of dissolution, we temporarily disentangle ourselves from the proliferation of our relationship with the forms and appearances of our life. A kind of spiritual holiday. In meditation practice this is a journey we repeat again and again, gradually refining the process as we go through it. When we look at the sadhana as I have described in Chapters 11-14, we see this cycle repeated each time we practise. We dissolve into the state of clear-light, dharmakaya, and then return in the aspect of the deity. This means we dissolve our ego identification and then arise in the aspect of our buddha potential time and time again. Gradually we come to a place where an inner alignment with our innate buddha-nature is so intimate and immediate that there is no longer a need to cycle through this journey, and we unite these two dimensions of being and manifestation simultaneously. Until this happens we need to repeat the cycle in the context of our practice. While we see this passage of death and transformation expressed in the heart of the traditional tantric sadhana, this does not necessarily convey how we experience it psychologically.

As I have explored in the previous chapter, while I was in long retreat this meditation process was gradually having a parallel psychological impact. I began to find that something in me was becoming increasingly agitated and anxious. My dreams were often disturbed, dark and frightening. I began to feel I was falling apart, disintegrating and losing my sense of solidity and stability. I felt a kind of existential anxious shakiness a lot of the time and being in isolation up in the mountains was becoming very hard. I had little to do other than meditate and go for walks in the foggy monsoon drenched forest. Everything was becoming very surreal and I was beginning to feel mildly depressed.

One evening I had the distinct feeling that I was actually going to die. I had lost a lot of weight through this process and was not feeling very strong physically. That night I decided to do a particular practice, a self-initiation, which I knew would be the best thing to do before dying. Eventually I lay down to rest and attempt to sleep. My anxiety level was high, but I was watching it with as much clarity of awareness as I was able. The whole process was on one level very scary and on another, I was just watching it unfold with a certain kind of objective fascination. I wanted to witness the death signs as they emerged, but at some point, must have fallen asleep. In my dreams that night I found myself deep in a hole in the ground. Before me a female figure was standing with her legs across this grave and I heard a voice say, "The waters have broken". I found myself making a particular mudra which symbolised the union of male and female, then I suddenly arose out of the ground and was standing as though I had risen from the dead. I awoke and to my amazement realised I was still alive. I seemed to be aware of every moment as it passed, and there was a huge sense of space and immanence as life emerged and arose within and around me second by second.

Soon after this I visited Gen Jhampa Wangdu and described my experience over the past months. His only comment was that I was very fortunate to have such an experience and that Tibetans pray to have this kind of thing. He said he was confident I had enough understanding of the dharma. He encouraged me to get back up the mountain and continue. I did as he said and made my way back up to my retreat hut.

At some point in the process of tantric practice we have to die and be reborn. We can see this symbolised in the skull images and this process is expressed in the evolution of deity practice. Here we are confronted with our relationship to psychological death as well as how we feel about our actual death. They cannot help but echo each other. Whether this process of death and transformation is comfortable or frightening will depend on each of us individually. For me that time in retreat was not easy, even so the result was, in retrospect, worthwhile.

Death and transformation are there at the heart of tantra. We can see this as a preparation for actual death. We can also experience it on the level of psychological death, where the ego loses its centrality of ground and has to let go into our deeper nature of wisdom and emptiness. This is a gradual process but can also have its nadir where we go through something of a crisis. If we learn through the practice of mahamudra to increasingly relax and let go of the holding we have to our sense of self, this process may not be dramatic. From my own experience, the more I was able to remain open and surrender, the less I grasped at and tightened around the sense of self that needed to die. In my experience, there were definitely times when I could do this, at others, I was just caught in my fears and anxieties. It was a painful but necessary learning.

Here we return to the point I was making within my exploration of mother tantra. Letting go is less easy if we fear that in doing so we will ultimately be annihilated and we will fall into a kind of abyss. As mentioned in the previous chapter, this is where we see that the dissolution of the ego into the ground of our nature echoes our original relationship to mother. She may have been a deeply holding presence or one that was anxious and unsafe. 'Mother clear-light', as this ground is called, is a neutral state but will be coloured by our early childhood experiences, which may make letting go very fraught. This psychological phenomenon explains why, for some of us, resting in the non-dual spaciousness of the nature of mind is not simple.

My fear and anxiety at this threshold of letting go, was a reflection my own struggle to find a deeper sense of openness and trust. This profoundly echoed my own experience of an anxious possibly even depressed mother, who's holding always felt to be a shaky ground, stimulating great anxiety in me. The idea of trust in letting go is something of a paradox in Buddhism, as ultimately there is nothing in which to trust. With time, however, we can gradually soften our holding, as we learn to open. Death is a return to that deep ground of dharmakaya, a coming home as we settle into the ocean. Once we go through this process and our holding to a sense of form dissolves into the space of non-duality, there is no anxiety, only peace and spaciousness. In my own retreats I found myself going through this experience many times, gradually becoming familiar with the sense of letting go and the peace that remained.

When we 'die' into the peaceful, spacious, formless nature of emptiness there may be a great temptation to simply stay there. That doesn't mean we necessarily can, as there is a natural movement of the mind towards form. But from that space we will also need to return to the relative world. Sometimes we may have a strong desire or even attachment to the peace of spacious awareness. I have known some who would prefer to just remain there if they could and have a deep reticence to being in this world. In one respect this is completely understandable, especially if this life is a struggle. For some of my psychotherapy clients, there was a sense that they did not actually wish to be born into this life in the first place. It is as though coming into form at the moment of conception was a struggle for them. There is, in this respect, a question: do we choose, or is this process one without choice? It is often said that the 'winds of karma' drive us whether we choose it or not. But for some who feel they do not have the life they want this apparent lack of choice can feel painful.

I have sometimes noticed in my own meditation that there can be a subtle sense of reluctance to come back out of the peace and spaciousness of emptiness into the realm of duality again. Why should I come back to the world of getting children to school, doing the washing up and the day's work? Wouldn't it be nice to just hang out in spaciousness? But, as Milarepa said, it is easy to meditate upon the sky, it is not easy to meditate upon the clouds. Our task is to work within the relative world of forms and appearances so that we can manifest and benefit others.

Within the absorption process when we abide in the state of empty, spacious awareness, there is a moment when we must bring a quality of intention to manifest in the world for the welfare of sentient beings. It is said in Mahayana teachings on bodhichitta that this is the quality of intention that differentiates the Bodhisattva from one who will become an Arhant. The Arhant is said to remain within that space and not return to a form. The Bodhisattva consciously makes the choice to return to the world of duality lifetime after lifetime, for the welfare of sentient beings. Whether it is at the time of psychological death or our actual death, what initiates the process of re-emergence is a willingness to re-engage with the relative world. As we re-emerge we are not going to be the same again and cannot predict or anticipate what this return will bring. What we will know is that we have touched the depth of our being and that our world has changed. Lama Yeshe once said, "Samsara shakes".

22

Re-emergence into Form

IN THE PSYCHOLOGICAL JOURNEY of descent, death and transformation, there naturally follows a movement of return. I have experienced this in my own path and I have seen it time and again with clients in the therapeutic context. We can see this as a psychological renewal and re-birth as we return into relationship with form, identity and the world. This psychological process is not something often spoken of within traditional Buddhist circles, therefore I feel it needs further explanation.

Psychologically, the process of re-emergence is one that needs to be undertaken carefully and at the right pace. As we return from a period of descent, death and transformation we slowly become aware of our sense of self identity again. Following the dismantling of the ego we discussed in the previous chapters, returning to a sense of our form in relationship to our life, as I found through my own experience, can be tentative and sometimes challenging. We may have let go of a lot of old patterns and ways of being and discovered aspects of ourselves that are new and significant. As a result, we may not be so sure who we are and how we respond and react to the world. This may be an uncomfortable and disorienting time. The danger will be that we push ourselves to become something too quickly. This may be because of outside demands, but it could also be because we have an impulse to find a form quickly so that we feel secure and in control again. It may be that we wish to express our new sense of self too urgently. These old habits are not helpful though. They simply re-instate another identity at a time when we have gone through a process of relinquishing one. We take shape too quickly and once again lock ourselves into a solid form rather than maintaining a degree of fluidity and openness. We cannot rush the process and we often need to take care to protect what is happening. Too sudden an emergence can be damaging or even traumatising. The time it takes to re-emerge is often greater than we think and needs to be handled carefully as a necessary aspect of the process.

When someone goes through a journey of descent and re-emergence in psychotherapy, the ordinary sense of identity has to be gradually restored. But they will not be as they were before. Often our values have changed, what is important to us may have changed, and things once meaningful may feel to have lost their meaning. We may also have discovered new aspects of ourselves, new resources, new strengths and capacities that were once buried or hidden. As we return we can bring these with us and begin to integrate them into our life.

My own emergence from years of retreat was a tough readjustment to life in a different reality. Living at first in London was extremely challenging. I had changed radically and as I returned to the West I had to gradually grow the capacity to live back in the ordinary world again. I felt supersensitive to the impact of the environment around me and needed to develop a kind of psychological skin. This, I began to realise, was not going to be a fast process and I needed to give myself time to adjust.

I am sometimes contacted by people who have also been through long retreat and had a very difficult time re-emerging following the kind of death transformation I have been describing. Many of them speak of their struggle to adjust and there is often an assumption that all should be fine and easy, but this is far from the case. Psychologically we may still be extremely vulnerable, like a dragonfly whose wings are not yet dry and so needs to wait before it can take flight. We will need to take care of ourselves and create an environment that is supportive and caring through the process. It helps to have people around that will understand this and be aware of the sensitivity and vulnerability that we may feel. It may be wise to get some more experienced support from mentors, counsellors or teachers who understand the process.

As we begin to form and move into the world again we do need to re-establish a stable sense of self. Without it we can become disoriented, feel highly vulnerable and even suffer the potential for psychosis. In Buddhism we speak of the 'emptiness of self' as the recognition that the self has no inherent, substantial and enduring nature. This does not, however, negate the necessity of a relative sense of self. As this relative self re-forms it needs to be more fluid and flexible, more permeable rather than narrow and contracted. We need a sense of cohesion and stability but not the habit of contraction, tightness and solidity that simply restores the ego-grasping that is the root of our suffering. Retaining a sense of spaciousness and fluidity as we re-emerge into the forming process means we can discover a very different sense of ourselves in the world. It can be both satisfying and empowering to see our new sense of being begin to manifest in our life in a way that is creative and truly congruent with our inner nature.

When we re-emerge, we can potentially bring something of the treasure we have found in the 'underworld' back into the upper world. This treasure may be the renewal of a quality that was long buried, or a vision of something we can bring into our life. It may bring a renewed sense of meaning that motivates us in a new creative way. It may bring a deeper wisdom that comes from the depth of our being. It can be a relationship to the source, the ground of our essential nature that we begin to express in the world through who we are. One of the ways this connection to the source is then expressed is in the form of the deity. In the depth we connect to the essential ground from which all the deities emerge and in the tantric tradition we can potentially bring this aspect of our nature up from the depths to manifest and be embodied.

In Buddhism, just as there is a path that takes us into our depths to open to the innate clear-light nature of mind, there is also the path of re-emergence. It is this re-emergence that requires us to return to relationship with the forms and interactions of the ordinary world. When Milarepa said, it is easy to meditate upon the sky, but not easy to meditate upon the clouds, he was implying that sometimes it may be tempting to be drawn to the peaceful state of emptiness where we are liberated from the complications of our relative world. The challenge he saw was to come into relationship with the dimension of forms and appearances and how we deal with them. If we see this in terms of ultimate truth or emptiness and relative truth or the world of manifest appearance, then the intention of our Buddhist practice is to recognise that they are two aspects of the same reality. A Buddha is considered to be one who brings together these two dimensions of being, unifying relative and ultimate truth.

We have seen that mother tantra is the expression of a path or process that deepens us into the experience of our ultimate nature. This journey is one that gradually unravels our relative form and identity as we descend into the 'unconscious' and eventually awaken our innate clear-light mind or mother clear-light. Following this it is important to consider the journey that returns us to the realm of form. In the tantric tradition this is associated with the path of 'father tantra', the path of re-emergence, embodiment and manifestation. It is the process whereby we begin to bring the insight of wisdom that has been awoken in the descending journey, to be actualised in our daily life. We see the gradual emergence of our form and identity, that can participate in the interdependent relationship of our ordinary world. From this emergence there is the possibility to act creatively to bring about an embodied expression of our innate wisdom nature. Emergence leads to embodiment and then to manifestation.

There is a Western psychological parallel to this process in relation to the father as the archetypal principle that enables embodiment in the world as a transition from the mother. Psychologically, the father principle is considered an important aspect of the emergence of both male and female children out into the world. When we have not had a satisfactory experience of a positive empowering father then our capacity to be in the world can often be impaired. While the father quality is usually experienced through a man, it could be embodied equally by either a man or a woman.

In the journey of re-emergence, embodiment and manifestation, our quality of intention becomes increasingly significant. At the heart of our tantric life is the quality of intention we know as bodhichitta. We can see this as the natural alignment with our desire to manifest our full potential in order to benefit others. Compassion and kindness combined with the willingness to serve the welfare of others act as a powerful motivation. When we surrender to this intention of bodhichitta we can begin to manifest our innate potential in the world.

The relationship between emptiness and the manifestation of form is dynamic. This dynamic is an aspect of our energy that moves us and has the natural propensity to manifest into form and expression when given the freedom to do so. It is unfortunate that often we block or limit that capacity out of, for example, doubt or fear. Then our creative potential becomes dammed up and is reflected in our physical and psychological health. Freeing this block is part of the process of re-emergence so that we discover our natural capacity for expression. When we align with the quality of bodhichitta we can begin to liberate the innate power and creative vitality within our energy-body. Once free, we can increasingly manifest this innate potential in the world through the quality of the deity. In kriya[35] or action tantra, the primary level of tantra, deities such as Manjushri, Chenrezig, Tara, and Vajrapani are all considered aspects of our nature that exemplify or express qualities of the Bodhisattva manifesting in the world. They are in this respect various expressions of the intention of bodhichitta to manifest in the world to bring benefit to others.

Re-emergance and the Diety

We could say that in the practice of tantra all deities are an expression of our innate clear light nature, our innate dharmakaya, emerging into form. When we make the journey of descent into clear-light we are going down to reconnect to the basic ground of our potential to emerge into form. We are returning to the source. The deities originate from this depth in our nature. When we touch this place, the gift we receive is the potential to embody certain archetypal qualities expressed through the form of the deity. It is as though we descend to release ourselves of our limiting obstacles and obscurations to reveal the jewel of our buddha-nature in the aspect of the deity. We are re-born as the deity and gradually return to the 'upper world'. All the deities, whether male or female, express this return to form. In this respect it is not the gender of the deity that is significant but rather the process we are passing through.

If the father archetype is connected to the capacity to embody our potential out in the world; in tantra it is the upward and outward movement of our energy into an embodied manifestation of activity for the welfare of others. This is where we learn to embody the potential of the energy-body and express its quality in the world. We could see this as the essential, creative nature that is at the heart of tantric practice.

It may be helpful to consider how we might experience the inner process of the expression of our energy coming into form. From a deep and subtle stirring of an inner spark of intention our energy begins to move and awaken. As we feel this movement it may bring with it a growing sense of something emerging. This may arise in the form of an image, an idea of some creative expression or a strong impulse in the body to perform certain activities. If we respond to these inner impulses a process begins to be initiated whereby it can come into expression though the body.

To give a simple example, I recently decided to lay underfloor heating in our meditation room, a job I had never done before although I am familiar with plumbing. I had a clear sense of how my quality of intention focused my energy as I prepared to do the job. I needed to spend some time visualising the entire process that I was going to go through before I started so that I would get the layout of the pipes and other parts correct. This visualisation gave my energy a kind of template I could then work to. As I began to bring this into the practical process I found my energy become strongly focused through my body to give me the capacity to engage in the work. I found it both invigorating and enjoyable to feel that vitality. There were challenges and difficulties in the process but these became part of the creative weave of my body and its energy as I came to manifest what I had envisaged. At the end of three days I was tired but I enjoyed seeing what I had completed and felt a deep sense of satisfaction. I could feel the transformation that had taken place internally and see its effect outside.

This example could be seen as analogous to what happens as we begin to embody the process of a deity practice as I have described in Chapter 16. The deity, as a manifestation of our buddha-nature, focuses and refines the energy-body enabling us to gradually cultivate its natural potential. This energetic quality comes into form as it is expressed through our physical body in the activities we manifest in the world. As this happens, our ordinary physical body becomes the vehicle for our sambhogakaya nature to manifest. It becomes our nirmanakaya or emanation body, that, like a lightening conductor brings our innate energy to earth.

The practices where we arise or emerge as a deity are not necessarily an aspect of father tantra as it would be traditionally understood. What I am describing, however, is the symbolic and psychological significance of emergence associated with the principle of the father, the masculine and form. What feels important is how this symbolic process can be understood from a Western psychological perspective that is echoed within the tantric tradition.

Recently I was teaching a group the practice of Manjushri, the deity considered to be the embodiment of wisdom, sometimes considered the Bodhisattva of wisdom. While in the tantric world most often the deities that embody wisdom are female dakinis, Manjushri holds a special place in how he embodies the manifestation wisdom in the world. He is what we might call the active expression of wisdom. He is an embodiment of, or creative expression of the wisdom that lies in the depth of our nature, particularly through the process of communication and creativity. His 'dragon-like proclamation of the dharma' is one way in which wisdom is translated into form through language and communication. But by language we should not limit this to speech alone as his name Manjugosha, literally smooth or gentle speech, might imply. Manjushri is also considered the deity associated with culture and the arts, where again he is an embodiment of the creative process that manifests emptiness into form. I have always found the relationship to his 'red-yellow' appearance interesting as it expresses the union of the elements of fire and earth, perhaps the two key elements within our nature in the process of creative expression. Fire brings with it the vision, inspiration and vitality of the creative process and earth its crystallisation into form.

For me, Manjushri has been a significant deity associated with the inspiration and expression of our innate clear-light wisdom manifesting into form. In embodying wisdom in form, we see the potential for all of our creative life to be rooted in our true nature, our buddha-nature rather than a relatively superficial reflection of the ego. This echoes Jung's view of how the archetypal nature of the collective unconscious, when expressed through our symbolic creative life brings deeper wisdom into form.

We could equally see this manifestation of wisdom-energy coming into form with the female deity Tara. She embodies our capacity to bring a particular quality of *all accomplishing wisdom*, unified with compassion into expression in the world. Her entire dynamic is to manifest whatever is beneficial for the welfare of others, symbolised in her stepping down onto a secondary lotus. As such we see again an expression of the upward, outward movement into form. Whatever deity we practice, it brings into manifestation and embodiment gifts from the depth of our nature. Each deity becomes a creative expression of our deeper nature and we become the vehicle for it to manifest into our life

If archetypally the path of the mother leads us into the unconscious and the innate nature of our being, then the path of the father brings this wisdom into form as a creative process. This dynamic also echoes a further consideration present within the tantric tradition expressed in principles of the masculine and feminine more generally. In the West we can become embroiled in all manner of definitions and interpretations of these two aspects of our nature, but in tantra there is a very clear way they can be understood. The feminine principle can be seen as the aspect of our nature that moves us towards the experience of emptiness, non-duality and space. The masculine principle moves us towards the experience of form and appearances. When we reflect upon this in our life we can see many ways in which this applies. The feminine moves us towards greater sense of space, openness, fluidity and flexibility. We are letting go of our form to become more in relationship to space and emptiness. With the masculine there is a natural movement towards the emergence of form, direction and intention as we shape and define our edges. This is the process of manifestation and expression.

This relationship between form and emptiness is reflected in these two paths where the journey of descent strips us of our clinging to form and the obscurations that veil the experience of our true nature. Once we have immersed ourselves in this state of non-duality, free of obscuring veils, we can return to the realm of form and appearances. As we re-emerge, we master the art of manifestation, refining and freeing the energy-body to its dynamic creative potential. On one level, this is the emergence of our capacity to manifest in the aspect of the tantric deities and their archetypal agency for activity in the world. On another level, this is the capacity to create and re-create whatever will serve the welfare of others as we engage with the world.

This process of emersion and re-emergence is practiced again and again as our innate nature is freed from the veils of obscuration to reveal its pristine quality. The journey of descent into the clear-light nature of our mind also purifies the energy-body which then emerges as what is called the *illusory body*. At first the impure aspect of this energy-body is subject to all the instability and unpredictability of our emotional and psychological life. As it begins to be purified it is the basis of an extraordinary capacity to manifest naturally and spontaneously in the qualities of the deities. In tantric practice we repeat this dissolving into clear-light and then the re-emergence of the illusory-body as the deity time and time again until all dualistic defilements are purified. Finally, our energy-body becomes the *pure illusory body*, the *complete enjoyment body* or sambhogakaya.

~~~~

In these chapters I have described a journey in which we encounter the depth of our nature with all of its pain and affliction as well as its extraordinary potential. This journey is one that we can begin to understand psychologically, and I feel, is important to recognise alongside or within our experience of tantric practice. When we do so it connects us to our own personal process and our own psychological reality. This is not always comfortable but is often a part of our experience within Buddhist practice whether we understand it or not. From my own experience, this was something I have gone through in a powerful often disturbing way within my practice even though it was not an aspect of traditional teachings. It was my psychological study and work that began to give me the insights that helped me see and understand the process I had been through. For this reason, it has felt important and necessary to include this exploration. If in doing so it gives the reader an insight into their experiences, thereby making it more possible to 'trust in the process', then I think this is worthwhile. It has been clear in my mentoring work with Western Buddhist practitioners that these kinds of problems and challenges arise. When addressed with psychological understanding they become a manageable aspect of the path. Without it there can be a huge potential for pain, confusion and disillusionment at times of what we might call spiritual crisis. For this reason, I feel it is crucial that we are also able to find the kind of mentoring support that can help us understand the journey we are on as we descend into the depths. This I would like to begin to explore in the next section.

Part Three

Guidance

Introduction

IN PART THREE I wish to look at an issue that is sometimes challenging for us in the West when we are seeking guidance in our practice. In the Tibetan tradition there is a strong emphasis on the relationship to a guru, or spiritual guide. He or she is seen as the root of the path and said to be of critical importance in the practice of tantra. This can present many of us with complications partly because it is not always clear how we find or make a relationship to a guru, lama or teacher. There can also be confusion between who is a guru and who is a lama. The Tibetan word lama is not synonymous with the Sanskrit word guru. Lama is an honorific term that is applied to those who are venerated as highly experienced practitioners and teachers, either Tibetan or Western, but this does not necessarily make them our guru. Within the Tibetan tradition, the term guru usually refers to someone who inspires great devotion and a sense of surrender to their guiding presence. A lama may become our guru if or when we enter into this specific kind of relationship. Often our meeting with lamas is in the context of many, sometimes hundreds of other students, monks and lay people. At these times we may make some kind of connection, but these lamas are often around only briefly and then fly away to some far-off land where they live. If we have the chance to meet them personally it may be brief, very formal, and can also be complicated by the fact that they may only speak Tibetan and we probably do not. This may not necessarily provide us with the guru relationship we are looking for.

As a consequence, when we are given the message that we need a guru to practice tantra this is not always straightforward. It is true we need an introduction to tantric practice which usually takes the form of an empowerment. We may be very inspired by this experience on one level, but does this automatically mean we have a connection to the lama that makes them our guru? There is often a kind of devotional wave that is present when large assemblies of students gather to meet a high lama. This can have a powerful impact upon us, but we may still be left with the question is this person my teacher, or my guru?

I have spoken with many people who find themselves feeling unsure about their relationship to a teacher, or do not feel they have found one. Some have described how without this relationship they are left feeling uncertain about the value of their tantric practice. They have wondered if there can be a way of practising if they do not find a guru in physical form. Some have also felt they needed more support to integrate the teachings or initiations that they have received from high lamas when they are seldom accessible.

It was this dilemma that initially motivated me to offer mentoring support to my students. A mentor does not replace the role of a lama and is not like the relationship to a guru. What a mentor can do through an ongoing personal connection is to provide crucial support for someone dedicated to the path but without a close connection to the lama from whom they have received teachings.

For this reason, in this section I will to look at the relationship to gurus, lamas, teachers, mentors and fellow practitioners, recognising where we need to have support for our practice. I will also look at the implications of the guru-disciple relationship in a Western context. First, however, I want to make a distinction between practice that is entirely guided by the authority of a teacher or lama, and that which might be seen as more *person-centred*, where there is a considered response to the dispositions and psychological needs of the student practitioner.

23

Personal Practice

IN THE WEST TODAY we have the extraordinary good fortune to be able to meet the transmission of a tradition that has been held intact over hundreds of years. While it originated in India, it is the Tibetans who have masterfully developed a system of practices and methods to accomplish realisations within tantra practice that are probably unique. Some of the greatest lamas have composed deity practices and written extensive commentaries creating a 'graduated path' to awakening that is thorough and systematic as well as highly elaborate and sometimes extremely complex. In order to enter into this path there has been a huge emphasis on the relationship between the teacher or guru and disciple. As Tibetan Buddhism has grown in the West there is still considerable emphasis on this relationship which has sometimes led to confusion and difficulty, in part because it is not the kind of relationship we have historically much experience of in the West. As new practitioners, most of us need guidance from those who have more experience than us. The Tibetan tradition and tantra in particular is complex, often obscure and opaque, so that understanding is mostly gained through oral instruction. A teacher or guide is vital in this as they carry the authority of the traditional teachings as well as being a holder of a lineage of transmission.

When I first became involved in this tradition it was to my amazement that I saw a way of practice that gave me a real sense that awakening was possible if I followed this graduated path. I could see there were clearly defined stages on that path and it seemed possible to gage where I was and where I needed to step next. It is a path that is often defined in terms of realisations that could be attained through specific practices if we apply ourselves diligently and with dedication. Many of the teachers I studied with emphasised that this step by step approach was quite linear and that until one attained a certain stage one could not move forward to the next. Others, including my own teachers Lama Yeshe and H.H.Dalai Lama in this, saw the path in a more circulating fashion where more advanced stages would support earlier ones and *vice versa*. I recall the Dalai Lama once saying to a group of Westerners he was teaching, that he wanted us to know the entire path, even the more complex advanced stages, because that understanding would give us confidence from the beginning.

This system of practice, cultivated and refined within the confines of Tibet clearly suits the way Tibetans practice, particularly in the monasteries. As Tibetan Buddhism has emerged in the West it is a rich resource for us to tap into under the guidance of teachers trained to hold faithfully to the tradition. Having spent many years studying tantra with highly revered teachers from various Tibetan schools, I feel huge gratitude for what I have been able to receive. As a Westerner receiving this transmission, however, I began to feel there were certain complications. While the Tibetan tantric tradition offers a well-defined path to awakening it did not clarify what might be seen as the underlying personal process that I would go through on that path. It offers us a very clear evolution of practices that lead to certain realisations. What can be problematic, however, is that the individual with his or her own psychological makeup and life process does not always fit into this path so neatly. Westerners, and I include myself, may try to fit into the traditional way of tantric practice, but find after some years that something is not working. We could, of course, conclude that we are doing it wrong, not understanding something, or perhaps not working hard enough. We may equally say that we do not have enough merit or that we need to purify more. However, what I began to see is that for this path to genuinely become a reality, it needs to address more specifically our Western psychological needs and differences. Our spiritual practice needs to relate to our individual psychological background if genuine transformation is going to happen. Without this relationship we may do a lot of tantric practice and yet be in danger of 'spiritual by-passing', and therefore not addressing our actual psychological problems.

I am aware that many of the key elements of the Buddha's teachings are appropriate for everyone across the generations and within all cultures. The understanding of impermanence, emptiness or bodhicitta are good examples. Even so the methods of practice and teachings that we meet today have been shaped and coloured by the Tibetans and therefore have a particular flavour that suits their psychological makeup. As this tradition comes to the West it meets a very different psychological disposition. From my own experience this has led me to ask the question, how do we make this complex system of teachings and methods of practice accessible to our Western psychological nature?

A further complication in the process of integration can be that the teachers we receive guidance from, especially Tibetans, may not be familiar with our psychological makeup. Why should they be if they have not grown up in the West? They have not been trained to understand of the kind of psychological or emotional wounding and trauma some of us may have experienced growing up in the West. Fortunately, increasingly there are both Tibetan and Western teachers who can begin to bridge these worlds and enable the tradition to become authentically integrated. This requires a capacity to bring together the traditional knowledge of practice with Western psychological understanding. As this happens we begin to see a blend of new ways of approaching tantric practice that are more specifically directed towards addressing and transforming our emotional process.

Having worked as both teacher and mentor over the past years, I have found that for the genuine integration of the traditional teachings into our life, they must be applied in a 'person-centred' way. To make different teachings and practices touch our psychological process they must be shaped in a much more personal way to respond to our individual differences. While there is a well-defined gradual path of methods for accomplishing certain realisations, how that is applied must be tailored to suit the individual.

While I was in India I received many commentaries on the primary tantric deity practices I was practicing in retreat. These teachings gave an extraordinary insight into the details of visualisations, the technicalities of the sadhana practice and their deeper meaning. What I needed, however, was guidance as to how to begin to shape my practice to suit my own personal disposition and capacity. I also began to have many questions about what to do when certain things began to happen in my meditation. This guidance only became possible when I was able to meet privately with Lama Yeshe or my retreat guide, Gen Jhampa Wangdu. Lama Yeshe in particular had the flexibility and openness in how he viewed practice to help me find ways to shape what I was doing to suit me personally.

When I eventually returned to the West and began to teach and mentor others I could see that this personal guidance had been crucial to the development of my practice. The dialogues I had the good fortune to have with both Lama Yeshe and Gen Jhampa Wangdu were a great help in that process. The difficulties and problems people brought to me I found reflected three things. One was that the way they were practicing, in its traditional form, did not always touch them. This particularly related to the complexity of tantric practice and is something I have addressed at length in this book in relation to the sadhanas of different deities. The second aspect was that they wanted to find a way of practice that directly helped in the resolution of psychological difficulties. The third was that the traditional view of the path did not always fit where someone was in their own life journey. These difficulties would often lead to grave doubts about whether they should be doing tantric practice and whether they were ready for it. Some I have spoken with came to a very disappointed or disheartened place that led them to give up their practices altogether. I could see that this response did not have to happen if it was possible to shape the way they approached practice to suit their personal capacities and needs.

Something that seems problematic is that many people I speak with believe there is a 'correct' way to practice and fear that if they not getting it right they will suffer some terrible karmic consequence. When we become involved in the tantric tradition, we inevitably have a sense that there are set ways to practice that have been handed down from teacher to disciple over hundreds of years and that this system has a great weight of authority. This authority is carried by teachers who, because of their position and experience, will often hold to a way of practice which is how things *should* be done if they are to bring the results that are sought. This can make us inflexible and rigid in how we approach our relationship to practice because we feel we have to get it right. It can lead us to fear the authority of the tradition in a way that can easily negate the reality of our individual experience, which I think is very unhelpful. When this happens, the process has become more authority-centred than person-centred and it doesn't recognise that we are all different with different capacities and difficulties. We are also very different to the Tibetans and will sometimes need other approaches to practice.

Within the tantric tradition there are many aspects of practice that need to be learned, especially within the deity sadhana. Many of the visualisation processes and rituals are very significant and need to be carefully studied so that we know what we're doing. These will often follow a certain formula that has been handed down for generations. Even within these practices, however, there are variations in how they can be approached, as was evident in Lama Yeshe's teaching as I have described earlier in this book. They are not absolutely rigid. In the process of mentoring I have found that I often need to be open and flexible, just as Lama Yeshe was, and begin to listen to what people individually respond to in their practice.

By practice I do not mean simply meditation alone, but how we are bringing the dharma into our life in general. Addressing the relationship between an individual's knowledge of dharma and its practical application is not always easy. Just because we have extensively studied traditional teachings it does not mean we are able to apply them skilfully in the immediate circumstances of our life. As a mentor I feel it requires considerably more than just knowledge of the dharma to support another in their path. To be more person-centred we need to be flexible in how we think about practice. I have found that when supporting others, I need to be responsive to where someone is and what they need. The traditional teachings are an invaluable resource of dharma understanding but this needs to be held skilfully and openly.

In my work, when I hear someone talking about their experience of practice, a question I find myself often asking is: "how is that for you?" This is an important enquiry into what effect any aspect of dharma practice is having on the individual. Are they finding it helpful? Are they connecting to the feeling of the practice? Is their practice having an effect upon what needs to change or heal psychologically and emotionally? These questions give space for an individual to have a sense of their own understanding and insight. It also validates that whatever a person's experience is, must be taken seriously. In response to this kind of question we may then consider whether the way we are practising, is actually beneficial or appropriate. It may also give a sense of what may need to be re-shaped to make it more effective in addressing particular aims or needs.

When I lead meditation retreats I find it extremely useful to ask the same question. Everyone experiences meditations in different ways. When I ask the question "how was that for you?" I can discover the way in which their inner experience is touched, what works for them and what does not. In a group setting it means we can learn from the experiences of others, opening new insights into our own meditation practice and new ways of approaching what we are doing.

There are also ways in which our relationship to the traditional view of the path can appear to come into conflict with where we are in our life journey. This can sometimes be confusing and give rise to some challenging re-assessments of how to integrate the path. A common example of this related to a mother with two children who was finding it frustrating and distressing that her dharma peers were all able to do long retreats when she clearly had no such freedom. It was some time before she began to accept that being a mother was also her practice.

Another example related to a young man who was struggling to engage with his life in a way that enabled him to find a livelihood to support himself. His understanding of the dharma gave him the feeling that this was wrong and that he should be renouncing this kind of worldly life. He was also worried that his attention to getting his life on track was about his ego and this should be abandoned. In our work together, I needed to reassure him that as a man in his early twenties this was the natural developmental process he needed to go through and that his desire to engage with the world was healthy. Psychologically I could see that at this stage of his life he needed to establish a stable sense of self in the world.

I occasionally speak with men in their early thirties who are in relationships where they have children or are about to have a child. A question that often arises is whether it is possible to practice as a parent or have they ruined their potential to awaken. There is frequently an underlying belief that the best path is that of the monastic and the lay path of the householder is inferior. This is a view that I recall hearing in my early years as a Tibetan Buddhist and it also created some conflict in my own life journey. I find myself responding to their dilemma from my own sense that the path of a parent is challenging but also very transformational. It can be a powerful way to open the heart and develop the qualities of love and compassion, because there is no choice but to let go of self-preoccupation and respond to the needs of others. There may be less opportunity to do a lot of meditation but there are many other aspects of the path that can develop profoundly as a parent. If we consider the six perfections of the Bodhisattva, certainly the first four: generosity, morality, patience and perseverance, are ideally practiced within lay family life.

There are also many people who have come to the Buddhist path later in life. I have had many students over the years who are in their late 60's and 70's. It has been very clear with most of them that while they may have a very natural capacity and dedication to enter into the tantric path, they cannot necessarily follow a way of practice that would be appropriate for someone in their 30's or 40's. Again, the need for practice to be tailored to the individual means that one cannot stick rigidly to the letter of the tradition.

We are all very different in how our spiritual journey unfolds and there are no rigid prescriptions in how this can be followed. In the Tibetan tradition there is a clearly defined path with stages and methods of accomplishment, which can sometimes appear complex and challenging for us in the West. For this path to touch us individually we need to be flexible and careful in how we approach it. For this we need guidance that is more person-centred and not just fixed in the authority of the system. Increasingly there are Westerners who have been on this path for a while and have grappled with its challenges. This is gradually leading to an understanding of what support and guidance we need to be able to integrate a more personal approach to practice. When teachers and lamas have thousands of students and are not easily able to engage in this more personal guidance, it will be the presence of mentors experienced in both practice and, when possible, Western psychological understanding that will be an invaluable resource.

24

The Role of Mentors

IN THE WESTERN BUDDHIST WORLD there is, I believe, an increasing need for those who are able to support us in our practice in a much more immediate, consistent and personal way. We need gurus and teachers to inspire us, but often the support many of us seek is some kind of regular mentoring. The role of mentor is one that has had a place historically within the Buddhist tradition as the *Kalyanamitta* or virtuous spiritual friend. This was a companion and guide that held a supportive role for those less experienced in their practice. Today this role feels increasingly important to support those that lack the presence of a guru and who may have become involved in often complex and challenging practices. The mentor may draw together elements of teacher and counsellor but also has its own qualities and characteristics. If we considered a spectrum with guru/lama (here I am implying that the words guru and lama are virtually synonymous) at one end and counsellor/psychotherapist at the other it, would be possible to place the mentor somewhere towards the centre. These roles and the relationships they offer are very different and it may be useful to define them more specifically to see where mentoring is significant. This may also begin to clarify what we personally need in our spiritual journey.

Let us consider a spectrum:
Guru/lama..............teacher..............mentor...........counsellor

We could look at each of these as roles that have a specific defining quality or characteristic. We could also consider them in terms of the kind of relationship they will tend to create in certain circumstances. This can be complicated by the way in which within each of these relationships there can be a considerable amount of projection. The nature of this projection may vary from one role to another but the fact of its presence makes these relationships psychologically more complex. It is often the reality of projection, be it unconscious or conscious, that can lead to both very beneficial as well as detrimental consequences. There may, for example, be considerable idealisation. There can be an unconscious tendency to project parental needs. There can also be the tendency to give away power and authority. There may equally be what in the psychotherapy world is called 'erotic transference', where we project sexual fantasies. When we take this into consideration it is clear we need, as much as possible, to become conscious of what the potential underlying psychological 'agendas' might be. When we don't the unconscious presence of these projections can be very problematic. Something that we could see as a common in any of these relationships, is the desire for a sense of trust, compassion and integrity.

If we start at the guru/lama end of this spectrum, it is useful to make a distinction between guru and teacher, although the line can of course become blurred. There is almost always a considerable idealised projection onto a guru that places them in a very important and powerful position in relation to our spiritual life. The guru carries the presence of the divine, they are avatars of higher truth. They are seen as the source of teachings, wisdom and of spiritual transmission that is only possible because of their depth of insight, beyond the scope of our ordinary experience. There is often a strong devotional element that invests a great deal in the guru. Traditionally in Tibetan Buddhism the guru is considered to be a Buddha and should be seen as perfect. This is a perspective that has increasingly become problematic in the West and even H.H.Dalai Lama questions its usefulness.

As I have said before, often the guru is somewhat inaccessible and may only be seen within the context of collective teaching. Seldom does one make a personal relationship to a Tibetan lama, and most personal or private meetings tend to be relatively formal and very brief, where disciples may ask for specific guidance around practice. In the practice of tantra the guru or lama maintains a relationship that is principally authority-centred, bestowing initiations and giving instruction on practice. Seldom do disciples question their gurus and challenge their authority.

At the other end of the spectrum a counsellor or therapist offers an entirely different kind of relationship. Possibly the most important aspect of the counsellor's role, as the Humanistic psychologist Carl Rogers suggested, is that it is person-centred. This means that a counsellor's relationship focuses on the person they counsel. Attention is given to the needs and psychological process of the client and in principle the counsellor tries to be an unconditional compassionate presence. The counsellor provides a holding space in which the client can express themselves, in a safe and non-judgemental environment. The counsellor may respond to this by asking questions or giving reflections that allow the client to discover a sense of resolution to issues that emerge through the interaction. One could see this as a considerably more passive role than the guru or teacher. The counsellor holds back his or her own personal material to create and maintain a relatively safe and contained, confidential space for the counselee to go through a process. Again, the term *process* is significant in that there is a natural psychological unfolding that occurs in our inner experience which needs to be respected in its own right. Often this process goes on beneath what we might consider as the spiritual path and is our own individual experience of that path. In this we are all different, it is our personal journey. The counsellor's role could be said to be to hold a compassionate supportive presence alongside that personal process.

As the opposite end of the spectrum to the guru, the counsellor is essentially person-centred, while the position the guru holds is mostly authority-centred. The guru may focus on the disciple and give direction based on wisdom and insights that are, in part, held within a doctrine, a system. A counsellor will focus upon the process of the counsellee as the central point of reference. There can be times when, as we get closer to a lama, they may respond more to our individual needs as a counsellor would. There will, however, always be a power imbalance in the relationship and authority will ultimately be with the guru.

The role of a teacher is also distinct from a guru. A teacher does not have to carry the same degree of idealised projection as the guru. We may revere and value highly our teachers as we learn from them and recognise their qualities. We may attribute a level of authority to them and allow them to guide us, but this is not in the same degree as the guru. In my own sense of the difference between these two, I have found I may have many teachers from whom I can learn a great deal, but the guru projection has only been carried by a few. Sometimes of course our teacher may become our guru, in which case there is greater charge to the relationship.

A relationship to a teacher may be one that is entered into and then parted from with relative ease. We may be with a teacher for a while and then find we need to move on and explore another place of learning. In the relationship to a guru one traditionally would not leave unless something disruptive occurred. If it comes to an end, the ending of the relationship to a teacher does not carry the same potential charge as with a guru. Those people I have known who have experienced a separation from a guru through some problem that has arisen, usually find the separation extremely painful. It goes to the very core of their spiritual life and their sense of trust and confidence in everything the guru represented. This does not happen in the same way with a teacher.

Teachers can potentially shift their relationship towards mentoring or even counselling more readily than the traditional guru. This is partly because it may be easier to make the shift in the focus of power and authority. Traditionally gurus do not readily step 'down' into the mentor or counsellor position as it is too great a leap. Teachers on the other hand, if they are not placed into too grand an idealised projection by a student, or if they do not hold themselves in too aloof or distant a place, may more readily make that shift of authority towards the counsellor or mentor.

Within this spectrum a mentor may be able to sit more readily in the centre where the role can be one of counsellor and teacher together. There may also be some middle ground where authority is held but not in a way that blocks more personal contact. Inevitably, if we enter into a relationship with a mentor we wish them to have a sense of authority based on their experience and understanding. What we do not need is for this to be the primary basis of the relationship. That authority needs to be held gently and skilfully unless it is required to be more strongly present. A mentor may, in this respect, be able to give over a sense of authority to the mentee so as to empower them in their path. It is a negotiated position that grows with mutual trust and respect.

Eastern lamas or gurus do not easily move out of the position of authority into a role more akin to counselling when in a one to one setting. This is very unfamiliar to them. There are some that begin to change as they spend more time in the West but meetings can still tend to remain relatively formal. I appreciated my own teacher/guru Lama Yeshe, who on occasions did something that seemed out of keeping with his usual role. When I asked his advice he would say, "What do you think?" or even, "What do you feel?". I found this surprisingly refreshing and very empowering to be given the space to say what I felt and have that supported. He would often say, "You trust your inner knowledge wisdom, dear!"

When a teacher can enter a middle ground as a mentor it can create a one-to-one relationship that is both valuable to the student and also enables the teacher to get to know more deeply the needs of the individual. This, I think is something that Western teachers may do more naturally. In my own work as a mentor, I have found that as I get to know the particular psychological dispositions of those I mentor I can help shape the kind of practice that will particularly benefit that person. It also gives the mentee a much safer ground to question and discuss what I teach when necessary. Guidance becomes a negotiated process. This experience then translates into the teaching situation where having greater knowledge of people's experience and background offers the potential to make teachings more psychologically relevant.

For a mentor to be in part counsellor is to become 'person-centred' so as to respond to the needs of the mentee, rather than 'authority-centred'. For a mentor to be in part teacher is to be able to then shape the process of guidance in the mentoring setting to suit the individual. This middle ground between teacher and counsellor can provide an invaluable space that is both creative and supportive, where there is a dialogue. It can be a place where mentor and mentee together enable a spiritual journey to be creative and grounded, relevant to the needs of the individual. This may bring a practitioner to a place where the dharma becomes genuinely integrated, relating to personal life issues in a way that has perhaps not been previously possible.

The reason I emphasise the role of mentor is that while it has been present in the Tibetan tradition it does not seem to have been given the emphasis I feel it needs particularly in the West. Within some of the Tibetan schools there has been a relationship more in the style of mentor, between meditators and their teachers where a dialogue would happen around how practice was evolving. This was something I began to feel with my own retreat guide, Gen Jhampa Wangdu, just before he died. Sadly, his death and that of my primary teacher Lama Yeshe was a huge loss for me in terms of that personal guidance. When we come to the practice of tantra I feel the need for mentors is really important. Tantra is a complex alchemical process that requires the presence of relatively experienced guides to hold that process. We do not always need very high lamas to do this and it is unrealistic to expect it when they may have many students and are continually traveling to teach. We need the more immediate and regular presence of people with experience and psychological understanding that can hold other practitioners.

It is for this reason the presence of mentors becomes an important intermediary on the path. We could say this has always been the role of the monk or nun and that the idea of *sangha* is exactly for this purpose. I personally don't think it is as simple as this and while we may get some support from our sangha, there needs to be a much clearer sense of what skill is needed to be a mentor. In my own work as a mentor, I have felt my psychotherapeutic background has been of huge value. I have also felt that it was not so much the amount of dharma knowledge I may have, as the actual years of experience that have made it clear where I have learned from my own struggles and challenges. Perhaps this suggests that there is a need to actually train mentors to be able to fulfil this role, something that may need to be a part of the future of dharma in the West.

It is my hope that as we move towards greater self-reliance as a Western Buddhist community, the place of the mentor will take an increasingly significant role. I feel it is important to stress in this process that simply having studied a lot of dharma in a relatively intellectual way does not make us good mentors. Dharma knowledge alone is not enough. Mentors need to have some kind of counselling or even psychotherapeutic training to be able to take on the role skilfully.

25

Devotion with Discernment

(Originally published as an article entitled "Our Teachers are not Gods.")

IN 1973 I FOUND MYSELF SEATED before a colourful brocaded throne in a meditation hall in a small Tibetan Buddhist Monastery near Kathmandu, Nepal. I was amongst a group of young Westerners waiting with some excitement for a Tibetan lama to enter. The atmosphere was electric with anticipation. After a few minutes there was a whisper, 'lama's here', we all stood up and most people bowed respectfully as a relatively young man entered the room, made prostrations and rose to the throne. What I suddenly realized was that I had had a dream of exactly this moment several months before when I was traveling in Canada. When he began to speak, I found myself immediately enthralled by his presence and playful humour. This man was to become an essential focus of my spiritual life from that point onwards. He became my 'guru'.

Like many Westerners at the time I was somewhat lost spiritually and very wounded emotionally. I would have given almost anything to find someone to guide me and give me a sense of meaning and direction that would make my life feel worthwhile. I believed and trusted that this Tibetan would do so. I also really wanted to be seen, so that I might have a sense of affirmation of my value and my nature. Part of this relationship to my guru was therefore a huge emotional investment. I became devoted in a way that was akin to falling in love and had a very idealistic view of how special he was. I recall sitting with other students, talking in a kind of romantic haze about all the qualities we felt he embodied.

Wearing my Jungian psychological hat, I can see that at the heart of this relationship was a massive projection. That isn't to say the lama was not extraordinary, but that extraordinariness was the hook for my projection. Jung saw that what we are unconscious of in ourselves we tend to project onto someone else. In the case of someone who becomes our guru we project an image of our 'higher Self' onto a person who can act as a carrier of that unconscious quality. When this begins to happen it is as though we become enthralled or beguiled by this projection. In the case of the projection of the Self onto a teacher we give away something very powerful in our nature and will then often surrender our own volition to be guided.

Something that was more problematic in this experience was that, like many of my peers, what I had projected was not just the inner guru, I had also imbued him with a quality of the ideal parent I dearly needed. In doing so I was giving away other significant aspects of my power, my own volition and my own authority and discerning wisdom.

Looking back, I can see that I had a lot of growing up to do. My desire to idealise the external teacher was actually supported by teachings I received on 'guru devotion' which said explicitly that we should try to see the guru as the Buddha and that he (or occasionally she) was effectively perfect. My idealism was blinding me to my teacher's human fallibility and was being reinforced by the teachings. I was even given the message that to see flaws in the guru would lead to dreadful suffering.

The danger with undiscerning idealised devotion to a guru is that we are trusting that this person will really hold a place of complete integrity and that he will have no personal agenda. I feel fortunate that with most of my own teachers this has been the case. What happens, however, when we start to discover that the guru is actually very human and has his own issues, his own flaws and his own needs?

Do we just dismiss this as our delusion or his crazy wisdom because he is, after all, Buddha?

In the 45 years that I have been involved in the Tibetan tradition it has become very clear that while there are some extraordinary Tibetan lamas with great integrity, they are not flawless. They may have profound insight but they also make mistakes, can have their own needs, and sometimes behave badly. As a psychotherapist I would go further and even suggest that a few of them actually have significant psychological problems. It is possible to have deep insights but struggle with the stability of their personal identity in the world. The exalted, almost divine, status of how certain *tulkus* or incarnate lamas are brought up, can cause them to become narcissistic and surprisingly self-centred. Occasionally this can lead to bullying and even cruel and abusive behaviour with students. It does not then serve any of us to simply ignore this behaviour of or go into a kind of naive denial that says 'it is my obscuration, the guru is perfect'.

H.H, Dalai Lama himself recently wrote in his book *The Path to Enlightenment*:
"The problem with the practice of seeing everything the guru does as perfect is that it very easily turns to poison for both the guru and the disciple. Therefore, whenever I teach this practice, I always advocate that the tradition of "every action seen as perfect" not be stressed. Should the guru manifest un-Dharmic qualities or give teachings contradicting Dharma, the instruction on seeing the spiritual master as perfect must give way to reason and Dharma wisdom. I could think to myself, 'They all see me as a Buddha, and therefore will accept anything I tell them.' Too much faith and imputed purity of perception can quite easily turn things rotten."[36]

Sadly, the unquestioning devotion some of us hold towards gurus has indeed occasionally turned things rotten. While the majority of Tibetan lamas and Western teachers are genuine in their integrity, there are a few that do not behave skilfully, and their students are extremely vulnerable to being abused and taken advantage of. It is in this respect necessary for us to wake up and not be beguiled by charismatic teachers and our own need to idealise. In our devotion to a teacher we can have a strong sense of respect, appreciation and indeed love, but not in a way that blinds us to their human fallibility. We need to retain our sense of discernment that recognises and faces when things are not acceptable or not beneficial. If this means a level of disillusionment, then so be it. At least we will end up with a more realistic and real relationship. Again, as H.H. Dalai lama once said, "Too much deference actually spoils the guru."

Recognising Boundaries

Possibly the most critical issue that arises in relationship to the teacher is the potential for a loss of appropriate boundaries. As a psychotherapist, there is consistent emphasis on the understanding of how teachers and therapists need to be clear around their ethical boundaries, especially because of the power imbalance in the relationship. When we consider the power we often give away to our gurus the assumption we make is that they will be skilful with us and not be abusive or exploitative. Unfortunately, this is often misunderstood by both teachers and students. Boundaries imply a teacher or guru will respect the needs and vulnerabilities of a student and not take advantage of them for his own needs. This can be materially, economically, emotionally or sexually. Materially it is very easy for teachers to exploit the devoted student who wishes to practise generosity towards them and so provide money, material goods, a home, work and so on out of devotion. Teachers can get very rich on the offerings of their disciples and in Tibet the estates of the highly revered tulkus were often extremely wealthy and powerful.

Emotionally, there can be a tendency for some teachers to actually feed on the devotion of their students. It can nourish a narcissistic need for love and to be seen as special that has been there since childhood. Possibly the worst form of exploitation is the sexual abuse of female students to satisfy a need of the teacher. It is this which is the most blatant form of abuse of boundary and power and can often be dismissed or denied within the context of a dysfunctional community of disciples.

For a relationship between a teacher or guru and student to be healthy psychologically and emotionally, ethical boundaries must be clear. I have seen in my work as a therapist and mentor that students who have experienced a teacher's confused or loose boundaries suffer greatly. Students may then find they have no one within their community to speak to about it because there is a taboo against 'criticizing the guru'. They may find that their community does not really want to know. The result is that the very heart of their spirituality has been betrayed.

Our teachers need to hold clear boundaries around their emotional and physical behaviour so that it does not become harmful to students. What can be problematic for us as Western Tibetan Buddhists is that some teachers, both Tibetan and Western, may not fully understand what this means. Within Tibetan monasteries boundaries were often implicit in the world in which they lived. Once Tibetan lamas move to the West they are not always held within their own culture and so it is totally dependent upon their own integrity to have clear boundaries. Sadly, this integrity is sometimes lacking, and lamas can become a kind of law unto themselves creating their own culture with boundaries that are arbitrary or absent. With both Western and Eastern teachers, the culture that grows around them can become like a dysfunctional family where a teacher becomes an all-powerful parent whose needs and wishes are paramount. Who then is going to provide the safe and trusting environment within which we can practice and grow?

Taking Responsibility

This brings me to a final thought which is about accountability and responsibility. Over the past 45 years it has been a privilege to be taught by some extraordinary lamas and to practise what they have given me. They have been the holders of possibly the most profound path to wisdom that has ever existed. They have brought this to the West in the hope that we may benefit from their knowledge and find our own experience. As a Westerner attempting to integrate the Tibetan tradition into Western life and Western psyche, one thing that I have begun to realise is that I cannot expect my Tibetan teachers to have all the answers. In the West we have a very different psychological upbringing and our emotional and psychological wounding is particular to our culture.

This has led me to recognise that there has to be a time when *we* begin to grow up and take more responsibility for our role in the integration of the Tibetan tradition to the West. We could say that this applies to all the Eastern traditions that come to the West but my particular experience is within the Tibetan tradition. Part of this growing up is the need to allow dharma understanding and practice to evolve in such a way that it can be genuinely accessible to Westerners with our different psychological needs. Just as Tibetans,

Japanese or Chinese shaped Buddhism over the years, it will also evolve as it comes to the West. In many ways this is going to be our responsibility.

There is also an important area of responsibility that needs to be taken into account in our relationship to our teachers. When I was in Dharamsala recently I recall hearing H.H.Dalai lama refer to a concern he had about tulkus in the West. When I heard him say this I had a question in my mind, which I wanted to ask – 'where is there accountability?' We may put our trust in our teachers with devotion, but if things go wrong then it is for us as practitioners to take responsibility for how we respond to it. If our teachers make mistakes, if they do not seem able to recognise the error, then it is up to us to address it and potentially to challenge them when necessary. If we see our teachers behaving in ways that are unacceptable it is up to us to name it and place a boundary if they cannot do so themselves. If teachers in the West do not demonstrate a skilful and appropriate boundary in their relationship to students, it is for students to hold the ethical ground when teachers do not. While the majority of lamas are impeccable, there are a few examples of lamas in the West behaving in ways that are potentially bringing Tibetan Buddhism into disrepute. Whether it is the accumulation of wealth and the establishment of cult-like organisations or the blatant sexual exploitation of vulnerable devoted students, it for us as Westerners to take responsibility for some sense of ethical integrity that says this is not acceptable.

Gone are the medieval days when fear could be used to say that someone who questions the guru will go to hell. We must begin to bring about a healthier culture of accountability and responsibility in our Buddhist world if Buddhism is really going to flourish and benefit sentient beings. The aim of the dharma is to alleviate our human suffering, not so that we can establish institutions and organisations that simply cultivate a dysfunctional culture where lamas are surrounded by infantilised devotees who don't question anything the lama does.

This need not happen if we respect the fact that our teachers need us as much as we need them. They need us to be honest, straight and real with them, not blinded by a haze of deferential idealism. They can then be real people with their own challenges and difficulties but with a great deal of wisdom to offer. If we can accomplish this then the Tibetan tradition has a chance to really flourish in the West with integrity. We can offer respect and even devotion to our teachers but with a real capacity for discernment and personal responsibility. In this process it would seem we have a long way to go. Our reverence for the Tibetans and their culture is so great we seldom want to risk questioning some of what goes on. We have a very challenging path to tread between our reverence for the Tibetans and the extraordinary gift they bring us, and growing up to be more responsible for how this comes into our life. Optimistically I think as the years have passed we are not so naive and begin to find our own way.

Epilogue:

Going Forward

As WESTERN BUDDHISTS we have much to learn about how to integrate Buddhism in all its variations into Western life and Western mind. There are inevitable complications in this process that we are having to find ways to resolve. We could continually refer to our Eastern teachers to tell us what to do and how to do it, but at some point, we have to begin to take the first faltering steps to stand on our own two feet. I feel this is beginning to happen. The Tibetans are the source of a transmission of a tradition that we are incredibly fortunate to receive and I feel huge gratitude for their gift of wisdom and guidance. However, as Lama Yeshe said, it will be Westerners that bring the dharma to the West. This, I believe, is because the dharma is going through a natural organic evolution as it settles into our Western life and it is *our* job, not the Tibetan, Burmese, Japanese or Thai masters that can do this for us. What we learn from them is extraordinary but we have to make it our experience.

In this book I have tried to respond to this challenge through my own explorations and practice. My relationship to the Tibetan tradition has been rich beyond belief, complicated without doubt, often a great struggle, but ultimately hugely valuable and inspiring. The way I now approach practice within the tantric tradition is the result of a process that has been necessary for myself and may not suit everyone. I do not wish to say that what I have written here is a definitive statement of how we should practise. It is a work in progress and a reflection of my own ongoing learning.

In the time I have been teaching others, I have seen many people struggle with their Tibetan Buddhist practice. This has been of great interest to me, and, in my own search to find resolutions and a way forward, it has been necessary to follow what my own teacher modelled so beautifully. He was a courageous, creative spirit that wanted to explore and experiment to genuinely see what would work for us. In doing so I feel he brought to life the essence of tantra in a way that I have seldom seen since. I feel deeply sad that he is no longer present to continue this work, but I have wanted to bring some sense of his spirit into my own. To this end I am hugely indebted for all he taught me. Above all, perhaps, I am grateful for his empowerment to be true to the essence of something he deeply cherished rather than become caught up in the complications of culture, of orthodoxy and intellectual systems that can become mechanistic and dry.

As I have guided others in the approach to practice described in this book, I have seen that tantra can really come alive in a profound way. This has given me confidence that we really *can* do this path and genuinely experience deep insights in our meditation. It has also confirmed for me that with careful and diligent practice this path can meet our Western mind and bring profound psychological transformation. This is often confirmed for me when, at the closing feedback of retreats, people describe how this has given them a taste of something extraordinary.

There are those who dedicate themselves to preserving the tradition and this is undoubtedly a noble and important task. For me, I feel that finding the essence of tantra is what will keep it a living experience. This is not easy to do and in some ways we can only gauge if we have the essence, if things really work and change us, opening us to our true nature, our buddha potential. While it is important to preserve the tradition, I also wish to continue the unfolding of its essence like the flow of a river, as a living expression of the depth of our nature. Tantra, I feel, is a living form that grows, changes and evolves. We can see this in the way it has moved through the centuries from India into Nepal, Tibet, China and Japan.

How this begins to manifest for us in the West is still very uncertain. I optimistically think that many of us have been practicing for long enough to have a clearer sense of how this could be. There is a journey ahead that is ours as Westerners to follow, if we have the courage to begin to grow up and individuate. This means taking increasing responsibility for our path with renunciation, bodhichitta and wisdom at its heart. Our Tibetan guides are an extraordinary resource for us as we go forward, for which I have huge gratitude.

Appendices

The meditations that follow are examples of a way of practice that cannot easily be transposed into a written form. It is through actual guidance that one receives what could be seen as the transmission of direct experience and the subtleties of how meditation touches us. If you wish to receive more direct guidance into this approach to practice then this is possible through attending retreats available through the Mudra website: www.mudra.co.uk.

Appendix 1: Body sweep meditation.

Appendix 2: Settling in a sense of ground.

Appendix 3: Opening into feeling and sensation with equanimity.

Appendix 4: Expanding awareness in the body.

Appendix 5: Becoming aware of the energy within the body.

Appendix 6: Becoming aware of the energy in the region of the chakras.

Appendix 7: Moving into the practice of mahamudra.

Appendix 8: The front-generation of Green Tara.

Appendix 9: Self-generation of Green Tara.

Appendix 1
Body sweep meditation
(Following the initial period settling on the breath, it is helpful to allow up to 2 minutes for each part of the meditation.)

Let us begin by resting on the natural arising a falling of the breath. Be aware of the sensations of the movement of the breath in the chest and abdomen.

With the quality of the out breath allow yourself to begin to rest and settle into the body. *(3-4 minutes)*

Then gradually bring your awareness to the crown of the head to become aware of sensation and feeling at the crown.

Slowly bring your awareness down to your face, down to your jaw and round to your ears to become aware of sensation and feeling in the whole of your face. Be aware of sensation around the eyes, the nose, the mouth and so on. *(We do this with a quality of bare awareness, without reflecting upon it.)*

Slowly sweep your awareness through your head to the back of the head. Pay particular attention to where your skull meets the top of the spine. Notice the sensations. Allow space around sensation.

Take your awareness down to the neck and throat. *(If as we go through the body if you notice any particular areas of pain or tension allow a sense of softening as you breathe.)*

Down to the shoulders. *(Take your awareness in to the muscles the joints the bones not just the surface of the skin.)*

From the left shoulder sweep down the left arm to the fingers of the left hand.

From the right shoulder sweep down the right arm to the fingers of the right hand.

From the shoulders again sweep down the length of your back and spine to the base of the spine and the sensations of your bottom on the cushion. *(Let your awareness go into the muscles the bones not just the surface of the skin)*

From the shoulders again sweep down through the front of the trunk; down through the chest and abdomen.

From the left hip sweep along the left leg to the toes of the left foot.

From the right hip sweep along the right leg to the toes of the right foot.

Finally, from both feet allow your awareness to spread back up through the body to become aware of the whole body. Rest with quite present awareness in the arising and passing of sensation and feeling as you breathe.

Whatever arises give it space to come and go. Don't become caught in it but simply witness its arising and passing in the space of awareness.

Whatever feelings or sensations arise allow them to be as they are, don't contract around them or push them away, don't judge them, allow them to come and go as you breathe.

~~~~

Appendix 2
Settling in a sense of ground.
(This meditation should take around 20 to 25 minutes)

Begin by resting upon the natural rising and falling of the breath. With an awareness of the quality of the out breath allow yourself to begin to rest and settle into the body. *(Allow 5 minutes for this initial settling.)*

As you breathe allow part of your awareness to go down to the root of the body to connect to a sense of ground. Become aware of the sensations in the base of your body, the weight of your body upon the cushion. The sensations in the pelvic floor. Let your awareness spread and open into that ground.

With each out breath let every cell of your body begin to relax more deeply into this sense of ground. Begin to open to the ground beneath, let the earth support you. *(allow this some 5 plus minutes)*

Notice if there is any tension being held in the body. If you do, allow a sense of melting and softening around that tension as you breathe.

As you settle more and more deeply be aware of any subtle sense of resistance to letting go and settling into the sense of ground. Notice any subtle holding that won't allow you to let go particularly in the pelvic floor and the perineum.

There may be the presence of a subtle level of feeling or emotion relating to settling in the quality of ground. Notice these feelings, just allowing them to be there without judgement. Give them space to open out and go where they need to go.

After some time begin to let your awareness rise from the ground up into the rest of the body. Coming up into the trunk of the body and then into the arms legs and eventually the head.

Allow your awareness to relax and open into the space of the body. Be aware of the arising of sensation and feeling. Allow whatever arises to come and go as you breathe, resting in a sense of ground.

Appendix 3.

Opening to sensation and feeling with equanimity.
(This meditation should take around 25 minutes)

1. Begin by settling on the rising and falling of the breath. Paying attention to the quality of the out breath - resting and settling into the body. (5 Minutes)

2. As you breathe take part of your awareness down to connect to the sense of ground in the body. Let your entire body relax into this sense of ground. (5 Minutes)

3. From the sense of ground gradually bring your awareness up into the trunk of the body slowly expanding out to the arms legs and head. As you breathe be aware of the arising and passing of sensation and feeling in the body with quiet present awareness.

4. Whatever is arising give it space to be as it is. Don't contract into it or push it away.

5. Allow your awareness to become more spacious around feeling and sensation to give it space to open. Maintain a quality of awareness that doesn't become drawn into the story of whatever feelings arise.

(Whenever you lose this awareness come back to the breath settle into the body again. Connect to a sense of ground and then open into feeling and sensation again.)

Within that awareness of feeling and sensation bring in a sense of acceptance and kindness that simply allows whatever is there to be there as it is. Don't become too focused on any particular feeling, simply let it be there within a more spacious awareness.

Try not to judge whatever is happening and whatever feelings are there, as though they should be different, even when strong feelings or emotions arise. Nothing needs to be done other than to stay aware and open.

Begin to notice that these feelings and sensations pass through and do not abide. As they arise let them go. As thoughts arise also let them go.

Remain with this relaxed open present awareness with the breath present but in the background.

~~~~

Appendix 4
Expanding awareness in the body.
(Begin in a similar way to the previous meditation up to stage 5. then continue:)

Once your awareness is beginning to settle, as you breathe begin to soften and open your awareness. Allowing your awareness to be more and more spacious within which sensation and feeling arises. Let the outbreath guide you in this, so with each outbreath allow a sense of softening and opening. (5 mins)

As you breathe be aware of the continual moment to moment changing nature of feeling and sensation. Recognise that nothing within the body or the body itself has any substantial enduring nature. Open to that awareness without conceptually reflecting upon it. Simply be with the fluid nature of what is arising. (5-10 mins)

Then as you breathe become aware of the subtle sense of your body's form and how you hold that form as a subtle contraction. Allow that sense of form to soften and open as you breathe. Breathe as though your whole body, every cell, is breathing, as though your skin is permeable. Be aware of the subtle filling and emptying of the breath. With each outbreath allow a sense of softening and opening, relaxing and letting go into spacious awareness. (5-10 mins)

Rest in that relaxed spaciousness with an awareness of the fluid changing nature of whatever arises moving though - feeling sensation, thoughts, images. Allow them to simply arise and pass through without becoming caught in them and without needing to do anything to them.

Appendix 5

Becoming aware of the vitality/energy in the body.
(Begin in a similar way to the previous meditations up to stage 5 then continue)

As you rest with an awareness of sensation and feeling begin to shift your attention to the vitality or energy that is there within or beneath sensation and feeling. This can be helped by a softening of awareness in sensation opening to the quality of its energy. This can also be helped by dropping the inner concept of what we experience is sensation and instead begin to see that is in fact energy moving. Be aware of the subtle vibration of that energy pervading your body.

If any noticeable emotions arise try to recognise the energy within that emotion allowing it to expand and move through rather than contracting around it and blocking it.

Whenever you notice the movement of energy in any part of your body try to give it the space to open out and move where it needs to go.

Once again as you breathe allow the energy in every cell or atom of your whole body to breathe as though your skin was permeable. As you breathe in feel a sense of filling with the energy of the breath and as you breathe out have a sense of letting go and emptying. Let the in breath bring a sense of freshness and clarity of energy, the out breathe releasing any tired or foggy energy.

As you do this allow your awareness to become more spacious pervaded by the felt sense of the vitality in your body. Let the feeling open and spread becoming more and more pleasurable. Notice any movement of the energy in your body and its feeling or emotional nature.

Rest in that spaciousness pervaded by the feeling of your natural vitality. Here feeling/energy is not other that awareness, awareness is not other than feeling/energy.

~~~~

Appendix 6

Becoming aware of the energy in the region of the chakras.
(Begin the meditation as before up to stage 5.)

When your awareness is settled gradually take your attention to the region of the root chakra. *(This means not directly into the chakra but the region around it)*
Give yourself time to gradually feel into the quality of the energy that lives there. Don't have any expectations as to what it may be. As you begin to be aware of the feeling quality allow it to be as it is without judgement or doing anything to it. As you breathe allow it space to open and rest with that awareness. (4 mins)

Then bring your awareness slowly up to the region of the navel chakra *(This can be either literally at the level of the navel or just below the navel at the Hara, Tantien, Svadistana)*
Give yourself time to gradually feel into the quality of the energy that lives there. Don't have any expectations as to what it may be. As you begin to be aware of the feeling quality allow it to be as it is without judgement or doing anything to it. As you breathe allow it space to open and rest with that awareness. (4 mins)

Then bring your awareness to the region of the heart chakra.
Give yourself time to gradually feel into the quality of the energy that lives there. Repeat the process of releasing and opening as you breathe. (4 mins)

Then bring your awareness to the region of the throat chakra.
Give yourself time to gradually feel into the quality of the energy that lives there. Repeat the process as before (4 mins)
Then bring you awareness to the region of the crown chakra.
Give yourself time to gradually feel into the quality of the energy that lives there. Repeat the process as before. (4 mins)

Finally let your awareness spread back down the centre of your body to be aware of all these five places. Rest with that awareness allowing a sense of space to be open and relaxed.
(It may be helpful to notice which chakra is the most pleasant and which the most uncomfortable. Simply allow this to be as it is without judgement))

Appendix 7

Moving into the practice of mahamudra.
(Begin this meditation through the stages 1-5 as before, then continue)

As you rest with an awareness of sensation and feeling let that awareness become more open and spacious. Notice the subtle changing nature of whatever is arising in the body and whatever is passing in the mind.

Allow your body to relax and settle into the sense of ground and your awareness to begin to expand and open.

When your awareness is relatively steady increasingly open to the sense of spaciousness. Gradually rest back into the space of awareness itself.

Be aware that feeling and sensation are not other than the space of awareness and the space of awareness is not other than sensation and feeling.

Whatever arises within that space of awareness give it gentle attention but do not interfere with it. Simply let it be as it is and notice its 'evaporation' back into the space of awareness.
(This helps sustain your meditation and enables a recognition of the empty nature of whatever arises be it feelings, sensations, thoughts or a sense of 'me'.)

~~~~

Appendix 8

The front-generation of Green Tara.
(Begin this meditation through the stages 1-5 as before, allowing perhaps 5- 8 minutes, then continue) (When I suggest remaining with a visualisation give it a couple of minutes to settle)

Within that space of awareness, in the space before you at
the level of the forehead there arises an 8 petaled white lotus.
In the centre of the lotus rests a circular white moon disc,
lying flat. In the centre of the moon disc stands a green flame
marked by a syllable Tam at its centre. *(rest with this for a short
while)*

From the flame and Tam green light radiates out in all directions
into the space around.

This light invites from Dharmakaya the essence of all the Buddhas'
wisdom and compassion in the aspect of millions of tiny droplets of
green light energy. Each droplet contains a tiny green Tara. These
absorb back into the flame and Tam like a green rainfall. *(remain with
this for a while)*

The flame blazes with light and suddenly transforms into the aspect
of Arya Tara. *(see front cover)*
Her body is green in colour with one face and two arms. She sits with
her right foot stepping down onto a secondary lotus. Her left foot is
held in closely. Her right hand is placed upon her right knee with the
palm facing towards you. It holds the stem of a blue lotus flower
blooming at the right side of her head. Her left hand is held at the
heart and holds between thumb and ring finger the stem of another
blue lotus flower blooming at the left side of her head. She is dressed
in robes of silk and ornaments of gold and precious jewels. Her hair
is tied in a topknot and loose across the shoulders. She has a crown
of five jewels on the forehead and her hair is adorned with flowers
and strings of pearls. She smiles with open interested eyes like a
loving mother for her only child and is surrounded by and aura of
light. *(rest with this for a while)*

Prayers
To you noble Tara who is the essence of our own innate Buddha
nature inseparable from that of all the Buddhas; you manifest for the
welfare of sentient beings; you are the source of blessings and
inspiration, healing and transformation; as our guide and protector
to you we go for Refuge.

We request you to bestow your blessings to cleanse and heal inner and outer obstacles, sickness, emotional afflictions and so on, that we may clear the obscurations that prevent us from awakening to our innate potential for the welfare of sentient beings.
(rest with this for a short while)

In Tara's crown is a white Om in her throat a red Ah, in her heart on a moon disc is a green Tam surrounded by her mantra.

Light of love and compassion emanates from her heart. It comes into your heart, healing and opening the heart, then filling your body.
As you breathe in, breathe this light into your heart, as you breathe out let it fill your body. *(do this for a few minutes to feel the connection to Tara in your heart)*

You hear the sound of the mantra in Tara's heart. Then begin to chant the mantra: Om Tare Tutare Ture Svaha *(Chant this for 21+ mantras.)*

When the mantra chant stops rest in the space of awareness for 5 to 10 minutes. Do not think or visualise anything, simply open to the space of awareness and its particular felt quality that remains.

Restore your awareness of Tara. She comes to the crown of your head and becoming smaller and smaller descends through your crown to become seated in your heart chakra, blessing your heart mind. Light fills your body blessing your body speech and mind. *(rest with this awareness)*

Dedication
May whatever positive wholesome energy developed through this meditation enable me to awaken to my full potential to be of value to every living being to help them also awaken to their full potential.

~~~~

Appendix 9
Self-generation of Green Tara.
(Traditionally this practice would not be done without some formal permission or initiation.)
(Begin this meditation through the stages 1-5 as before, allowing perhaps 5- 8 minutes, then continue)

While resting in the space of quiet present awareness begin to be aware of a small green syllable Tam resting in your heart chakra. If a Tam is unfamiliar imagine a small sphere of green light the size of a pea.

Green light begins to radiate out from the Tam (sphere) filing your body. It radiates out from your body into the space around. This light is not ordinary light as it passes through the space in matter. It radiates out through the walls of the building in which you sit. Gradually it expands out into space around becoming more and more expansive.

All relative appearances lacking inherent substantiality, by nature empty, begin to melt into light. That light absorbs back eventually into the building. This melt into light and dissolves into you.

Then your ordinary appearance, ordinary identity and your body melt into light and dissolve into the Tam in the heart.
The Tam gradually dissolves upwards until all appearances dissolve into emptiness like a clear sky. Let go into non-duality, into dharmakaya.
(Rest in this space for as long as you can- this could mean 5 to 20 minutes)
Within the space of awareness a subtle intention arises to manifest for the welfare of sentient beings.

Where you are seated suddenly an 8 petaled white lotus arises. At its centre is a moon disc lying flat. Standing in the centre of the moon disc your consciousness arises as a green Tam.

Light radiates out from the Tam into the space around. It invites the blessings of all the Buddhas, which returns in the form of light and dissolves into the Tam.

Instantly you arise as Arya Tara. Your body is green in colour with one face and two arms. You sit with your right foot stepping down onto a secondary lotus. Your left foot is held in closely. Your right hand is placed upon your right knee with the palm facing outwards. It holds the stem of a blue lotus flower blooming at the right side of your head. Your left hand is held at the heart and holds between thumb and ring finger the stem of another blue lotus flower blooming at the left side of your head. You are dressed in robes of silk and ornaments of gold and precious jewels. Your hair is tied in a topknot and loose across the shoulders. You have a crown of five jewels on the forehead and your hair is adorned with flowers and strings of pearls. You smile with open interested eyes like a loving mother for her only child and are surrounded by and aura of light. *(rest with this for a while holding what is known as divine pride)*

In your crown is a white Om, in your throat a red Ah and in your heart a green Tam standing on a moon disc with the mantra encircling. From the Tam light emanates into the space inviting the blessings of the Buddhas in the form of light which dissolves into you.

From your heart a radiant light of love, compassion and wisdom emanates. It goes out to those you live amongst and work amongst, those that inhabit the planet and to the planet itself. This light heals and liberates others from their suffering and its causes, it also heals the planet. With this visualisation chant: Om Tare Tutare Ture Svaha *(Repeat this as many time as you can)*

Finally rest in the space of awareness in the aspect of your radiant rainbow-like body of Tara. *(Rest for some minutes)*

Dedication
May whatever positive wholesome energy developed through this meditation enable me to awaken to my full potential to be of value to every living being to help them also awaken to their full potential.

~~~~

Tibetan Terms

Chenrezig	The Buddha of compassion
Dag tsin	Ego grasping
Dzog chen	Lit. Great completion; meditation on the natural clarity of the mind
Dzog rim	The completion stage of higher tantra
Gyu	Lit. Continuity; Skt. Tantra
Je nang	Permission to practice
Kum nye	System of physical healing exercises
Kye rim	The generation stage of higher tantra
Lama	Skt. Guru; A teacher
Lam rim	Graduated path
Lung	Skt. Prana; energy-wind
Lung ku	Energy body
Ma rig pa	Lit. Not seeing; Ignorance
Nam tok	The minds discursive chatter
Nge jung	Definite emergence - renunciation
Ngon dro	Preliminary practices
O sel	Clear-light - extremely subtle nature of mind
She ne	Skt. Samatha; calm abiding
Tangkha	Tibetan icon

Tig le	Skt. Bindu; Elemental fluid drops in the body
Torma	An offering cake often sculptured into elaborate forms.
Tsa	Channel within the energy body, meridian.
Rang tong	Lit. Self empty; an approach to the wisdom teachings of Buddhism rooted in philosophical understanding of emptiness
Rig pa	Awareness
Rig tong	Awareness and emptiness
Rinpoche	Lit. Precious; the name given to a reincarnated lama
Shen tong	Lit. Other empty; an approach to the wisdom teachings of Buddhism based in meditation on the nature of mind
Trul kor	System of physical exercises associated with the practice of tummo
Tsongkapa	The originator of the Gelgpa school of Tibetan Buddhism
Tummo	Lit. Wrathful female; the practice of generating psychic heat at the navel
Tulku	A reincarnated lama, usually called Rinpoche.
Wang	Empowerment
Yidam	Heart/mind bound deity

Sanskrit Terms

Asana	Posture used within Yoga
Arhant	One who has become liberated from the cycle of existence.
Bodhichitta	The awakening mind or heart; the intention to awaken for the welfare of sentient beings.
Bodhisattva	One who is engaged in the path to awaken for the welfare of sentient beings.
Chakra	Lit. Wheel – conjunction of channels in the central channel of the energy-body

Dakini	Highly evolved female tantric practitioner; a female being associated closely with the natural environment eg. the 5 elements.
Dharma	Lit. Truth or True; The Buddha's teachings.
Dharmakaya	The wisdom or 'truth body' of a Buddha
Guru	Tib. Lama; teacher
Guru yoga	Devotional practice in relation to a teacher or deity
Kryia tantra	Action tantra; the first level of tantra
Kundalini	Psychic energy in the central channel
Maha anutara yoga tantra	The highest level of tantra
Mahakala	A fierce dharma protector; a manifestation of Chenrezig
Mahamudra	Meditation on the minds innate clarity
Mahayana	Lit. The great vehicle; the northern Buddhist
Madhyamaka	A philosophical system that emphasises the 'middle way' between eternalism and nihilism.
Mantrayana	The path of secret mantra, another name for Tantra or Vajrayana
Sadhana	Method of accomplishing the deity
Samatha	Tranquil abiding
Samaya	Commitment
Sambhogakaya	The 'enjoyment body' or purified energy body of a Buddha
Samskara	Habitual karmic pattern
Sutra	The Buddha's doctrinal teaching
Tantra	The Buddha's esoteric teaching
Theravada	Buddhist school based in the Pali cannon, common to Thailand, Shri Lanka and Burma
Vajrayana	Diamond vehicle; another name for tantra

Notes

1   For more information I refer the reader to: *The Changeless Nature, The Mahayana Uttara Tantra Shastra.* by Asanga and Arya Maitreya. (See Bibliography)

2   *Lung* in Tibetan is the same as Prana in Sanskrit, Chi in Japan and Qui in China. We could potentially translate it as 'energy wind' or perhaps spirit.

3   The view of some of the earlier mahasiddhas such as Naropa and Ghantapa suggests that it is not possible to attain Buddhahood without working with the energy of the subtle body.

4   Reggie Ray, *Touching Enlightenment*, Sounds True.

5   Shantideva, *A Guide to the Bodhisattva's way of Life.*

6   Rythmic healing; A healing movement practice created by the late Ruth Noble.

7   Rob Preece, *Feeling Wisdom;* Ch 8.

8   Rob Preece, *The Psychology of Buddhist Tantra*; Chapter 3.

9   Peter Levine, *Waking the Tiger* and *In an Unspoken Voice.*

10 Trulkor exercises: These exercises are found particularly with the teaching on the Six Yogas of Naropa. They are often strong physical exercises intended to clear blocks in the energy body and to awaken the heat of Tummo in the navel chakra.

11 H.H. Dalai Lama, *Mahamudra in the Gelug Kargyu Tradition*, Part III chapter 3.

12 H.H. Dalai Lama, *Mahamudra in the Gelug Kargyu Tradition*, Page 123, pp2.

13 H.H. Dalai Lama, *Kindness Clarity and Insight*

14 Khenchen Thrangu: *Ocean of the Ultimate meaning.* Page 92, pp2.

15 H.H. Dalai Lama, *Mahamudra in the Gelug Kargyu Tradition*, Page 100 pp2, Page 143 pp 3.

16 Song of Mahamudra; Tilopa: Do nought with the body but relax; Shut firm the mouth and silent remain. Empty your mind and think of nought, Like a hollow bamboo, rest at ease your body.

17 Lama Yeshe, *The tantric path of purification,* Page164, pp2.

18 The word Gyu in Tibetan is often translated as Tantra in sanskrit but in English means *continuity*. This term can particularly relate to

the meaning implied by the continuity of transmission of a lineage of a deity practice unbroken from its origins.

19 Lama Yeshe, *The bliss of inner fire*, page 80.

20 Michael Washburn, *The Ego and the Dynamic Ground,* The emergence of the ego from the dynamic ground – primal repression, Ch 2. Page 50.

21 Lama Yeshe, *Becoming the Compassion Buddha*, Chapter 8.

22 H.H.Dalai Lama, *The Path to Enlightenment*, page 71.

23 Rob Preece, *Preparing for Tantra*, page 136.

24 Lama Yeshe, *Becoming the Compassion Buddha*, Pages 116-118.

25 Rob Preece, *Wisdom of Imperfection*, Chapter 10, Spiritual Flight.

26 James Hillman, *Insearch: Psychology and Religion*. Chapter II, Page 50 pp2.

27 Anthony Storr, *Jung, Selected Writings*, Pages 341-343.

28 Herbert V. Guenther, *Kindly Bent to Ease Us*, Page 150-151 pp3.

29 C. G. Jung, *The Archetypes and the Collective Unconscious*, pages 208-9.

30 James Hillman defines daimons as " . . . figures of the middle realm, neither quite transcendent Gods nor quiet physical humans . . . . [T]here were many sorts of them, beneficial, terrifying, message-bringers, mediators, voices of guidance and caution." James Hillman, Healing Fiction, Barrytown, NY: Station Hill Press, 1983, page 55.

31 C. G. Jung, *Symbols of Transformation*, Page 232.

32 Rob Preece, *Psychology of Buddhist Tantra*. Chapter 6, Entering the Vessel.

33 "Free and secure space". This is a term used by the Jungian Sand-Play therapist from Switzerland called Dora Kalff who I met in 1976. She defined the sand tray in which patients placed objects in the process of therapy as a free and secure space in which whatever needs to be expressed can be expressed.

34 Silvia Brinton Perera, *Descent to the Goddess; A Way of Initiation for Women*, 1932.

35 Kriya tantra is seen as the first level of tantric practice. There are four levels known as Kriya, Charya, Yoga and Anutara yoga tantra.

36 Dalai Lama, Tenzin Gyatso, *The Path to Enlightenment*, page 71.

Bibliography

Arya Maitreya and Asanga. *The Changeless Nature, The Mahayana Uttara Tantra Shastra.* Trans. Ken and Katia Holmes. Eskdalemuir, Dumfriesshire, Scotland: Kagyu Samye Ling, 1985.

Allione, Tsultrim. *Feeding Your Demons.* London: HayHouse, 2008.

Brinton Perera, Sylvia. *Descent to the Goddess, A way of Initiation for Women.* Toronto, Inner City Books, 1981.

Chang, Garma C. C. *The Hundred Thousand Songs of Milarepa.* New York: Harper Colophon, 1970.

-------. *Six Yogas of Naropa.* Ithaca, NY: Snow Lion Publications, 1986.

Dalai Lama. *Stages of Meditation.* Ithaca, NY: Snow Lion Publications, 2001.

-------. *Essence of the Heart Sutra.* Trans. & Edited by Thubten Jinpa. Wisdom Publications, Boston, 2005.

-------. *The path to Enlightenment,* Ithaca, NY: Snow Lion Publications, 1994.

Dalai Lama & Alexander Berzin. *The Gelug/Kagyu Tradition of Mahamudra.* Ithaca, NY: Snow Lion Publications, 1997.

Dowman, Keith. *Buddhist Masters of Enchantment: The Lives and Legends of the Mahasiddhas.* Trans. Keith Dowman. Rochester, VT: Inner Traditions, 1998.

-------. *Sky Dancer: The Secret Life and Songs of Lady Yeshe Tsogyel.* Ithaca, NY: Snow Lion Publications, 1997.

Dzogchen Ponlop. *Wild Awakening: The heart of Mahamudra and Dzogchen.* Boston: Shambala, 2003.

Edinger, Edward F. *Ego and Archetype.* Boston: Shambhala Publications, 1992.

Evans-Wentz, W. Y. *Tibetan Yoga and Secret Doctrines.* 3rd. edition. New York City: Oxford University Press USA, 2000.

Guenther, Herbert V. *The Life and Teaching of Naropa.* Oxford: Clarendon Press, 1963.

-------. *The Royal Song of Saraha: A Study in the History of Buddhist Thought.* Boston: Shambhala Publications, 1973.

-------. *Treasures on the Tibetan Middle Way: A Newly Revised Edition of Tibetan Buddhism Without Mystification.* Boston: Shambhala Publications, 1976.

-------.*Kindly Bent to Ease us. Part one: Mind. Longchenpa.* Emeryville, California: Dharma Publishing. 1975

Gyatso, Kelsang. *Clear Light of Bliss: The Practice of Mahamudra in Vajrayana Buddhism.* Glen Spey, NY: Tharpa Publications, 1992.

Gray, David. B. *The Chakrasamvara Tantra, The Discourse of Shri Heruka.* New York, The American Institute of Buddhist Studies, 2007.

Hillman, James. *The Dream and the Underworld*. New York: Harper & Row, 1979.

-------. *Insearch: Psychology and Religion*. Dalas: Spring Publications, 1967.

Jacobi, Jolande. *Complex/Archetype/Symbol in the Psychology of C. G. Jung*. Trans. Ralph Mannheim. Princeton: Princeton University Press/Bollingen Foundation, 1971.

Jung, C. G. *Alchemical Studies*. Ed. and trans. Gerhard Adler and R. F. C. Hull. The Collected Works of C. G. Jung. Vol. 13. Princeton: Princeton University Press/Bollingen Foundation, 1983.

-------. *Archetypes and the Collective Unconscious*. Ed. and trans. Gerhard Adler and R.F.C. Hull. The Collected Works of C. G. Jung. Vol. 9, Part 1. Princeton: Princeton University Press/Bollingen Foundation, 1981.

-------. *Psychology and Alchemy*. Ed. and trans. Gerhard Adler and R. F. C. Hull. The Collected Works of C. G. Jung. Vol. 12. Princeton: Princeton University Press/Bollingen Foundation, 1980.

-------. *Psychology and Religion: West and East*. Ed. and trans. Gerhard Adler and R.F. C. Hull. The Collected Works of C. G. Jung. Vol. 11. Princeton: Princeton University Press/Bollingen Foundation, 1970.

-------. *Symbols of Transformation*. Ed. and trans. Gerhard Adler and R. F. C. Hull. The Collected Works of C. G. Jung. Vol. 5. Princeton: Princeton University Press/Bollingen Foundation, 1977.

Khenchen Thrangu Rinpoche. *Essentials of Mahamudra*. Boston: Wisdom, 2004.

-------. *An Ocean of the Ultimate Meaning, Teachings on Mahamudra*. Boston: Shambala, 2004

Levine, Peter. *Waking the Tiger, Healing Trauma*. Berkeley, North Atlantic Books 1997.

-------. *In an Unspoken Voice, How the body Releases Trauma and Restores Goodness*. Berkeley, North Atlantic Books, 2010.

Long Chen Rab Jampa, H.H Dudjom Rinpoche, Beru Khyentze Rinpoche. *The Four Themed Precious Garland*. Dharamsala: Library of Tibetan Works and Archives, 1979.

Phabongka Rinpoche. *Commentary on the Heruka Body Mandala* (in Tibetan). Unpublished translation.

-------. *The Sadhana of Chakrasamvara* (in Tibetan). Unpublished translation.

Preece, Rob. *The Alchemical Buddha*. Devon, UK: Mudra, 2000.

-------. *The Psychology of Buddhist Tantra*, Ithaca: Snow Lion Publications, 2006.

-------. *The Wisdom of Imperfection*, Ithaca: Snow Lion Publications, 2006.

-------. *The Courage to Feel,* Ithaca: Snow Lion Publications, 2009.

-------. *Preparing for Tantra, Creating the Psychological Ground for Practice*. Ithaca: Snowlion, 2011.

-------. *Feeling Wisdom, Working with Emotions using Buddhist Teachings and Western Psychology*. Boston: Shambala Publications, 2014.

Rabten, Geshe. *The Essential Nectar: Meditations on the Buddhist Path*. Boston: Wisdom Publications, 1984.

-------. *The Preliminary Practices of Tibetan Buddhism*. Dharamsala, India: Library of Tibetan Works and Archives, 1974.

Ray, Reginald. A. *Touching Enlightenement, Finding realisation in the body*. Boulder, Sounds True, 2008.

-------. *The Awakening Body, Somatic meditation for discovering our deepest life*. Boulder, Shambala Publications, 2008

Rosenberg, Larry. with David Guy. *Breath by Breath, The Liberating Practice of Insight Meditation*. Boston: Shambala 2004.

Sonam Rinchen, Geshe. *The Three Principle Aspects of the Path*. Ithaca, Snowlion Publications, 1999.

Storr, Anthony. *Jung, Selected Writings*. London, Fontana Press, 1983.

Tarthang Tulku. *Kim Nye Relaxation, Part 2: Relaxation Exercises*. Berkley: Dharma Publishing, 1978.

Tsongkhapa. *Three Principal Aspects of the Path*. Trans. Alexander Berzin. Dharamsala: Library of Tibetan Works and Archives, 1982.

Washburn, Michael. *The Ego and the Dynamic Ground, A Transpersonal Theory of Human Development*. Albany: State University of New York Press, 1995.

Yeshe, Lama Thubten. *The Bliss of Inner Fire: Heart Practice of the Six Yogas of Naropa*. Boston: Wisdom Publications, 1998.

-------. *Introduction to Tantra: The Transformation of Desire*. Boston: Wisdom Publications, 1987.

-------. *Mahamudra*. Boston: Wisdom Publications, 1981.

-------. *The Tantric Path of Purification: The Yoga Method of Heruka Vajrasattva Including Complete Retreat Instructions*. Boston: Wisdom Publications, 1995.

-------. *Becoming the Compassion Buddha, Tantric Mahamudra for Everyday Life*. Boston: Wisdom Publications, 2003

37488723R00155

Printed in Poland
by Amazon Fulfillment
Poland Sp. z o.o., Wrocław